THE HISTORY OF
BABYLONIA AND ASSYRIA

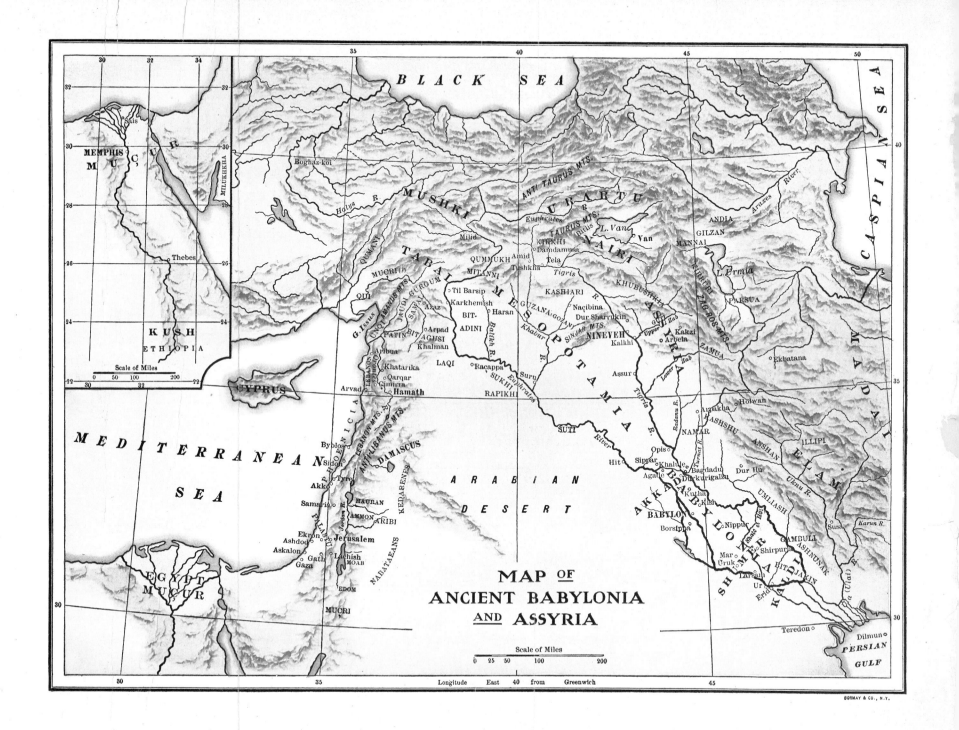

MAP OF
ANCIENT BABYLONIA
AND ASSYRIA

Scale of Miles
0 25 50 100 200

Longitude   East 40 from Greenwich

THE HISTORY OF

BABYLONIA AND ASSYRIA

BY

HUGO WINCKLER, Ph.D.

Professor in the University of Berlin

TRANSLATED AND EDITED BY

JAMES ALEXANDER CRAIG, Ph.D.

Professor of Semitic Languages and Literatures in the
University of Michigan

REVISED BY THE AUTHOR

NEW YORK

CHARLES SCRIBNER'S SONS

1907

COPYRIGHT, 1907
BY CHARLES SCRIBNER'S SONS

Published September, 1907

PREFACE BY THE TRANSLATOR AND EDITOR

Dr. Winckler is *facile princeps* in the field of historical research covered by the following volume. He has not only the great advantages of being one of our foremost Semitic linguists, and a specialist in Assyriology but is also naturally endowed, as few men are, for the constructive work of the historiographer. Perhaps to no one of the present generation of Semitic scholars, more than to him, are the workers in the various fields of Semitic Literature and History indebted. He has been for a quarter of a century not merely a rehearser of verified facts in this new and difficult domain but an indefatigable discoverer of new facts which, with his brilliant historical imagination, he has always known how to illuminate.

It was, therefore, a matter of self-congratulation when the present editor secured his consent to revise his *Geschichte* in the light of the knowledge gained since it was published in 1899 as a contribution to the *Weltgeschichte* of Dr. H. F.

Helmolt. Not only were important additions
made to the work as it was first presented and
modifications of many portions thereof introduced, but the author has also carefully reviewed
the translation and has made use of this opportunity to add further corrections to the original
text.

I have endeavored to give an accurate rendering
of the original and, at the same time, a readable
English translation, which I hope will not too
often betray an unconscious influence of Teutonic
modes of thought and expression. Here and
there I had introduced a sentence or two of my
own, for purposes of further elucidation, without
indicating that they were not the author's. To
the footnotes I have added I have generally
affixed my name. I have not considered it necessary to distinguish, as is often done, between the
spellings *Ashur,* the god, and *Ashshur,* the land,
of Assyria.

I trust that the historical order followed in
this work will be found to justify itself in the use
of it. The leading rôle played by Babylonia in
the history of the ancient Orient during the four
milleniums of her history, in the field of politics
as well as of culture, not only excuses the plan
adopted, but also entitles this ancient land to a
treatment of her history apart from that of
Assyria, advantageous, from some points of view,

as the combined treatment may be. In fact it is
only by the method here followed that the student
who is not already familiar with the progress of
the history of the two states can readily gain a
correct understanding of their peculiar characteristics and relative importance in the history of
civilization.

It is with the earnest hope that this new and
revised edition may be found more adequately
to meet the wants of that growing body of
students in our colleges and theological seminaries
who perceive the almost unique importance of
this study in relation to our knowledge of the history of civilization, its culture, art, and religion,
that the editor has undertaken the work of translation which called for a special knowledge of the
subject.

Helmolt's entire work, the *Weltgeschichte,* to
which, as above stated, the present volume in its
original form was contributed, was published in
English some years ago by Wm. Heinemann
in London under the title ''The World's History,''
and by Dodd, Mead & Co. in this country, with
the consent of both of whom this work is published.

JAMES A. CRAIG.

UNIVERSITY OF MICHIGAN,
    June, 1906.

CONTENTS

BABYLONIA

CHAPTER VIII

CHAPTER IX

CHAPTER X

CHAPTER XI

CHAPTER XII

CHAPTER XIII

CHAPTER XIV

ASSYRIA

THE NEW BABYLONIAN–CHALDEAN KINGDOM

CHAPTER I

CHAPTER II

CHAPTER III

I—BABYLONIA

BABYLONIA

CHAPTER I

THE REGION OF WESTERN-ASIATIC CIVILIZATION

OF the two civilizations which sprang up almost
contemporaneously with one another, the one in
the valley of the Tigris and Euphrates, the other
in the alluvial lands of the Nile, the Babylonian
unquestionably exercised the greater influence.
The culture of Greece owed much to Babylonia,
and European civilization became, in turn, heir
to her achievements through the Greeks. It is
not yet possible to discover all the lines of communication along which the thought of the East
passed over in historic times to the mainland of
Greece. It is still less possible to determine the
prehistoric paths by which Babylonian ideas
reached European nations and others beyond the
bounds of Babylonian empire. Nevertheless, it is
sufficient to point to the single word μνᾶ (the
Babylonian *mana,* or weight of sixty shekels) as
presumptive evidence of an influence that was far-
reaching. The timepieces that we carry in our
pockets, and place upon our mantels, are constant
witnesses to the scientific influence of Babylonia.

The faces of our watches are divided into twelve
periods corresponding to the old Babylonian division of the day into twelve double hours (*kasbu*).
It was from this *kasbu* that the mile, as a measure
of distance, was derived, the old mile representing the space traversed in two hours. The routes
by which these products of ancient Semitic
thought were transferred to the West lie, at present, quite beyond the bounds of our vision, but
the agreement that exists, even in matters of
detail, between the Babylonian mythology and
that of the ancient Germans, and other peoples as
well, precludes the possibility of their independent
development. "The common endowment of the
race" is an hypothesis that fails utterly to
account not only for the main features in which
these mythologies are agreed, but also, and more
especially, for the evident accord in unimportant
particulars.

The decipherment of the cuneiform inscriptions
and the hieroglyphs of Egypt has extended our
historical knowledge of Western civilization to a
period almost twice as remote as that previously
known. The history of Greece was known to us
from the seventh or eighth century B.C. The
oldest records of Babylonia and Egypt have lifted
the veil that shrouded the centuries of the fourth
millenium before our era. The period that separates their authors from that of Lycurgus and

the foundation of Rome is, consequently, as long as that which lies between us and the historical beginnings of Hellenic life.

Babylonian civilization and history was not confined to the region watered by the Tigris and Euphrates. A civilization so advanced as that of Babylonia could not exist without attracting to itself the assistance of neighboring lands and carrying thither its own achievements. Thus we see, even in remote antiquity, Babylon reaching out toward Palestine, Armenia, Elam, and even to Arabia. Her merchants went forth in the pursuits of commerce, her soldiers to war and victory. The products of her artists and artisans were laid in foreign markets. Her superfluous population found homes on alien soil. There, however, they were often exposed to attack from barbarous neighbors and often succumbed to their superior numbers. Generally speaking, therefore, the history of the outlying countries and peoples is vitally connected with the history of Babylonia. It is no mere accident that we possess little or no knowledge of these peoples beyond that which has come to us from the Babylonians. The gaze of all these outlying peoples, and the direction of their movement, was toward the old culture-land, and that irrespective of the existing relation, whether ruled by the latter or imposing their rule upon it. Emphatic testimony is given to this fact in the extensive spread of the cuneiform writing, the pre-eminent achievement of the Babylonian intellect. Throughout the whole of Western Asia it became the medium of intellectual exchange. Everywhere, so far as we are at present able to see, we discover it. It was used in Elam, in Armenia, and even in Asia Minor, the home of the Hittite script, which still remains undeciphered. The peoples of Palestine were familiar with it, and through it with the Babylonian language and thought. It was studied at the court of the Pharaohs, and in the fifteenth century B.C. it was the medium of diplomatic and political correspondence between Egypt and the states of Western Asia.

Inasmuch, then, as the development of Babylonia conditioned the historical and cultural advance and political character of Western Asia, the task of presenting its history is many sided, especially so when this history is to deal with a civilization extending over three thousand years, developing in the midst of barbarian neighbors, and subject to the most varied succession of incursions from without. Babylonian civilization was not confined to a single people—on the contrary, it was enjoyed and transmitted by peoples, of different homes and blood, who entered in succession the great plain of the Tigris and Euphrates and there, under the influence of its dominant culture, started upon a fresh career. The same was true of the neighboring lands which felt in a measure the effects of this civilization, though with regard to these our knowledge is much more defective owing to the scantiness of our material.

Just as the great civilizations have developed along the great natural highways of communication, the great rivers, so the great movements of peoples originate in the treeless plains which afford grazing for the herds by which man lives in the nomad stage.

But great though the extent of this territory may be, to which the nomad lays claim, it is, nevertheless, able to yield support to only a comparatively small population. As the people multiply they are compelled to seek fresh fields for support, and naturally the simple, vigorous sons of nature are enticed by the attractions of civilization and the hope of easy victory over men who through the seductions of refinement have lost in virility.

As regards Babylonia there were three of these original centres which contributed to its population: the steppes of Europe, whence migrations took place over the Caucasus, around the Caspian Sea, or to the west through Asia Minor; the steppes of Central Asia to the northeast; south and southwest Arabia.

Of these three regions the first is of minor importance owing to the unfavorable conditions for numerical growth; the second, Central Asia, occupies a more important place. This, however, was true of both these centres: every wave of migration which went out from them toward Babylonia struck first upon the border states that stood under Babylonian influence, *viz.:* those of Asia Minor, where the Hittites had developed their peculiar life, and those of Syria, Armenia, and Elam. Babylonia was consequently protected, in a measure, by these buffer-states from incursions from both of these quarters. On the south and southwest it was different. Arabia, with its extended steppes, touched immediately upon Babylonia, and Arabia from time immemorial was the home of nomad tribes possessed of overmastering predatory instincts. The only natural boundary between the two lands was the Euphrates River. The roving nomad could sweep over the plain and skirt the cities on the west bank unhindered; that, too, even when a sturdy arm checked his passage to the rich pasturage on the east. The boundary which the Babylonians were compelled to defend was an extended one, and ran in parts through dreary wastes. It rarely happened, therefore, in olden days, any more than now, that the rulers of Babylonia were able to command a sufficient force to repel the impetuous rush of nomads and prevent them crossing the river. It was from this quarter that the old homeland of culture was exposed to the most frequent and permanent incursions, each, in turn, to spoil its predecessor of its title to sovereignty over the fertile plain. So far as our knowledge reaches, Arabia is the home of that family of people which, on linguistic grounds, we designate as Semitic. The history of Babylonia is, therefore, for the most part Semitic; the history of its neighboring peoples, so far as they were subject to her influence, is also Semitic. In so far as it was modified otherwise from without we must look to the other two main regions already referred to as the centres whence the influence proceeded. It was in *Babylonia* that the Semites achieved their greatest attainments. There they developed all that their natural endowments under the given conditions could effect; there Semitic history, so far as it is a history of civilized people, discovers its field of movement. Even Islamism has its proper seat there, but we can no more speak of a Semitic-Islamic civilization, indeed even less, than of a Babylonian-Semitic: the Arabs succeeded by virtue of the Persian-Byzantine culture.

The actors in Babylonian history, so far as it falls within our vision, are Semites. Their speech was preponderatingly Semitic despite the non-Semitic elements of admixture in the population. But our historical knowledge, it need not be stated, does not reach back to the beginnings of Babylonian civilization. History begins with *written tradition.* Written tradition, however, presupposes a long period of development during which the transition is made, on the one hand, from the first crude efforts to body forth an idea in written form to the achievement of a serviceable script, and, on the other hand, from incoordinated efforts in thought to the development of the reasoning powers. These stages must have been left behind before events could be handed down by written records. It is a long step from the pictographs of savages to written narratives of wars and records of temple-building, such as we find in old Babylonian inscriptions of the fourth millenium B.C., and to the records of administration drawn up in systematic form during the same period. Possibly the peoples who surmounted the difficulties of the early stages labored longer to accomplish their tasks than the three or four thousand years through which we can follow the cuneiform script in its use and development. We shall see that the oldest documents, at present known to us, are of Semitic origin—the work of Semites who came into Babylonia from without and, through war with one another, united in forming greater states. These records, however, show distinctly the influence of the old civilized stock that was in possession of the country prior to the Semites. It is to them, therefore, we must ascribe the origin of Babylonian culture and the invention of the cuneiform writing—for us they are *one* people, for we see them only through the veil of prehistoric time. Of their rise, growth, and fortunes, which must have been as varied and changing as those of the Semites of Babylonia, whose history fills the next three thousand years, we know nothing.

CHAPTER II

THE SUMERIANS

THE oldest records we have are written in a non-Semitic language—"the language of the Sumerians," as they are called in the later texts. This language is all that we know of this ancient people, the inventors of the cuneiform writing and the originators of Babylonian culture. This, however, is the weightiest and most convincing testimony to their importance. For, long after Sumerian ceased to be a spoken language, when the most varied peoples had settled in the Babylonian plain and had passed again in turn from the stage of its history, as the old Sumerians themselves had; when the rôles of the different Semitic peoples were ended, when Persians, Macedonians, and Parthians still ruled there—almost to the beginning of the Christian era—the Sumerian language continued to be cultivated in Babylonia in connection with the sacred cult. It enjoyed there the dignity accorded to Latin as the tongue of the learned and of the church in the Middle Ages and in more modern times, and maintained itself in this rôle for a period more than twice as long.

If then, up to the present, no Sumerian speaks

to us out of his own inscription, if the past of this remarkable people belongs to the prehistoric age, though its final achievements descend in an uninterrupted chain of tradition into our own time and civilization, it, nevertheless, comes nearer to us in the preservation of its speech than it could have done by any other of its intellectual feats. Inscriptions and religious texts in the Sumerian language have descended to us from the fourth millenium B.C. The oldest of these inscriptions are those of the kings of Lagash. But, in addition to these, other inscriptions in Semitic-Babylonian language have come down to us from their immediate predecessors, contemporaries, and successors. These are written by Semites, and as we shall see later, by Semites who consequently form, so to speak, a second layer of the population. We must assume that about the end of the fourth millenium the Sumerian speech had wholly, or almost wholly, disappeared from vulgar use, and at this time played practically the same rôle as Latin at the time of the Merovingians. We can readily comprehend how the language, maintained only by artificial means in the succeeding centuries, should have suffered a fate similar to that of Latin in the Middle Ages. A rejuvenation through the evolution of classic ideas, such as came to the Latin with the Renaissance, was foreign to the Oriental mind. Sumerian, and its

idiom known as Akkadian, suffered constant
deterioration in later times. Semiticisms were
freely incorporated. The later the texts the
stronger is the impression that they are composed
of shortened and inflected Sumerian expressions
by rejecting the original and totally different
syntax. This Sumerian exhibits the same characteristics as the Monks-Latin, and even those of the
macaronic compositions, though, in the latter case,
the linguistic hybridations were often humorously
meant, whereas this mongrel Sumerian was always serious. It will be readily understood that
we are but imperfectly acquainted with the proper
pronunciation of this old language when it is further borne in mind that the older the texts the
greater is the number of ideographs employed in
them. These ideographs, or symbols, though they
suggest the meaning of the word, or expression,
do not tell us how the latter was read. While,
therefore, the meaning of the old inscriptions can
be made out with at least approximate, if not
always absolute, certainty through our knowledge
of the meaning of the signs, the pronunciation, in
so far as it is discoverable, depends upon the
information supplied by the scribes of later
centuries.

Notwithstanding the fact that we are in possession of numerous texts there remains much in
connection with the language that is still unknown

or obscure. Enough, however, is established to
enable us to comprehend in a general way the
character of the Sumerian, the oldest language
of civilization. It is *agglutinative,* in structure
essentially like the Turkish, and consequently
wholly unlike the Semitic. The following sentence may serve as an illustration:

egal Ur-gur ungal Ur gal e-An-na in-ru-a-ka-ta=
palace + Ur - gur + king + Ur + man + e-Anna + he built + genitive particle + in=

in the palace of Urgur, the king of Ur, the builder
of (the temple) E-anna. The genitive relation,
which, in English, is expressed by "of" between
palace and Urgur, and appears in the same place
in Semitic languages, is here thrown to the end,
where it is expressed by *ka.* The whole sentence
is, therefore, somewhat after the manner of German word-formations, a kind of *compositum.* In
the same way, the preposition "in," which is so
important for us, since it designates the place and,
therefore, stands at the beginning, is here found
last of all (*ta*). We may note further the expression of the Semitic participle by the circumlocu-
tion gal . . . in-ru-a=man . . . +he built.
The effort to establish a relationship between this
language and any of the ancient tongues, even of
the different ones spoken by surrounding peoples,
or those of the present day, must be renounced.
What has already been said with respect to its

pronunciation is in itself suggestive here. Phonetic decay had already reached an advanced stage. The majority of words consist of only simple syllables with a vowel and consonant, or of one compound syllable, a consonant, vowel and consonant; but most of the latter have lost the final consonant, becoming thus open syllables. Moreover, a large number of words which were originally different are phonetically indistinguishable. The Sumerian language has, therefore, undergone a similar process of detrition to that found in the Chinese. The question of the linguistic relationship of the Sumerian to the languages of other peoples is a very enticing one for the linguist. But at present we know far too little of the structure and vocabulary of this tongue to anticipate much success for investigations of this problem. It is easy enough to pose it, but it is almost impossible to solve it so long as we remain ignorant of the history of the people who spoke it. Moreover, a literature in which thought is prevailingly expressed by suggesting ideas (or by a succession of signs representing ideas), and not by sounds, fails to supply the primary data necessary to the determination of the development of a language phonetically. Future investigations are as likely to fail of important results in settling the precise linguistic relationship of this old speech as have those hitherto attempted.

Of the history of the Sumerians we know nothing. The same is true of early Egyptian life. In the first historical period of the Old Kingdom, when the Semites appeared in Babylonia, civilization was fully developed; but scarcely anything is known from the inscriptions of the earlier times when civilization was in its infancy and youth. We may nevertheless, by looking to later times, and allowing ourselves to be guided by the analogy of similar conditions, draw at least one conclusion with reasonable certainty—the development of these civilizations was not realized in an idyllic age on the fruitful banks of the Euphrates and Nile. Foes and friends met together. The same relationships as we find among the peoples of both lands in later ages, such as are found among all civilized peoples between whom communication is not prevented by insurmountable barriers, must have existed in the gray dawn and early development of Sumerian history. Then, too, trade had its movements hither and thither, kings must have exchanged letters, and clashed in arms, and one people bowed subject to another's yoke.

CHAPTER III

THE EARLIEST IMMIGRATIONS OF SEMITES

As soon as the darkness of the distant past is illumined by the light shed from historical inscriptions, the oldest monuments which speak to us directly, not by way of inference, show us Semites settled in the plain of the Tigris and Euphrates, where they have already won the mastery and exercise lordship. The name Semites is now commonly employed to designate that family of people which speaks the same language as the Hebrews, who, in the genealogical table of Genesis X. are counted with the descendants of *Shem*. It is puerile to point to the correctness of this table for a justification of this designation, or to its errors, to prove its unfitness. The principles which guided the biblical compiler were by no means those of the nineteenth century with its emphasis upon language. Even language is very defective and much overrated as a means for the determination of racial origins and connections; but insufficient as it is, it was little considered in the ancient Orient. Lately, however, it has been discovered that Elam, the first mentioned

son of Shem (x., 22), which hitherto has been
regarded as erroneously classed with the Semites,
not only used the cuneiform script but also wrote
a form of Babylonian similar to that employed
in Canaan.   Unexpectedly, too, our discoveries
show this to have been the case in the age of the
first Babylonian rulers of whom we know.   The
French excavations in Susa have also shown that
Susa and Elam were then considered to belong
to Babylonia, and that it was not until later that
the "Elamite" language was used in writing.
The genealogical table is, therefore, correct as
regards Elam if we read it as the writer intended
it.   That it should have put *Lud, i.e.,* Lydia,
before Aram excites surprise, and the opinion is
unanimous that we have a scribal error here.
Besides Arpakshad, the best suggestion is that
Lullu ought to be read.   Lullu was the name of
the border land between Assyria and Babylonia
and Media.   The proposal made by Jensen to read
Lubdi for Lud (לבד for לוד) is less worthy of
attention, as this name, so far as we know, was
given only to a region situate between northern
Mesopotamia and Armenia.   It is, nevertheless,
possible that it was once employed more com-
prehensively to designate the northern part of the
Babylonian territory of Armenia.

The home of the Semites was Arabia.   The
consideration of any other centre is excluded on

geographical grounds. Up to the present day the purest Semites are to be found in Arabia. There, under similar conditions, they live on the same plane of development as their tribal relations who in the fourth millenium won for themselves the fertile and cultivated lands of Babylonia. The eyes of the descendants still look longingly in the same direction despite the gloomy contrast between its present impoverishment and neglect and the richness and cultivation of the ancient days.

The only routes along which the nomad tribes of Arabia could migrate led toward Syria and Palestine. The ocean set bounds to their movements in other directions. Migrations westward or eastward would presuppose the use of ships, and this a transition from the nomadic life of the desert to settled homes. The fisherman, at least, must needs have pitched his tent, but large numbers are never nourished by the fisherman's craft. From South Arabia, therefore, no exodus of importance occurred. It was only when the Sabæans, and the peoples united with them, had developed a semi-civilization of their own that settlers crossed over from South Arabia into Abyssinia and Africa, and of this movement very little is known.

We are able to determine, approximately at least, the course and the time of these migrations since we have a fairly accurate knowledge of the beginning and end of the last of them and a corresponding certainty with regard to the first. They are the natural result of overpopulation. They must, consequently, recur with a certain periodicity under similar conditions of life and society. This *a priori* consideration is amply supported by the inscriptions. We have definite knowledge of *four main Semitic migrations* northward. The last, *the Arabian,* we may take first, as it stands in the clearer light of later history, and culminated in the conquests of Islam. It began about the seventh or eighth century B.C., when the influx of Arabs into Syria is known to have taken place. This was preceded by the *Aramaic,* the beginning of which we can also approximately discover. As early as the fifteenth to the thirteenth century we find Mesopotamia overrun by Aramaic nomads. The first advances of these tribes must have antedated this period. Prior to the Aramaic was the *Canaanitic-Hebraic* (Amorite). If, in view of what has been said, we allow in round numbers a thousand years between these great movements we shall arrive at a date for this latter one which is supported by the monuments. About 2400 to 2100 B.C. we find that Western Asia, Babylonia, Egypt likewise, are in possession of a people best described as Canaanite. Another thousand years, or more, earlier than this the *Babylonian Semites* have entered into the full inheritance of the old Sumerian civilization.

These are the four great groups of Semitic peoples whose successive movements most vitally affected the history of Western Asia. One must bear in mind, however, that computations such as the above are only approximate—the estimate may be a century too high or too low for any, or all, of the groups. To set definite limits to any great migration, however tempting, is manifestly impossible. In all such movements of great masses one people is driven before another, and the last part of a group is still on the move when the first contingent of the next takes up the march, as, for example, in the case of the Hebrews and Aramæans about the middle of the second millenium B.C.

THE PRINCIPAL CITIES

It is to be supposed that the Semites who entered Babylonia found there on arrival a highly developed civilization. This they accepted, and possessed themselves of the superior advantages which it offered as barbarians always do in similar circumstances. Our earliest sources make mention of a number of cities whose gods and their worship were held in high reverence. Centrally situated at the converging points of the great highways they remained throughout the

course of history marts of business and fosterers
of culture. The majority of them were pre-Sem-
itic settlements, which were completely Semitized
on the arrival of the Semitic nomad wanderers.
To us they are Semitic cities, just as Cologne
and Augsburg are German.

The most important of these cities lying along
the Euphrates, beginning with the most southerly,
are *Eridu* (*Abu Shahrein*), the seat of the worship of Ea, the god who bestowed upon man all
the elements of civilization; *Ur* (*Mugheir*), where
Sin, the moon-god, was worshipped in southern
Babylonia; *Lagash* (or *Sir-pur-la,* as the ideogram is read phonetically). The modern *Telloh*
represents the ancient site. It was here the
French consul De Sarzec made his important discoveries. There is also a city whose site is not
yet known, and whose name, written ideographically, is not yet read, but from whose rulers several
inscriptions have come down to us. Since the
second sign in the name was erroneously connected with the sign for *bow*[1] (*Ban*) the name

---

[1] *Vid.* Hilprecht, Old Bab. Inscriptions, Pt. II., pp. 51–56, where
the author, owing to this erroneous identification, reads *gish Ban
ki* and then connects it with *Harran* because of *Albiruni's* statement that Harran was crescent in form, and in view of Sachau's
sketch. Radau, Early Bab. History, and others, have read Gish-
Uḫ(?) and identified it with the modern *Djokha.* Its territory ad-
joined that of Lagash with which it came into frequent conflict over
the state boundary. Finally the delimitation was effected by means
of a canal, which was constructed from the Euphrates to the sacred
territory of Nin-girses, the god of Lagash.—*Craig.*

"Bow-city" was given to it. But the sign is
rather the one which later represented the war
chariot and it might, therefore, more correctly
be called the city of the War Chariot; *Isin* (formerly read Nisin and also *Pashe*), likewise yet
undiscovered, in later times the seat of a Babylonian dynasty; *Larsa* (*Senkereh*), the seat of the
southern Babylonian sun-worship; *Nippur* (Nuf-
far), the city of the god Bel, where the Americans
have excavated with so much success; *Uruk*
(Warka), the seat of the Nana-Ishtar cult. The
latter two from their position looked toward North
Babylonia and exercised a corresponding political
influence. In North Babylonia the most important cities are *Babylon,* the city of Marduk, but it
was not until later that it rose to pre-eminence;
Kish (Uhaimir?); *Cutha* (Tel-Ibrahim), the city
of Nergal; farther north *Sippar* (Abu-Habba),
the seat of North Babylonian sun-worship. It is
known to us chiefly by the excavations of Rassam
and more recently of Scheil. *Abu Habba* is the
Sippar of Shamash, the sun-god. But there was
another Sippar (of *Anunit*) whose site is unknown though it was probably not far distant
from the former and, therefore, a sort of pendant
to it. The modern *Deir* has been thought to represent its site. It is doubtless identical with the
otherwise named Sippar of Arura. In one inscription we read also of a "Sippar of the desert"

and called the "Old Sippar" in which designation there probably is reference merely to the more ancient ruins of the city. *Dur-ilu,* with its worship of Anu, the sky-god, is still unidentified. It commanded the passes leading into Elam and was, therefore, the first city to bear the brunt of the Elamite attacks: *Upi* (Opis), on the Tigris, was the most northerly of the large Babylonian cities. Others we need not mention here. Farther to the north the Mesopotamian steppe begins, and here as we go northward on the Tigris we pass the larger cities: *Ashur* (Kalʻa-Shergat), *Caleh* (Nimrud), and *Nineveh,* which in later times became the capital of the Assyrian kingdom. Lying to the east, toward Media, lay *Arbail* (Arbela, the modern Irbil) commanding the eastern region of Assyria between the upper and lower Zab. Here, too, was the junction of the highways leading to Media and the regions around the Urumia Sea. To return again to the country between the two rivers, we note the mountainous region of the *Singara,* the Sinjar Range, which in former times must have counted many cities even though no trace of them remains in our historical records. The valleys of the *Khabur* and *Balikh,* further westward, which run from north to south, offered the necessary physical conditions for larger settlements in the great Mesopotamian plain. Numerous mounds enclosing the remains of ancient cities dot this entire region and, doubtless, hold their treasures for the future pick and spade. The most important of all, and one that succeeded in maintaining a prosperous existence until late in history, was *Harran* on the upper Balikh. It was the northern seat of the cult of the moon-god: *Arban* and *Tel-Halaf* will be referred to under Assyria.

These are by no means all of the important cities of Babylonia. With the exception of the more arid portions of these regions it is scarcely possible for us to overestimate the numerous towns and villages which dotted the plains and hillsides. Babylonia, especially in its prosperous periods, like Egypt, tilled its soil more after the style of the gardener than that of the agriculturalist, and this form of husbandry supports a greater population and lends itself to concentration. The cities above named are those only which on account of their political and religious importance were prominent in the life of the nation. They are, moreover, in part, those in which the excavations have been conducted which have given us a knowledge of the land. Numberless other mounds hold the secrets of their forgotten past.

CHAPTER IV

THE BABYLONIAN KINGDOM

THE EARLIEST TIMES, CIR. 3000 B.C.

The Semitic Babylonians on entering the country took possession of it in the same way as history teaches us their kinsmen obtained their possessions in later times—the Chaldæans in Babylonia, the Hebrews in Canaan. They pressed forward into the open country, asserting themselves there in the face of a half-hearted opposition. Gradually the cities fell into their hands, and, therewith, they were masters of the land. Formerly wandering nomads they now became dwellers in cities. The old civilization they took over without reserve. Political changes of great importance followed of necessity. Formerly they were free nomads under the leadership of a sheikh, now they became *subjects* of a king. The leader knew better than his "brothers" whom he led how to use the institutions which he found at hand to his own advantage.

We must, consequently, assume the existence at first of a number of city-kingdoms corresponding to the old centres of culture, which had been founded long before our knowledge of them

begins. Each of the invading tribes took possession of one city or another for itself. As nomads,
the different tribes were natural enemies unless
there existed between them a blood-covenant.
Now again, the kings were scarcely in possession
of their new kingdoms before the old feeling of
hostility asserted itself among them. New wars
had to be waged. Here one emerged from the
fray of battle victorious, another fell, until at
length, and gradually, the numerous petty city-
states were fashioned into several larger kingdoms. This accomplished, the old *status quo* of
the Sumerian age, so far as relates to the cultural necessities of the land, was once more
regained.

It is natural to expect that the oldest monuments of the Semitic period will be found in the
inscriptions of the kings of the different large
cities who were at war with one another. This
expectation is confirmed by the latest discoveries.
Few as these inscriptions are, in proportion to
what remains to be unearthed, they are nevertheless quite sufficient to substantiate the correctness
of our inferences, from the natural order of development, as to conditions of life in the primitive
period.

The oldest inscriptions which have come down
to us are from the kings of *Lagash* in South
Babylonia, of *Ur, Uruk,* and *Kish* farther to the

north, and of the city whose name we are unable
to read,[1] all of which were engaged with one
another in a war of subjugation. All these are
to be assigned to a period before 3000 B.C., speaking generally from 3500 B.C. down to about 3000
B.C. During this time the wars of the Semitic
city-kings were fought. To enter into a detailed
narrative of their conflicts would be a thankless
task, and the recital of the unspeakable combina-
tion of signs which make up their heroes' names,
the correct pronunciation of which is still an
enigma, would convey no meaning to the non-
specialist. The outcome of these wars was
greater kingdoms. The king of the conquering
city became the sovereign of the conquered
princes, who thenceforth bear the title of *patesi*.
All these kings, especially those in the South, still
wrote in Sumerian; indeed, Sumerian continued
to be used much longer as the literary language
in South Babylonia than in North Babylonia—
almost a thousand years longer. We have numerous inscriptions from patesis of Lagash, that is,
from vassal princes of a ruling king. They belong
to the closing period of the fourth millenium B.C.,
and the last of them were contemporaries of the
South Babylonian "kings of *Sumer* and *Akkad*"
to be mentioned shortly.

Some of the earlier of these South Babylonian

[1] *Vid.* p. 23 and note.

patesis were subject to North Babylonian kings,
two of whom, *Shargani-shar-ali* (Sargon I.) and
his son *Naram-Sin*, we are acquainted with
through their own inscriptions. The first of these
still calls himself "King of Agade," a city in
North Babylonia. Thus it is seen that the South
was subjugated by the North. The inscriptions
which relate to his reign and that of Naram-Sin's
prove that these kings extended their conquests
over all Western Asia to an extent, at least, equal
to that to which they were carried at any time
under Babylonian influence. They ruled not only
Babylonia and Mesopotamia[1] but also Syria and
Palestine. Sargon is said to have embarked upon
the Mediterranean. He records that in an expedition which lasted for three years he conquered
regions beyond the sea. We do not know whether
he here refers only to Cyprus, but the conquest
would appear to have been more far-reaching
than that. One thing is certain, namely, that this
was no mere plundering exploit, but a lasting subjugation. He expressly states that he erected his
monuments of victory in the subjugated territories, and established an organized government
in tho land. Captives were taken thence to Baby-

[1] A monolith with an inscription of Naram Sin was discovered
at Diarbekr, near the headwaters of the Tigris to the N. E. of Mt.
Masius. Another was found in Susa, but, as the inscription of the
Elamite king, Sutruk-Nakhundi, which was carved upon it later,
states, it was found in *Sippar*.

lon. There Babylonian laws were imposed, and
thither Babylon's mandates were carried. Most
noteworthy of all, Babylonian governors and
officials sent their official reports to the king
couched in his own tongue. Two thousand years
before a word of Greek was heard in the Mid-
land Sea natives of its isles were familiar with
the cuneiform script and read the language of
Babylon. The traces of Babylonian influence
there in ancient times are not wanting.

That wars were waged with the barbarians of
the North lay in the very nature of the situation.
Arabia, Dilmun (in the Persian Gulf), Magan
(bordering on South Babylonia and the Persian
Gulf), Melukha (on northwest of Arabia) likewise were called to arms against the forces of
these kings. Thus, nothing short of a great Babylonian kingdom was founded, extending over the
greater part of Western Asia, vying in extent
with the dominions of Assyria in her most flourishing period. The names of Sargon and Naram-
Sin are, therefore, linked with an early golden
age in the history of Babylonian Semites. Their
Semitism is attested even by their inscriptions,
which in contrast to those of South Babylonia are
written in Semitic. Their date is about 3000 B.C.[1]

---

[1] The date usually assigned, on the basis of an inscription of
Nabuna'id (555 B.C.), to Naram-Sin is 3750 B.C. and to his father,
Sargon, cir. 3800 B.C. The arguments presented in favor of setting
aside Nabuna'id's statement are insufficient, and, to my mind,

Their contemporaries were *patesis* of Lagash. Conspicuous among them is Gudea, from whom several long inscriptions have come down to us. These bear witness, as do those of Sargon and his son, to the widespread rule of Babylonian power and civilization. In the accounts of his buildings, on which he dwells with pride, he tells us whence he procured the various materials for their construction. Cedars were brought from Mount Amanus, dolerite stone for his statues from Magan. This bears witness to the extension of peaceful intercourse at this period, and makes at the same time for the spread of Sumerian culture in the preceding days, when similar conditions existed. The ideas and political achievements of this and the preceding age continued to exert great influence down to the latest times, even when their origin was but little understood. When Nabuna'id, the last king of Babylon, found an inscription of Sargon's son, Naram-Sin, and appealed to the scholars of his court for information as to its age, they had not the historical data at hand to make a correct computation. They roughly ascribed it to 3200 years before his own time, or to *cir.* 3800 B.C., thereby exceeding its real age by 800 years or more. [The number is

plausible as they are, there is a strong preponderance of probability derived from other sources that Nabuna'id had adequate data for his reckoning.—*Craig.*

reached by a method of reckoning which prevailed
everywhere in antiquity; it is based upon astro-
logical cycles—40 x 80 years. Forty is the num-.
ber of the vernal constellation of the Pleiades, and
eighty is also a customary cycle, and was known
to Mohammed as *khuqub*. The *savants* of the
king doubtless intended by adopting this method
to appeal to his vanity. A reign that began a
new epoch was illustrious as introducing a new
world era; and so it happened, but not in the way
the court flatterers intended. Cyrus came and
with him a new epoch for the Orient.]

The more or less isolated facts known to us of
these times do not furnish sufficient material for
the framing of an adequate picture of them. It is,
moreover, a matter of minor interest, even in
connection with a more minute treatment of the
history of Western Asia, to follow in detail the
wars waged between these city-kingdoms and
their varying fortunes, now winning the prize of
victory, now bemoaning the fate of the vanquished.
As it was in Islam after the fall of the Caliphate,
and in Syria almost always when it was not under
the rule of a greater power, so it was here. We
have to do for the most part with kings of uncertain names whose deeds had significance only for
their own age. It is still impossible to bring the
majority of the events recorded in their inscrip-

tions into sure and satisfactory relation either chronologically or geographically. At present they are of importance only to the specialist.

Of more general interest is the question as to the general development of Babylonia, in view of these mutual hostilities. It is very plain that a state of strife was general at the time. So far as our present knowledge extends only Sargon and Naram-Sin ruled over a large West Asiatic Kingdom. How far the rule of the kings of Kish, Uruk, Lagash, etc., reached cannot in each case be determined. It is true that Ungal-zag-gi-si of Uruk records that he marched from the lower sea to the upper sea, that is, from the Persian Gulf to the Mediterranean.[1] We must, therefore,

---

[1] The location of the city *Az* would have an important bearing on our knowledge at this point if it were certainly known. E-anna-du, patesi of Lagash, narrates that he conquered Uruk, Ur, and Larsa. And immediately following (ll. 12–19) he adds that he destroyed the city of Az and killed its patesi, destroyed Milimme and exterminated Arua. The last two are unknown. Judging from the connection with Uruk, Ur, and Larsa we would naturally look for Az in Babylonia. The mention of a patesi as ruler of the city also points in that direction. It is to be noticed, however, that while these are only subjugated Az is destroyed, and, as a rule, this extreme measure was adopted only with cities that lay without the bounds of the kingdom. Especially important is Gudea's statement that he brought *shirgal* (*parutu*)-stone for mace-heads from Mt. Ur-in-gi "and (near?) uru-*az*-ki on the upper sea." The city must, therefore, have been on the Mediterranean coast. With this agrees what we know from Sennacherib that *shirgal*-stone was used for mace-heads before his time, and the mace-head of Gudea shows that the *shirgal*-stone was limestone from the Lebanon and Anti-Lebanon. This is further confirmed by the inscriptions of Tiglath-pileser III. The writing uru-Az-ki, or uru-ki-Az (brick of Eannadu 5, 4), likewise favors an extra-Babylonian location for this city.

conclude that these city-kings ruled at times over
large territories; at all events we are compelled
to think that this period did not belong to the
primitive age of civilization, or that Babylonian
cities and rulers then broke forth from their nar-
row boundaries for the first time. Even in these
days of hoary antiquity there emerge practically
the same conditions in this respect as existed
later during the wars of Babylonia with Assyria,
or at the time of the fall of the Caliphate.

A further question arises, *viz.*: to what body of
Semites do the kings of this time belong? Incessant change and internecine wars point to a period
of dissolution or disorder. The conditions are
such as must have marked the beginning of the
Canaanite immigration or the close of the period
during which the first Semites held the country.
The movements which we describe as immigrations are not completed at once and do not imply
the immediate subjugation of the old inhabitants
by the new intruders. The *fait accompli* is preceded by many attempts and reverses and often
by centuries of intermittent struggle. In civilized
lands the population is never, ethnologically
speaking, of unmixed stock. When, therefore, in
times of warfare we see first one city then another
victorious, the victors in this instance may belong
predominantly to one layer of the population, in
that to another. We must then conceive of it as

a transitional period, the period of the gradual
influx of the new Canaanite hordes in the face of
the determined opposition by the older Babylonians. In this connection we must bear in mind
that the character of the political régime of a
civilized state is dependent not upon its ethnic
affinities but upon its civilization. The Normans
who conquered England very soon—counting still
by centuries—became Englishmen. The ruling
houses of England and Russia are English and
Russian despite their German descent.

The transitional period which we are inclined
to assume for the earliest rulers was, consequently, strongly influenced by Canaanites. The
state of things which confronts us is much the
same as that which we shall meet again in Babylonia in consequence of the Chaldean immigration. It ended with victory for the Canaanites
and their subsequent spread over the whole land.
With the first dynasty of Babylon the victory is
complete; and also in the time of the later kings
of Ur. We must consequently regard Urgur and
Dungi, and their contemporaries, the last patesis
of Lagash, as ruling at a time when the Canaanite
was already in the land.

The transitional and unstable character of the
age is further attested by the noteworthy facts in
connection with the development of the arts.
The sculptures and writing of the first king of

Lagash, Ur-Nina, are in part so crude that we might imagine ourselves face to face with the beginnings of civilization. But the character of the script, nevertheless, proves that the first stages of development then belonged to a distant past. Soon after this monuments of much better workmanship appear. Eannadu, the grandson of Urnina, left behind him a monument, the so-called "Stele of Vultures," in which we note a great advance in the artist's work. The statues of Gudea manifest not only an aptness for technical work of the first order, but also an artistic comprehension on the part of the artist in all that is unconventional, which puts him in the same class with the brilliant artists of the old empire of Egypt. Futhermore, they show the development of a conventional idea in body-pose and arrangement of dress, which, with the execution of the work, presuppose centuries of patient study. Thus we are forced to conclude that the crudity of Urnina's art finds its explanation in a *temporal decline of culture* in Lagash as a natural result of conquest, or of other unknown causes.

Although it is at present impossible to assign Sargon and Naram-Sin to their proper chronological places, so much at least is certain they belonged to the same centuries as the patesis of Lagash. Their sculptures and inscriptions show the same delicacy of execution, though to some extent there is an individuality of style, and their writing has a particularly definite character which is the certain result of long use for monumental purposes. They both employ Semitic instead of Sumerian in their inscriptions in common with the North Babylonian kings of Kish, whose writing is likewise strikingly similar to theirs. As a general rule Sumerian was employed as the official language in inscriptions of South Babylonia, whereas in the North the Babylonian-Semitic prevailed. And this was the case not only in Babylonia itself but also in subject lands, and in those which had yielded to the spell of her civilization during the time of the North Babylonian rulers. A dedicatory offering, which probably came from Sippar, contains an inscription of a king of Gutium (Armenia south of Lake Van), which is written exactly like those of Naram-Sin. Another from a king of the Lulubi, in the Zagros, shows the same character.

The picture which, with the help of the material at our disposal, we have sketched of the most important events, and the chronological succession of the kings suggested, are presented with many *reservations* which admit the possibility of fundamental changes. It may not be amiss at this point to enter briefly into a few matters of detail.

We know, for example, from an inscription found at Nippur of a king who calls himself

"lord (?) of Kengi," that is, Sumer or South
Babylonia, "and . . ." The name of the city
which should follow is broken off. It is impossible to determine his date and no reasons exist for
placing him before those that follow. The inscription reads:

"To the God Bel, the lord of lands, *En-shag-
kush-an-na*, the lord (?) of Kengi, king of . . .
the spoil of Kish, the wicked of heart, presented."

The inscription relates to a victory over the
city of Kish, whose kings according to inscriptions
referred to below were rulers of Babylonia. *Man-
ishdu-shu*, the king of Kish, is known from a short
inscription and also from a lengthy one upon an
obelisk found in Susa. As it contains the record
of a land-survey of North Babylonian territory it
was doubtless brought to Susa from its original
site. The name of *Uru-ka-gina*, son of En-gil-sa,
patesi of Lagash, appears upon it. It is *possible*
to identify this ruler, the son of a patesi, with the
well-known Uru-ka-gina, *king* of Lagash. Me-
salim, a son of his, is also mentioned, and he may
be identified with great probability with the Mesa-
lim to whom *Ungal-kurum-zigum*, patesi of
Lagash, dedicated a mace-head.

Another king of Kish from whom we have
inscriptions is *Urumush*. He tells of victories
won over Elam and a border people known as the
Bara'se. And one named *Ur-zag-uddu* calls him-

self "king of Kish and king of . . ." He also consecrated an object of some kind to Bel of Nippur. Furthermore, a lance-head was found in Telloh, below the strata of Ur-nina, belonging to *Ungal-da* (?)-*ak* (?) king of Kish.

One or two other kings of Uruk are also known to us from the inscriptions of Nippur, who likewise can be assigned to this period only in a general way. The determination of their relation to one another or to those previously mentioned is not possible.

The one who left behind him the longest inscription is *Ungal-zag-gi-si*, "king of Uruk, king of the land, son of U-Kush, patesi of the city of the War Chariot." He lays claim to the old culture cities of Ur, Larsa, and the city of the War Chariot, and boasts of subjugating all lands from east to west and of having marched in triumph from the lower sea (the Persian Gulf) to the upper sea (the Mediterranean).

Two other kings, *Ungal-ki-gub-ni-du*, and *Ungal-si-kisal*, co-regent, and probably son of the former, claim sovereignty over Uruk and Ur.

CHAPTER V

FROM Lagash we have in addition to some older and as yet undeciphered inscriptions those of Ur-nina, the son of *Ni-gu-du,* king of Lagash. He was succeeded by his son *A-kur-gal,* who in turn was followed by his son *E-anna-du I.*

A very important stele of victory, the so-called stele of vultures, and several inscriptions of E-anna-du have been discovered. In these he calls himself as well as his father patesi. It appears, therefore, that after Ur-nina Lagash lost its independence. Once, however, E-anna-du calls both himself and his father king, and since he reports victories over other cities he must at times have regained his independence. He conquered the mountains of *Sumashtu.* That is, Mesopotamia and Syria, and also the North Babylonian city *Gish-gal,* the city of the War Chariot, Uruk, Ur, Larsa, Az, Susa (?) and others—in short, an entire kingdom. The king of Opis appears to have been his chief opponent, and he may originally have been his sovereign with both Opis and Kish under him. E-anna-du subdued Kish and

41

assumed sovereign title over it. Opis appears to have risen again to power after the defeat of its king.

E-anna-du was succeeded by his brother *En-anna-du,*[1] and a cone inscription of his son and successor, *En-temena,* affords us a glance at the conditions of the time and the relations existing between several of the rulers and states. It tells of a certain boundary dispute that had existed. Me-salim, the king of Kish, of whom we have previously spoken, had marked off by a stele the boundary line between Lagash and the city of the War Chariot. These cities were, therefore, neighbors, and also his vassals. *Ush,* the patesi of the city of the War Chariot, removed Me-salim's stele and made an attack on the territory of Lagash, but was vigorously attacked and driven back by Me-salim, who exercised over him sovereign authority. Under E-anna-du I., the uncle of En-temena, the delimitation of the boundary was again effected, by means of a canal, in co-operation with *En-a-kalli,*

[1] The genealogy is:

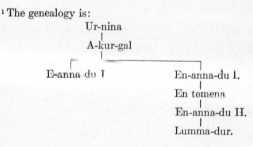

the patesi of the city of the War Chariot, and
Me-salim's boundary stone,[1] which had been
removed by Ush was restored to its place. Then
Ur-lumma, another patesi of the city of the War
Chariot, and probably the successor of En-a-kalli,
entered upon fresh hostilities against En-anna-du,
the brother and successor of E-anna-du, and
destroyed the boundary stones. The war appears
to have been waged at first chiefly by E-anna-du,
then by En-temena who came off victor, putting
Ur-lumma to rout and appointing *Ili,* a former
priest, as patesi in his stead in the city of the War
Chariot. En-temena's inscription then tells us, in
Col. IV., that he commanded Ili to construct certain canals and buildings and imposed upon him a
tribute of 36,000 *gur* of grain.

We see from this that Me-salim was king of
Kish and suzerain of Lagash (and the other cities
of Babylonia) prior, at least, to E-anna-du. And
since we know, from the "mace-head" inscription,[2] the name of the patesi of Lagash who was
subject to him we must, accordingly, assign him
a place before Ur-nina. Furthermore, we find
Lagash enjoying a more independent position and
defending its rights after the victories of E-anna-
du. It now appears as the suzerain of another
state which up to that time stood upon an equality

---

[1] Probably similar to that of Man-ishdu-shu, discovered in Susa
(p. 39).

[2] P. 39.

with itself. When, nevertheless, its patesi does not assume the title of king, it must on its part have recognized a higher *imperium*. It is possible, however, that this relation was now only a formal one, such as appears to have existed prior to Hammurabi between the kings of North and South Babylonia, and occasionally between the king of Egypt and his provincial princes.

En-temena was succeeded by his son, *En-anna-du II.*, and he in turn by his son, *Lumma-dur,* who is known to us from his own inscriptions. At this point the succession of the patesis of Lagash, so far as we know it, is interrupted. We are tempted to put next in the line of its rulers *Uru-ka-gina,* the *king* of Lagash. The general appearance of his inscriptions at least suggest this rather than priority to Ur-nina. But we are well aware that nothing is more certain than the inconclusiveness of arguments based upon such data. Uru-ka-gina takes at one time the title king of Lagash, at another king of *Girsu.* The site of Girsu is not yet determined; but it always stood in close connection with Lagash. The adoption of different titles proves, however, that the reign of Uru-ka-gina was not free from the usual civil strifes.

Within this chronological gap must fall also the reigns of *Saryon* and *Naram-Sin,* for they cannot be placed very much before *Ur-gur of Ur,* and the next series of patesis, as proved by documents, is immediately connected with them. We have seal impressions that were appended to dispatches sent by a patesi of Lagash to Sargon and Naram-Sin. This patesi, *Ungal-ushum-gal* by name, was "servant" to both, and his son *Ur-e* was in all probability his successor. Another patesi of Ur, *viz., Ur-utu,* appears as contemporary of Ur-e; thus the same relation of Ur to the North at this period is established. The next patesi of Lagash was *Ur-ba'u,* of whom we have a number of statues and inscriptions, which were found in Telloh (Lagash). *Nam-makh-ni,* who married Ur-ba'u's daughter, was also a patesi of Lagash, and doubtless Ur-ba'u's successor.

The next patesi known to us is *Gudea,* who cannot have been separated by a great space of time from Nam-makh-ni. He is the best known of the rulers of Lagash. We possess several of his statues, a large number of smaller monuments, two long inscriptions and numerous short ones. Lagash must have been a flourishing and wealthy city during his régime. His inscriptions tell of the buildings which he erected, for which he imported the material from all parts of the world known to him.[1]

Ur-ningirsu, Gudea's son, united to his patesiate the honors of priesthood. He exercised the functions of the latter office under *Dungi,* the son

[1] P. 34, note.

of Ur-gur of Ur. At this point, then, the chronological nexus between the princes of Lagash and
their overlords is again discovered. It would
appear that Ur-ningirsu first held the patesiate,
and that, for reasons unknown to us, he was
deposed from that office. Convicted or suspected
of inability to rule, he was not, however, deemed
unworthy of the priesthood. At all events his son,
Gal-ka-ni, possibly also his grandson, *Khala-lama,*
still held rule under Dungi as patesi of Lagash.
Khala-lama has left us a short inscription upon
a fragment of a statue which he dedicated to the
goddess *Bau* for the life of Dungi, which proves
that they were contemporaries. The title patesi,
however, is not clearly assumed in the inscription
by Khala-lama, though it is given to his father.[1]

The last of the patesis of Lagash known to us
from inscriptions, is *Ur-ningul,* who brings us
down to the time of the kings of "Ur and the
Four Quarters of the World."

During the last few pages we have diverged
somewhat from the main course of our story for
the purpose of introducing a few details as side-
lights upon the historical situation. Let us now
return to the larger movements of history. In

---

[1] The inscription reads: "To the mother of Lagash, the goddess
Bau, his mistress, for the (preservation of the) life of Dungi, the
powerful king, the king of Ur, the king of Shumer and Akkad, Khala-lama, the son of Gal-ka-ni, patesi of Lagash."—*Craig.*

learned circles and in political life the geographical names and political titles of these earliest times continued long in use, and even in the latest period were greatly in favor. The wars of the Semites, whether or not they were the continuation of Sumerian conditions, resulted in the formation of two great kingdoms in Babylonia. The one had its seat of empire in South Babylonia, and its kings bore the general title *"king of Shumer and Akkad."* The other was in North Babylonia, and its kings called themselves *"kings of the Four Quarters of the World."* Farther still to the north, with its chief city (possibly Harran) in Mesopotamia, another kingdom developed whose kings assumed the title *"kings of the World."* Between these three kingdoms wars were waged and frequently one king triumphed over the others. Thus we see here a further development of the period of the city-kingdoms. Only a few details of some of these rulers have come down to us. We know, however, that their titles maintained their significance down to the last days of Babylonian independence. All the later kings of Babylonia and Assyria, each according to his possessions, adopted them.

Within the sphere of Babylonian culture, at this time, stood Elam, Anzan, and Suri, now at war with her, now her subjects, as we can most plainly see from the testimony derived from the Assyrian period. Anzan, and Suri, from which came the later name Lyco-Syria, began on the west of Elam and stretched in a northerly course around the Mesopotamian plain, thus reaching virtually from Media to Cappadocia. To the northeast was the barbarous people known as the *Umman-Manda,* or Manda hordes, the Babylonian Scythians. On the north, practically corresponding to Armenia, lay Gutium, or the territory of the "Kuti," from one of whose kings we have an inscription in the Semitic language and in the style of the time of Naram-Sin. It relates to the dedication of an object set up in Bablyonia, probably in Sippar, and is similar to the dedications made by foreigners to the Greek oracle. In Asia Minor, beginning with Cappadocia, lay the region of the *Khatti,* or Hittites, who came to the front later. The northern part of Palestine was known soon after as the "West-land." The statements, already referred to, about Sargon, whether historical or not, prove that the Mediterranean was navigated. Arabia on its western side was known as *Melukha,* and on the eastern as *Magan,* and appears to have been more accessible to the ancient Babylonians than it was later to the Assyrians or to us of modern times. Southward, the Persian Gulf must also have been navigated, for Dilmun, the island Bahrein, came within the bounds of Babylonian interests, and monuments

with cuneiform inscriptions have been found
there. It is, moreover, scarcely conceivable that
Gudea brought the stone from *Magan* by any
other means or route than the sea. As Naram-
Sin's expeditions prove, Dilmun, Magnan, and
Melukha fell more within the Babylonian horizon
(as, indeed, they did in Islamic times) than they
did when Assyria was at the height of her power.

The numerous monuments of this period evince
technical skill of the highest order. The earliest
inscriptions and monuments of the kings of
Lagash are naturally very crude, so markedly so
that we are tempted to attribute lack of skill to a
decline consequent upon the Semitic invasion. But
there quickly followed a new stage comparable to
that of the Old Empire in Egypt. The inscriptions
of Sargon and Naram-Sin are distinguished by
a beautiful script, and so excellent is the technical
execution of Gudea's statues that archæologists
once thought it necessary to assume a Greek influence. A vast number of documents of this period
relating to the administration of temples and
lands have been recovered. They belonged originally to the Lagash archives.

Such was Babylonia in her sphere of influence
and cultural attainments 3000 B.C. and earlier.
Possibly at that time she reached the zenith of
her development. The age of the beginnings of
civilization, the age when the Sumerians stood

upon the level of the Italic peoples in the eighth century B.C., of the Slavs from the eighth to the twelfth century A.D., had then long passed away, leaving to history neither monument nor message.

CHAPTER VI

THE last inscriptions of the patesis of Lagash, who are known to us, and who were immediate successors of Gudea, contain dedications to new kings from whom we have numerous inscriptions from the cities of South and North Babylonia. These rulers call themselves "king of Ur, king of Sumer and Akkad." Their inscriptions, at least those from the southern cities, are, like those from Lagash, written in Sumerian. We have, in these facts, evidence of a complete change from the preceding time. The sceptre of sovereignty has passed from the north to the south. *The kings of Ur rule Babylonia* instead of the kings of Agade—inscriptions found in North Babylonia show that it, as well as the South, passed to their dominion.

This kingdom of *Sumer and Akkad* was ruled over by three dynasties. The first is known as the Dynasty of Ur, so-called in accordance with its title and seat of government. Chief among its kings were

UR-GUR AND HIS SON DUNGI

3000 B.C. Their numerous inscriptions contain only records of the building of temples in all the

51

important cities of Babylonia, in the South as well as in the North. As regards their political deeds and power they convey no direct information. It is nevertheless clear from the expulsion of the North Babylonian rulers that they came into possession of their territory. Dungi in one of his North Babylonian inscriptions written in Semitic calls himself "king of the Four Regions" as Naram-Sin does. Apart, therefore, from the internal revolution, the Babylonian domain of power and culture remained as it was before. Just as Dungi in North Babylonia had previously done so his successors call themselves in their inscriptions, found in the South, "kings of Ur, kings of the Four Regions," and omit the title "king of Sumer and Akkad." Their seat of government must consequently be looked for in the North. The political centre moved steadily toward the capitals of Sargon and Naram-Sin, and the South, with its adherence to Sumerian thought and modes of life, lost proportionately in importance. Even the names of this dynasty, and all the following ones, are purely Semitic in form. It would, therefore, appear that Dungi's successors, like Naram Sin, were North Babylonians, who resided in the South. About 2600 or 2500 the dynasty came to an end. The supremacy passed into the hands of less vigorous rulers whose capital lay farther to the North.

THE KINGS OF ISIN—2600–2500 (?)

The second ruling-house is called the dynasty
of Isin, after its capital. Its kings call themselves
"kings of Isin," "kings of Sumer and Akkad."
Here again we have evidence of another revolution. Even the *names* of the kings bear witness
to this fact. For, notwithstanding their use of
Sumerian in their inscriptions, in common with
their predecessors and successors, they departed
from the previously established custom in the
South of giving to their own names a Sumerian
form, it is evident at once that theirs are Semitic
like those of the northern kings, Naram-Sin and
others. The last of these kings was called Ishmé-
Dagan ("Dagan heard"). His complete title
was, "Ishmé-Dagan, the governor of Nippur, the
prince of Ur, the Uddadu of Eridu, lord of Uruk,
king of Isin, king of Sumer and Akkad, the
beloved spouse of the goddess Nana." It is clear
from this compound that the name of the deity
Dagan is "Canaanitic"; and we have even at
this early period Canaanites before us, a fact of
importance as we shall see when we come to
discuss the first dynasty of Babylon. Five kings
of this dynasty are known at present, ISHBIGIRRA,
GAMIL-NINIB, LIBIT-ANUNIT, BUR-SIN, ISHMÉ-DAGAN.
The close of the dynasty we may assign approximately to 2500–2400 B.C.

THE DYNASTY OF LARSA—2500-2400

The third and last series of the independent rulers of Southern Babylonia exercised sovereignty from Larsa, the capital, from which the dynasty derives its name. Three of its kings are known to us, *viz.*, NUR-RAMMAN, SIN-IDDIN, and RIM-SIN, who succeeded in turn to the throne. From the time of these and the preceding kings a great number of business documents have come down to us, and these, since they are dated according to important events, furnish us with much valuable information about the military movements and other significant undertakings of the times. But no royal inscriptions giving a historical résumé have been found. Instead of them we have only the usual building and dedicatory inscriptions. *Rim-Sin,* the last king of the dynasty, was an Elamite—not a Babylonian. He expressly states in his inscriptions that he was the son of the Elamite *Kudur-Mabuk,* who appears to have subjugated the entire domain of Babylonia as far as Phœnicia, and left his son upon the throne of Southern Babylonia as the last "king of Sumer and Akkad."

Elam was the most powerful opponent that Babylonia had, as is sufficiently apparent from the records of earlier times. At this time she must have descended with irresistible force, for the whole land of Babylonia and its dependent states became the vassals of Elam. When we bear this in mind, together with what has just been said of the probable *Canaanite* connection of the last dynasty, and with what we shall presently discover to have been the facts in connection with the first dynasty of Babylon, it will be evident that the rôle of the "Babylonian Semites" has come to an end. *The first post-Sumerian period* of Babylonian history has already passed, and we find ourselves in a time when new conditions are emerging into view. Other peoples are entering into the land, or are already there. The old wars are waged again, and once more there is no Babylonian kingdom. The powerful neighbor's star is, for a time, in the ascendant and a heavy hand is laid upon the old culture-land—conditions which in later times frequently reoccur.

CHAPTER VII

THE FIRST DYNASTY OF BABYLON—"CANAANITE"

With respect to the changes which occurred in the different dynasties previously described much remains uncertain and unknown. We are but imperfectly informed both as regards the exact time and the causes and conditions which produced them. In the period to which we now come the case is altered. The essential aspects of the change which followed these dynastic struggles emerge in the clear light of history. It was a change which culminated in new relations which were the natural outcome of the preceding wars.

At the same time that the Southern Babylonian kings of *Larsa* and some of their predecessors of the dynasty of *Isin*[1] held sway there ruled in Northern Babylonia, in Babylon, or by preference in *Sippar* (owing perhaps to its connection with Agade, the capital of Sargon I.), a succession of princes which, following the Babylonian king-lists we designate *The First Babylonian Dynasty.* After the time of Sargon and Naram-Sin, when

[1] The exact situation of *Isin* is not yet determined, but it evidently lay to the north of Erech.—*Craig.*

the North was predominant, as we have already
seen, kings of the South as early as the second
dynasty of Ur lay claim in their titles to sovereignty over the North. Numerous business documents have been recovered from this period, and
it is noteworthy that in them the rulers of Northern Babylonia are never called kings. It is not
until the later subjugation of the South that the
royal title is ascribed to them. The ready inference to be drawn is that the northern rulers exercised sovereignty as vassals of the kings of the
South. The Southern Babylonian kings of Isin,
similarly to the kings of the dynasty of Ur, and
contrary to Naram-Sin, took up their residence
again in the old capital of Sumer and Akkad, and
left the rule of the North to the independent man-
agement of their vassals in Babylon. That, at
least, was the *formal* state of affairs. It is, however, a very frequent occurrence in such relations
that the alleged sovereign is dependent upon his
vassals who possess the power, while the title
alone is his. And it is quite possible that there
existed between the "kings of Sumer and Akkad"
and their "vassals" in Northern Babylonia a
relation similar to that between the Caliphs of
Bagdad and the Buyids, or other Sultans. The
same relation existed under the kings of the
Larsa dynasty. The last of these kings, the Elamite, Rim-Sin, was overthrown by the fifth king of

this first Babylonian dynasty after the vassal relation had become weakened, doubtless long before, and at the time was virtually ineffective. With this change a new political era was ushered in. The independence of the South was destroyed for all time. Thereafter, the kings of Babylon rule the Southern Babylonian kingdom and bear the title "king of Sumer and Akkad," a title which no later ruler bore alone with the exception of a few late and unimportant cases in which there was a division of inheritance. The political significance of the South thus came to an end. As under Sargon and Naram-Sin, now it became a province of the North Babylonian kingdom. From now on the kingdom of Babylon was the determining power. It had previously, probably with the fall of the Isin dynasty, taken possession of the North Babylonian kingdom whose rulers called themselves "kings of the Four Quarters of the World." From this point on Babylonian history virtually becomes a history of Babylon.

But the house which transferred the rule to the city of Babylon, from which both the land and its culture were destined to be named as the result of this development of affairs, was not Semitic-Babylonian. It was *Canaanite.* The evidence is to be found in the names which compose it. These names, eleven in number, and the dates are procured from a Babylonian king-list, and are:

SUMU-ABI, *cir.*	2400–2375
SUMU-LA-ILU, *cir.*	2374–2353
ZABU, *cir.*	2352–2328
ABIL-SIN, *cir.*	2327–2303
SIN-MUBALLIT	2302–2268
KHAMMU-RABI	2267–2213
SAMSU-ILUNA	2212–2183
ABESHUA	2182–2165
AMMI-SATANA	2164–2151
AMMI-TSADOQ	2150–2116
SAMSU-SATANA	2115–2101

During the last ten years a great many documents belonging to the time of this dynasty have been recovered. From them we are afforded a glimpse into the economic life and ethnological connection of the ruling population of the time. The names of the kings, as we have already seen, prove that the great influx of people which had poured into the land was of Canaanite[1] origin. The conclusion is further corroborated by the numerous names which appear in these letters and contracts. The greater proportion of them are such as we meet with in the Old Testament. This great wave of immigration, which may have spread over a considerable period, broke upon the highlands of the West and one portion of it

---

[1] By the use of the term *Canaanite* it is not intended to suggest that the conquest was made by Canaanites, but only that the character and language of this body of immigrants was maintained in greater purity and for a longer time by that portion of the same stock which took contemporaneous possession of Canaan.

flowed into the rich alluvial lands of Babylonia.
There, in the meantime, had been a repetition of
the same events which had occurred during the
first immigration of the Semites. The advancing
nomads pressed into the cities from the surrounding plains; a ruling population different from that
formerly in possession now took its place, and
these new inhabitants, like their predecessors,
adopted the Babylonian culture and passed
through the same experiences. This is the light
in which we were inclined to view many of the
phenomena appearing during the last South Babylonian dynasty. This, then, is the *second* period
of Babylonian history, and at the same time the
end of the political domination of Western Asia
by Babylon. The same immigration reached
Syria and Palestine, and it is possible that a portion of it entered Egypt, a fact which would
account for the explanation of the Hyksos and
the powerful Semitic influence noticeable in
Egypt from that time forward. Babylon still
held at this time rule over the West. The tribes
and princes of Palestine were tributary to the
kings of Babylon. The territorial limits of power
remained unchanged and were preserved despite
the confusion of tribal movements. The interior
Orient was still Babylonian, and the conception
which we must form of the importance of Babylonia for the rest of Asia Minor at this time corre-

sponds essentially with that which we have presented of its influence a thousand years earlier.
The Orient in possession of the *"Canaanites"*
presented virtually the same aspects as the Orient
of *Semitic Babylonia:* it was completely under
the influence of Sumerian culture which was
now further modified by this second influx of
Semites.

The rule of this first dynasty of Babylon meant
a new era ethnologically and politically for Babylonia. The political organization effected by the
many wars through which the country passed,
and of which we have but a limited knowledge,
became normative for the future. North Babylonia with its central point, Babylon, the capital
of the new rulers, exercised upon the future of the
country an influence similar to, but much greater,
than Bagdad later wielded in Islam. From now
on the "kingdom of Babylon" is the province
Kar-duniash as it was later called, with *Babilu,*
the holy city of the god Marduk (Merodach),
the seat of authority in the Babylonian world of culture. In the history of the world Rome alone can
be compared with Babylon when we consider the
important rôle which this city of Marduk played
in Western Asia. As in the Middle Ages Rome
exercised its power over men's minds and, through
its teaching, dominated the world, so did Babylon
from this time in the ancient Orient. Just as the

German kings strove to gain for themselves world-sovereignty in papal Rome, as the heiress of world power, so shall we find later a similar claim by the kings of Assyria who look back to Babylon. The influence of this dynasty appears most conspicuously in the admiration in which it was held when Babylonian independence was hastening to its close. When after the fall of Nineveh Babylon again rose to political independence under Nebuchadrezzar, and, for the last time, appeared as mistress in Western Asia every exertion was put forth to represent the new kingdom as a rejuvenation of the ancient empire of Khammurabi. His was the golden age to which the latter looked back with reverence, and proudly judged itself to be a *Renaissance* of that splendid period. It was in Babylonia, as it was in later Judaism, which saw in the rule of David the zenith of Israel's glory. Even in the royal inscriptions the development of more than one and a half thousand years was ignored and, with the painful accuracy of pedantic schoolmasters, the royal scribes imitated the forms of the signs and characteristic orthography of Khammurabi's age.

But we must not be misled by the extension of Babylon and the Babylonian empire during this period. It would be a serious error to look for the culmination of Babylonian civilization during the rule of this dynasty. On the contrary, even the execution of the monuments furnishes evidence that we are dealing with an epoch of decline. The monumental art of Sargon and Gudea, figures so dimly visible through the haze of antiquity, exhibit achievements of classic excellence when placed by the side of the work of the artists of the first dynasty. Babylonian rule and intercourse were never so widely extended as then, and the general intellectual measure as well as the artistic products of this second epoch are markedly inferior. This second Semitic invasion of Babylonia resulted in deterioration in the highest elements and evidences of national progress, notwithstanding the material and political improvements made, especially during the reign of Khammurabi.

As it was in Italy with the descent of the *Germanen*, and in Western Asia with the intrusion of the Turks, so it was here. Babylonian history moves from now on along a descending plane. As long as the Semitic people dwelt there they enjoyed the fruits of previously won culture—they created nothing new, they rather corrupted what they found.

The regulation of commercial life at this time has been amply illustrated by the discovery of the Hammurabi code of laws in *Susa*, whither it was carried, like the stele of Naram-Sin,[1] by the same

[1] P. 30, note.

conqueror. It is the oldest code of laws known.
One may, therefore, be inclined to attribute to
Hammurabi and his age a lofty rôle in the historical development of the race, and they are
doubtless entitled to this recognition. But we
must, nevertheless, not forget that there previously existed a high culture and social development which must not be underestimated because
we know less concerning it. Fragments of laws
exist which antedate Hammurabi's age which
reveal an organized life not inferior in its cultural
development to that attested by his code. The
earlier period has the merit of initiative and
attainment, the later adopted and imitated and not
infrequently imitated badly.

One general characteristic of the social life of
that earlier time which distinguishes it from that
of the later is, perhaps, discoverable in the fact
that religion, and the organized forms of human
society dictated by it, were much more funda-
mentally effective, whereas from now on the
temporal power appears in the forefront. Hammurabi professes to have received his laws from
the hand of the god *Shamash,* but it is no longer
"divine law" that the code presents. It is clearly
the "law of the king" which assigns to the hierarchy, as to other classes of society, its appro-
priate position, according to it no recognition of
leadership. Babylonia at this time occupied a

position midway between the earlier state and the later one of military rule in Assyria, which arose partly upon the ruins of the old Babylonian civilization as Oriental cities arose upon the *tells* of ancient settlements.

CHAPTER VIII

In both the "king-lists" the first dynasty is succeeded by a second, called *the dynasty of Shishku,* likewise of eleven kings. Notwithstanding that numerous documents of the time of the first dynasty have come down to us very few have been recovered from the time of the second. This in itself is a sufficient indication that the same condition existed then as we shall be obliged to chronicle frequently in the history of Assyria. Periods of retrogression and impotence are generally shrouded in obscurity. Babylonia has now, in fact, entered upon a time when many and fruitless struggles are put forth to maintain herself as a World-Power. Her best efforts prove abortive. She is forced to retreat until, finally, every shred of political independence has been wrested from her; but, all the more clearly shines out her superiority in the works of civilization and science.

The names of the eleven kings of this second dynasty are known to us almost entirely from the king-lists. They are, for the most part, put into Babylonian form, or, rather, Sumerian and, consequently, appear almost as strange to us as those of the oldest kings of Ur. In reality, however, these new conquerors of Northern Babylonia had not hitherto been established in the South.

Inasmuch as the movement of civilization was always from the south northward the region at the mouth of the two rivers, and along the Persian Gulf, was naturally more open to migrations. We shall see that, at a later time, this territory was a sort of border-land of Babylonian civilization which was first seized by those who aimed at conquests in the north. The Babylonians called it *The Sea-Land*. Its position corresponded, at times, to that of ancient Sumer in so far as the latter had definite geographical and political boundaries. The cultural significance of the Sea-Land was not, however, co-extensive with that of Sumer.

It lay in the nature of things that a people resident here, and that was constantly adding to its strength by fresh accessions from Arabia, was ever upon the alert for the favorable opportunity of political weakness or disintegration in the North. The lust and perhaps necessity of expansion was there, and, at the opportune moment, the march up-stream began. The course of events is the same as was frequently witnessed in later times in the case of the Assyrians and Elamites; the same as so often exists where a powerful and

conquering state stands face to face with a rich
and powerless one.

Thus, it would seem, Babylon now fell under
the domination of a dynasty which ruled according to the king-lists 368 years. About 1000 years
later there ruled another dynasty of the Sea-Land,
the first of whose three kings, Simmash-shikhu, is
connected by descent with the former dynasty.

In the last millenium B.C., when Chaldean tribes
were in possession of large parts of Babylonia it
was the Sea-Land that formed the strongest of
their numerous "kingdoms." In the time of Sargon, king of Assyria, we shall find as his adver-
sary Merodach-baladan, the king of the Sea-Land,
who for a long time successfully disputed with
him the throne of Babylon. He calls himself the
offspring of Irba-Marduk, who, therefore, must
have reigned before him. Moreover, during the
reign of the following Kassite dynasty we know
of kings of the Sea-Land who bear Kassite names
and probably were related to the Babylonian royal
family. The name *Simmash-shikhu* (clearly Kassite) points to the same relationship. The existence of an independent state at the mouth of the
two rivers barred Babylonia from the Persian
Gulf, whereas in the time of Gudea her commerce
still found there an easy outlet to adjacent as well
as distant lands. The presence of this state and
its temporary rule over Babylon herself proves

that Babylonia has fallen from her former greatness.   Henceforth, it is an inland state whose
claim to importance rests upon the strength of
its ancient culture and historical traditions, not
upon its actual national power.   Thus weakened,
her boundaries were open to every ambitious
conqueror.

The names of the eleven kings and the few
facts known about them at present may be added
to this meagre sketch of the dynasty which ruled
from *cir.* 2100–1732:

AN-MA-ILU 51? years.
KI-AN-NI-BI 55? years.
DAM-KI-ILI-SHU[1] 30? years.
ISH-KI-BAL 15 years.
SHU-USH-SHI-AKHI 27 years.
GUL-KI-SHAR[2] 55 years.
KIR-GAL-DARA-BAR 50 years.
AI (Malik)-DARA-KALAMAMA 28 years, son of preceding.
E-KUR-UL-ANNA 26 years.
MELAM-KURKURA 6 years.
EA-GAMIL 9 years.

[1] This name is met with also outside of the king-lists in the
date of a contract-tablet, and in a fragment of an inscription of the
Kassite period where the king appears in a rôle that would suggest
that it was he who actually established the rule of this dynasty.
And Simmash-shikhu is said to have been a descendant of his.

[2] So the name appears in the lists.   According to an inscription
of the time of the *Pashe* dynasty he reigned as king of the Sea-Land
696 years before Nebuchadrezzar I.   The name is there written with
an old sign Gir (instead of Gul) which apparently was sometimes
written in a complicated way by the ancient scribes.

The sum of the regal years amounts to 368.
In the lists the dynasty is called the dynasty of
Shish-ku in opposition to the first which is called
the dynasty of *Tintir* (Babylon).   Shish-ku appears also to have been a name of Babylon which
may have been introduced intentionally by this
dynasty in reference to the cult of the capital.

CHAPTER IX

THE THIRD DYNASTY OF BABYLON—THE KASSITES
CIR. 1700–1130

THE third ruling house was also a foreign one, and, unlike the preceding, issued from the East, from Elam-Media. Kassite soldiers were found in the service of Babylonia during the first dynasty, and the people whose kings were now to occupy the throne of Babylon for the next five centuries called themselves *Kashshu* (Kassites). Their descendants still existed in the high ranges of the Zagros in the time of Sennacherib. They had several strongly fortified cities and numerous smaller ones, all of which fell before the army of Sennacherib on his second expedition. Their appearance in Babylonia at this time must have resulted from a great movement which, starting from the east and northeast, overran the civilized countries as they went, as the Turks and Mongols did in later times. Of that portion of this stock which flowed into Babylonia we have but a limited knowledge. For the relations which were established between them and Media and other countries we must await further discoveries. At all events, the influx of these barbarous hordes was of no inconsiderable proportions. From now on we meet frequently in Babylonia with Kassite names even among families of aristocratic birth. To the mixture of races in Babylonia a new element was, therefore, introduced, and in the "confusion of tongues" of Babel there resounded the well-known Kassite vocables with which we have become acquainted through the word-lists and proper names. The Babylonian dynastic tablet ascribes to this dynasty 36 kings with a rule of 546 years. It lasted accordingly from about 1700 to 1130. The names of the majority of these kings have been preserved, and we have a considerable amount of information from royal inscriptions, and other documents, relating to the events of this period. But great gaps in the story remain.

We are afforded a glimpse into the development of affairs during the early years of the dynasty by an inscription of

AGU-KAKRIME

who, it seems almost certain, was the sixth in succession. He calls himself "king of Kashshu and Akkad, king of the great land of Babylon who settled with numerous people the land of Dupli-ash[1] (on the border of Elam), king of Padan and Alman (bordering on Media), king of Gutî

---

[1] Commonly read *Umliash*. The ideographic writing is Ab-nun-na-ki, *i.e.*, large abode. In the inscription V. R. 33 col. 1, l. 36 the text reads mât *Ash*-nun-na-ak.—*Craig*.

(Northlands?), the king who rules the four quarters of the world." These titles which differ entirely from the customary ones, and the precedence given to the Kassites, show that this king was one of the earliest of the new rulers. Karaindash, who reigned a couple of centuries later, adopts the usual titles and closes the list with "king of Kashshu," and his successors omit it altogether. These barbarians, like the rest, soon adopted the old civilization, and became Babylonians.

That the weakened condition of Babylonia must have preceded the conquest may be assumed as certain. The kingdom of Khammurabi must, therefore, have gone the way of its predecessors before the barbarian hordes could enter in and possess the land. Its strength must have been broken; disturbances must have arisen and decay followed. We have testimony to this effect in the inscription of Agu-kakrime, already mentioned. There we learn that Agu-kakrime brought back to Babylon the statues of Marduk, and his spouse Tsarpanit, from the land of Khani. A couple of centuries later a region in Western Media, on the confines of Assyria, bore this name.[1] Changes in geographical boundaries and names of countries were wont to be made quickly at this

---

[1] We have an inscription of a king, Tukulti-mar, which cannot be definitely assigned to the land of Khani, but is of a late period, with a dedication to the sun-god of Sippar.

time. The country of *Mitani* was also known as Khanigalbat, the last part of which is probably to be referred to the so-called Hittite language, of which nothing is known as yet.[1] Since we see in the conquest of Mesopotamia by the Mitani the result of a forward movement of the "Hittites" it is natural to connect these two names of countries and regard them as the designations respectively of the eastern and western parts of one temporary state (Khani) whose existence explains the later kingdom of Mitani. We have, therefore, here, as we have in the union of Anzan and Suri in old Babylonian geography, a precursor of the later Median kingdom. We are possibly justified in connecting with this view of the case the fragment of an oracle-text according to which Marduk was captive in the land of *Khatti* (the Hittites) for twenty-four or thirty-four years. And, as Khani-galbat belonged to Khatti, the latter must, at that time, have reached to Western Media and there included the region

[1] Many attempts have been made to decipher the few so-called "Hittite" ideograph-inscriptions, but neither the methods nor the results justify the claims to success made by the decipherers. The most exhaustive and, in some parts only, seemingly plausible, of these efforts is that of Professor Jensen in Z. D. M. G. The Hittite language is now known, since Winckler's explorations and excavations at Boghaz-köi, the Hittite capital, in 1906, to have been written in cuneiform and syllabic. Some 2500 fragments of tablets, among which are a score of lengthy and complete tablets, have been found. If the ideograph-inscriptions are also "Hittite" the key to their decipherment may now be found.—*Craig*.

known as *Arbach.* This view of the situation
would enable us to see clearly how the two great
streams of migration, the one, the Hittite, moving
from the west, the other, the Kassite, coming
from the east, cease, modify each other, and at
the same time by their counter effects influence
the old civilization. The case of the Chaldees and
Medes from the eighth century to the sixth was
similar to that described.

This weakness of Babylonia and the complete
assimilation of the "Canaanite" population appear more clearly in two other phenomena of
this time. The third Semitic immigration, the
Aramaic, occurred during this Kassite period,
approximately from 1700–1100, and, further,
Babylonia's supremacy over the West was contested, and, finally, wrested from her hands by
Assyria, a new power ambitious of conquest, which
was rapidly developing from a city-kingdom.
The future was reserved for these two. The Kassites, the previous rulers of Babylonia, shared
the fate of that empire and must now relinquish
their power. As the march of empire was at first
from the south toward Babylon, so now it moves
further, along the Tigris, to Assyria. This fact
constitutes the pivotal point around which the history of Western Asia turns, from about the sixteenth century, when Assyria appears as the
rising power upon the field of history.

During the Kassite dynasty the struggle began between Babylonia and Assyria for supremacy over the old cradle of civilization. The varying changes of fortune which accompanied this struggle we can follow, thanks to the ever increasing sources at command, more clearly than we could the events of the earlier period. This war between the old and the new kingdoms and its result is of paramount importance in the political history of the future. The history of Babylonia and that of Assyria concern us, therefore, primarily, in so far as they touch and are interwoven with one another. That which we have to consider is two different developments running parallel to one another which can be pursued most easily when presented together. On the other hand, Babylon asserted her independence as a state almost continuously, long after she had fallen from power, and, even at the last, rose again victorious. Moreover, at the beginning of this struggle she was the superior power, and when she stood directly under Assyrian influence she never ceased to have a history and development of her own. If we wish, therefore, to do more than recount the wars between Ashur and Babylon, if, indeed, we wish to do justice to the importance of Babylon as the seat of the old culture, so frankly recognized by Assyria herself, we must follow the history of this independent state by itself.

We have already seen to what territory Agu-kakrime, the Babylonian ruler, laid claim. His power extended no longer over Mesopotamia and the West. The reasons for this we shall see when we come to treat of the development of these regions. In the next inscription known to us after Agu-kakrime's, *viz.*, that of

KARAINDASH I.,

sovereignty is asserted likewise only over Babylonia. We shall see that the first attempts to bring Mesopotamia again under the sceptre were made when Assyria, the ruling power there, was forced to retreat. In Palestine Babylonian rule gave way to Egyptian. It would appear from the manner in which Karaindash's successors speak of him in their letters that he was the head of a new family in the Kassite dynasty. His date was about 1500. That which we know of him, apart from his inscription already mentioned,[1] is that he formed a treaty with *Ashur-bel-nisheshu,* the king of Assyria, and carried on a correspondence with the king of Egypt. This last fact is attested by a letter which one of his successors,

[1] This inscription is preserved upon a brick and is published iv., R. 36, 3, and in K.B. iii., s. 153. It reads: " For the goddess, Nana, the mistress of E-anna (house of heaven) Karaindash, the mighty king, king of Babylon, king of Sumer and Akkad, king of Kash-shû, king of Karduniash, built a temple *in* E-anna" (probably temple area in city of Erech or Ur). Otherwise he can mean only that he restored the old temple.—*Craig.*

Burnaburiash, sent about sixty years later to the
king of Egypt, Amenophis IV. The discovery
of the collection of tablets to which this letter
belongs is one of the most surprising and important that has been made in the Orient. To tell
the story is at the same time to write of history.
In 1887 there were found in Tell-Amarna, the
site of the ancient capital of Amenophis IV., in
Middle Egypt, about 180 miles from Memphis on
the east bank of the Nile, more than three hundred
cuneiform tablets and fragments of tablets. They
are a remnant of the national archives of Egypt
and consist chiefly of letters which were sent to
the kings of Egypt, Amenophis III., and his successor Amenophis IV., by kings of Western Asia
and by the Syrian and Palestinian vassal-princes
of Egypt. Among them are letters from the kings
of Babylon, Assyria, Mitani, which lay to the
north of the Euphrates between the Balikh tributary and its western boundary; from the kings of
the Hittites and others. These letters constitute
the most valuable documents we possess for the
history of Western Asia during this period, and
frequent reference to them will be made in what
follows. The letters from Babylon, with which
we are at present interested, say nothing of her
greatness and power. Nevertheless, the existence
of the whole collection speaks in unmistakable
language of the controlling influence of Babylon

in earlier times—it is written in the cuneiform script, and with three exceptions in the Semitic-Babylonian language. And, what is of still greater significance, two of the letters from the king of Egypt, one addressed to the king of Babylon, the other to one of his own vassals in Northern Palestine, are in the same script and language. *The cuneiform script and the Babylonian language were at that time the literary means of communication throughout Western Asia. And a knowledge of the language implied a study of the literature.* This is abundantly proven by the discovery among the tablets of a couple inscribed with a Babylonian myth, which was written in Babylon, and apparently used as a text-book in Egypt.

The two kings, eleven of whose letters sent to the Egyptian kings have been recovered, were

KA-DASHMAN-BEL AND BURNABURIASH.

The former corresponded with Amenophis III., the latter with his successor, Amenophis IV. It is possible that they were brothers and that the younger overthrew the elder. The letters give no information of great national occurrences. They relate chiefly to marriages between the royal houses.

The Pharaohs have taken Babylonian princesses to their harem, but to their Babylonian friends they are not so generous with their own daughters—princesses, at least, could not be given to Babylonians. It would require the pen of a Mark Twain to deal adequately with one point that bulks large in these letters, *viz.*, the presents. The Babylonian king, like other kings, evinces in his persistent demands upon the Pharaoh all the characteristics of the *baksheesh*-begging Oriental. That which he sends is always declared to be trivial—the gold that he gets is tested in the purifying fires of the crucible and found wanting, and more and better is demanded.

From the historical point of view the relation of these two old centres of civilization to one another disclosed by the letters is more important. Babylonia (and even Mitani) sends as presents such products of her industry as artificially wrought lapis lazuli, so highly favored in Babylon. Egypt, on the contrary, sends gold. It seems almost as if diplomatic dealings were intrusted to oral explanation and argument and the astuteness of well bribed court officials, for political questions are rarely touched upon. Letters reflect the life of a people. Even kings engaged in trade, and, it seems, were exempt from customary taxation. Business men from Babylon, who were in the king's service, appear in Akko, where, apparently, they are about to embark for Egypt, when suddenly they are arrested and maltreated for reasons unknown.

The Babylonian king demands of Pharaoh the immediate release of the men and indemnification as well, since Akko lies within the latter's territory. In only one instance does a political dispute arise. At the expense of Babylon plans for territorial expansion had been formed by the Assyrian king, Ashur-uballit, and these were recognized at the Egyptian court of Amenophis III. and support promised. Burnaburiash protested against this procedure on the ground that Assyria was a vassal state under him and, therefore, could not be treated with independently. He pointed to the conduct of his father, Kurigalzu, who, when he had been urged by Canaanite subjects of Egypt to join them in an uprising against her, had promptly declined to participate in the plot. But in Egypt too much confidence was not placed in the ardent friend of Egyptian gold, and his assurances of loyalty can scarcely have been accepted with unquestioning faith. When the Phœnician princes wished in their rivalry to discredit one another at the Egyptian court they were wont to raise the cry of treason, and to declare that their rivals were intriguing with the king of Mitani, of the Hittites, or of Kash, *i.e.*, the Kassites of Babylon. The situation referred to in the case of Kurigalzu is exactly the same as we meet with again in the time of Sargon and Merodach-baladan II. The Canaanites asked the support of the Babylonians against Egypt, and urged them to unite with them in their designs against her. On the other hand, Merodach-baladan sent his ambassadors to Hezekiah[1] to induce him to join forces against Assyria. Later Taharka and Sennacherib, Nebuchadrezzar and Necho (and in 587 Hophra) constituted the support and hope of the Canaanite states.

As a matter of fact we have evidence that shortly afterward, when the death of Amenophis was followed by disturbances in Egypt, Babylonia attempted to regain the West. Despite the anxiety manifested in the letter of Burnaburiash to Amenophis IV. over the territorial seizures of Assyria, and the fact that he waged wars with her, he married his son Karaindash II.[2] to the daughter of the energetic Assyrian king, Ashur-uballit. Her son

KADASHMAN-KHARBE

succeeded to the throne, a fact which shows the influence of Assyria. It was under him that Babylonia sought to regain a firm foothold in the West. At this time Assyria had a strong grasp of Meso-

---

[1] 2 Ki. 20, 12; Isa. 39.

[2] This was doubtless the name of the father of Kadashman-kharbe. He is once called in the synchronistic history Kara-*khar*-dash, the scribe having misread his original, which, as this proves, was written the same as that of Chronicle P which also has *in* not *khar*. The two signs are very similar in this document, and in another passage the same sign was read *in*.

potamia and this compelled Babylonia to send
her army straight *through the Syrian desert.*
Kadashman-Kharbe sought to make the desert
road secure by chastising the nomad tribes which
roamed there and which were called the *Suti.* He
made wells, and also erected military posts and
settlements and filled them with Babylonians. He
thus established a highway of communication with
the West and made the circuitous route through
Mesopotamia unnecessary. This scion of the
Assyrian house was apparently a determined
opponent of Assyria such as later was never lacking. It is possible that his plans were based upon
what previously existed. At all events, he recognized that the wisest course was to satisfy his
threatening rival with territory still to be conquered and, in the meantime, to deprive it of value
by diverting from it the trade so important for
Babylonia. Therein lay the solution of the disputed question of the time as to who should
possess Mesopotamia. Kadashman-Kharbe might
have come to a peaceful understanding with
Assyria about the determination of the territory
which affected both their interests if his plans
had succeeded, and thus have proved his ability
to strengthen his power by mightier weapons than
those of war, especially where industrial Babylonia was face to face with the military power,
Assyria.

SHUZIGASH

Kadashman-Kharbe cannot have reigned long. He was murdered in an insurrection excited by the Kassites, but we are not informed what was the immediate motive of the act. At bottom it was possibly due to the fact that the kings and the ruling classes of the Kassites had, in the meanwhile (after 1400), become Babylonians in all essential respects. The Kassites who at the distribution of spoil came off empty-handed, or who had lost their share through the accidents of business or industrial life, formed a party of malcontents who longed for the old times when the Kassite was lord and the Babylonian was plundered. We find, at least, that the insurrectionists raised a man of common origin to the throne, who is called in the two chronicles *Shuzigash* and *Nazibugash,* "the son of nobody." To Ashuruballit, the grandfather of Kadashman-Kharbe, who was still active on the throne of Assyria, this was a welcome incentive to secure the upper hand by the extension of his kingdom. As the avenger of his grandson and the restorer of order he appeared in Babylon, quelled the insurrection, and placed his great-grandson,

KURIGALZU,

while still in his minority, upon the throne.

But the might of circumstance is stronger than

the bonds of relationship and good deeds of doubtful intention. As long as Ashur-uballit lived, and during the reign of his son, Assyria continued to struggle for possession of Mesopotamia. But when Adad-nirari I. drove out thence the Mitani, and long after Kadashman-Kharbe's undertakings had proved abortive, Babylon saw her opportunity again to gain Mesopotamia and thus insure her connection with the West. As Assyria was now in possession of it war broke out between her and Babylon. The clash of arms between the two states began in the reigns of Kurigalzu and Adad-nirari I.

We have an interesting bit of information of a war waged by the Babylonian, Kurigalzu, against Khurbatila, the king of Elam, in which he worsted and took prisoner the latter on Babylonian soil. Elam was, therefore, the invader. Kurigalzu must have followed up his victory. On the reverse of an inscription dedicated, by a subject of Dungi of the ancient dynasty of Ur, to the goddess Nana of Erech appears a dedication of Kurigalzu's as follows: "Kurigalzu, king of Karduniash,[1] captured the palace of the city of Shasha[2] in Elam, and presented this tablet to Belit (the god of Nippur) for his life." This tablet was, accordingly, carried off at some time from Erech by Elamites, and now on this victorious expedition

---

[1] Kassite name of Babylon.   [2] i.e., Susa? or Shushan.

of Kurigalzu's against Elam, found again in a temple,[1] more than 1200 years after it was dedicated in Erech. Then it was rediscovered a few years ago by the American expedition, and brought to Constantinople. Books are not the only things that have their fate!

These wars prove that the conditions already exist which are always apparent in the future; Babylonia is the prize coveted by both Assyria and Elam. For the present she is able to cope with both, and, if at times worsted, at others she proves superior. The contest is waged through the following centuries to the fall of Assyria. In later times Babylonia was a vassal state of the one or the other.

Even at this time the same shifting of national fortune can be traced. Soon after Kurigalzu, as we shall see in the history of Assyria, Babylonia and Babylon fell into the hands of Tukulti-Ninib, king of Assyria. Not long before, during the year and a half that

NADIN-SHUM

reigned, Kidin-Khutrutash, king of Elam, invaded Babylonia and laid waste Dur-ilu, the Babylonian city situated on the western terminus of the highway from Elam. He then conquered Nippur, which was especially favored by the Kassite

---

[1] If the Elamite temple was in Susa it was doubtless the temple of the goddess Shushinak mentioned by Ashurbanipal.

kings, and where, doubtless, at times they chose to reside. A similar expedition was undertaken by the Elamite during the reign of the second successor of the Babylonian king,

ADAD-SHUM-IDDIN,

who was enthroned by Tukulti-Ninib. This time it was Isin that suffered. Many an elegiac verse mourns in the tone of the penitential psalms the devastation of the land and especially of certain cities. In the centuries of Babylonian history the same thing, it is true, frequently occurred. But these songs of lament suit this period admirably, and if they did not originate then they are revisions of older ones which now resounded in the temples of Babylon. The remaining kings of the dynasty ruled for the most part under the protection of Elam.

It is clear that we have again come to the end of a period. The Kassites have long ago become Babylonians and now have played their rôle on the stage of history—the Kassite dynasty draws to a close. There remain only four kings, and

MARDUK-APLU-IDDIN,

Merodach-baladan I., was the only one of these who appears to have successfully opposed Assyria and asserted himself over Mesopotamia. The change of the dynasties indicates, as always, a time of tumult and weakness, and brings to the throne a royal line whose work it is to withstand Assyria and renew the struggle for Mesopotamia.

The American expedition at Nippur has proved that this city of "the Lord of Lands," *Bel-Mâtâte,* was especially favored by the Kassites. This may have been due to some similarity that existed between their national cult and that of Nippur. They had a strong predilection for names compounded with *buriash,*[1] that is, *Bel-Mâtâte.* On the other hand, we may, perhaps, discern therein efforts intended to counteract the preponderating influence of Babylonia which had been greatly strengthened by the dynasty of Khammurabi. It was necessary for it to overcome Nippur since it rose to power over the dynasties of Isin and Larsa. But the "kings of Isin" also appear to have attributed the same importance to Nippur as the Kassites.

The thirty-six Kassite kings, so far as they can be determined at present, and the most important events of their time are the following:

GANDISH. His name appears also as Gaddash, and Gande, on a fragment and votive tablet, reigned 16 years.

AGUM-SHI (an abbreviated name), his son, reigned 22 years.

GU-YASHI (otherwise read Bibe-yashi) reigned 22 years.

---

[1] *e.g.,* Burna-buriash, "servant of the Lord of Lands"; Nimgirall-buriash, "a Saviour is the Lord of Lands"; Ulam-buriash, "sprout of the Lord of Lands"; Kadashman-buriash, "my protection is the Lord of Lands"; Nazi-buriash, "shadow of the Lord of Lands."

USHSHI [otherwise read Dushi, Abu (ad) shi] reigned 8 (?) years.

ADU-METASH reigned — years.

TASHI-GURUMASH reigned — years.

AGUM-KAKRIME, successor of preceding (p. 72), reigned — years.

. . . lacuna.

KARAINDASH I., belongs to a new family(?); the beginning of relations with Egypt; alliance with Assyria, reigned — years.

. . . lacuna, one or more kings, reigned — years.

BURNA-BURIASH I., contemporary of *Amenophis III.*, compact with Puzur-Ashur of Assyria relative to certain territory, reigned — years.

KURIGALZU I., relations with Egypt under *Amenophis III.*, and with Assyria under *Ashur-nadin-akhi*, reigned — years.

KADASHMAN-BEL, brother of preceding; correspondence with Amenophis III., with whose death the end of his reign practically synchronizes. There is extant a copy of an inscription of his that was made by the scribes of Ashurbanipal's library, which contains the dedication of a wagon to Bel of Nippur, reigned — years.

BURNA-BURIASH II., son of Kurigalzu I.; he wrested the throne from his predecessor, maintained a friendly correspondence with *Amenophis IV.* Four of these letters are now in the British Museum, and two in Berlin. *Ashur - nadin - akhi*, contemporary king of Assyria, extends his dominions, reigned — years.

KARA-INDASH II., son of Burna-buriash II., married Muballitat-sherua, the daughter of *Ashur-muballit*. *Bel-nirari* and *Pudu-ilu*, probably ruling in Assyria, reigned — years.

KADASHMAN-KHARBE I., the son of Karaindash II., and Muballitat-sherua, attempts to establish communication with the West by repressing the Suti and opening the way through the Syrian desert inasmuch as Mesopotamia is in the hands of the Mitani. In a rebellion, probably incited by Kassite distrust of Assyrian influence, he was murdered. Reigned — years.

SHUZIGASH, or Nazibugash, was placed on the throne by the rebels; deposed and killed by Ashuruballit. Reigned — years.

KURIGALZU II., son of Kadashman-Kharbe, who was yet a child, was appointed in his stead by his great-grandfather, *Ashur-uballit*. Appears to have had a long reign. War with Khurbatila of Elam; *Bel-nirari, Pudu-ilu, Adad-nirari I.*, his contemporaries in Assyria. Reigned —[1] years.

NAZI-MARUTTASH, son of the preceding. War with *Adad-nirari I.*, over territory on the east of the Tigris; defeated by Adad-nirari. Reigned 26 years.

KADASHMAN-TURGU; *Adad-nirari I.* rules in Assyria, and now after expelling the Mitani from Mesopotamia and causing the retreat of Babylonia, he takes possession. *Shalmaneser I.*, a contemporary. Reigned 17 years.

KADASHMAN-BURIASH waged war with *Shalmaneser I.*, chiefly over Mesopotamia. Reigned 2 years.

KUDUR-BEL reigned 6 years.

SHAGARAKTI-SHURIASH, contemporary of *Shalmaneser I.* Reigned 13 years.

---

[1] In Winckler's *Untersuchungen zur Alt-orientalische Geschichte*, s. 146, where the king-list "b" is published in the original, the number 22 is plainly written before the *lacuna* where the name of Kurigalzu II. should appear.—*Craig.*

BITILIASHU,[1] son of Shagarakti-Shuriash, succeeded. About this time *Tukulti-Ninib*, King of Assyria, invaded Babylonia and conquered Babylon. Reigned 8 years.

BEL-NADIN-SHUM I.[2] During his reign *Kidin-Khutrutash*, the King of Elam, invaded Babylonia, took the cities of Nippur and Dur-ilu, wasted the land, and deported many of the inhabitants. Reigned 1 year, 6 months.

KADASHMAN-KHARBE II. In his reign Babylon was in turn conquered by the Assyrian King, *Tukulti-Ninib*, under whose supremacy Kadashman-Kharbe continued to rule. Reigned 1 year, 6 months.

ADAD-SHUM-IDDIN. In the early part of his reign he was apparently deposed by the Elamite king, *Kidin-Khutrutash*, and after he had succeeded in regaining the throne, probably with the aid of Assyria, the Elamites again overran the country. Isin was spoiled and Nippur, Babylon, and other cities plundered. The hymns of the time lament the desolation wrought. About the same time the Assyrian power was overthrown by a rebellion in Babylonia, and *Tukulti-Ninib* lost his life in an insurrection in Assyria under the leadership of his son. Thus the two reigns ended contemporaneously. Reigned 6 years.

ADAD-SHUM-UTSUR ascended the throne and reigned 30 years.

---

[1] In the "king-list" the name is abbreviated to *Bitil*, or Bibe, as others, who read the full name Bibeyashu, would transliterate it.—*Craig.*

[2] Or Bel-shum-iddin. The object more commonly stands before the verb.—*Craig.*

MELISHIKHU.[1]   This was a time of weakness and unrest in
Assyria which was followed by fresh attacks by Babylonia.   Reigned 15 years.

MERODACH-BALADAN I. took Mesopotamia; *Ninib-apal-
Ekur* and *Ashurdan* ruled in Assyria.   Reigned 13
years.

ZAMAMA-SHUM-IDDIN.   *Ashurdan* invaded Babylonia and
plundered three of its cities.   Elamites attack Babylonia and Bel-nadin-shum was dethroned.   *Kudur-
nakhundi* the son of the king[2] of Elam was placed on
the throne and wasted Babylonia.   Reigned 1 year.

BEL-NADIN-AKHE.   Babylon subject to the over-lordship
of Elam.   Later there appears to have arisen a conflict
with Elam.   Bel-nadin-akhe was apparently forced to
turn to Assyria, but failed to receive the necessary
support.   Contemporary of *Ashurdan*.   Reigned 3
years.

According to a summary item in one of the king-
lists this Kassite dynasty had 36 kings and lasted
five hundred and seventy-six years and nine
months from *cir.* 1700 to 1130.

[1] Kassite compound=Arad-Marduk "servant of the god Marduk"
in Babylonian.— *Craig.*

[2] His name is not given.   If it was not *Kidin-Khutrutash* it must
have been *Shutur-nakhunde* from whom, and his son, *Kutur-nakhunde*,
we have inscriptions from Elam.   It is possible that it was the
Elamite who ruled after the dynasty of Bazi (p. 98) and who is
said in chronicle S to have been a descendant (*lip-pal-pal*) of *Shutur-
(nakhunde).*

CHAPTER X

THE following dynasty is called in the king-lists the *dynasty of Pashe,* the name of a quarter of Babylon. Nebuchadrezzar I., the prosperous king of this dynasty, expressly speaks of himself as the offspring of Babylon. It is, therefore, clear that this line of kings lays claim to national origin. It consisted of 11 kings who held the throne of Babylon for 132 years. The conditions which brought the new house into power, as we may gather from the picture of the times, so far as they are at present discernible, are what we had reason to expect. As at the end of the Kassite dominion, the conflicts with Elam and Assyria were continued and the struggle for the recovery of Mesopotamia, or for sovereign rights there, was renewed. Of the first two or three kings of the dynasty we have no information whatever, except that the first ruled 17 years and the second 6 years.

The third[2] or fourth king,

[1] *Pa-She.*

[2] Hilprecht, Old Bab. Inscr. I. Pt. i., 38 ff. argues, inconclusively however, that Nebuchadrezzar was the *first* king of this dynasty, and Rogers, Hist. Bab. and Ass., I., 426, states that he was the *sixth;* but the inconclusive data do not favor so late a succession.—*Craig.*

NEBUCHADREZZAR I.,

waged victorious war with Elam and acquired possession of Mesopotamia and the Westland. He extended once again, and for the last time, the sovereignty of Babylon to the shores of the Mediterranean. The war with Elam proves that the pitiful condition of affairs that obtained when Kidin-Khutrutash attacked Babylonia had grown worse under Nebuchadrezzar's predecessors and the last of the Kassite kings. Even the statue of the god Marduk had been carried off in triumph to Elam. It may be that this occurred at the time of the deposition of Bel-nadin-akhe and was, therefore, connected with the change of dynasty. The deportation of the god implied the loss of national independence and degradation to a state of vassalage. Just as Marduk had now to do obeisance in the temple of a foreign god, so the Babylonian ruler was no longer a king, but only a servant of the Elamite sovereign. As long as the divine statue was absent from Babylon Nebuchadrezzar, therefore, did not call himself king but only governor. It was not until he had recovered the statue of Marduk, which presupposes a decisive victory over Elam, that he took the title "king of Babylon." The statue had been in captivity thirty years. The length of his reign corresponded, accordingly, with the thirty years

after the close of the Kassite dynasty. Hymns
lamenting the absence of Marduk from Babylon
and celebrating his return have been preserved
for us. Whatever the outcome of this victory
may have been it is at least evident that for some
time a check was put upon the advance of Elam.
Our further knowledge of events connected with
this dynasty is gleaned from sources which tell of
the wars with Assyria. In the history of Assyria
we shall see that the success of Nebuchadrezzar's
reign continued to exert an influence long after,
and that the advantages gained by Assyria, which
paved the way for the conquest of Babylon by
Tiglathpileser I., were not enduring.

The list of the kings of the *Pashe* dynasty may
be restored, in some instances provisionally, in
others with reasonable assurance, with the help
of the king-lists and other available documentary
sources, as follows:

MARDUK-AKHI-IRBA(?). The name is broken off. *Ashur-
dan*, king of Assyria and probably vassal of Elam.
Reigned 17 [1] (?) years.

NINIB-NADIN-AKHI, the father of Nebuchadrezzar I.(?).
Mutakkil-Nusku, probably as vassal of Elam, reigned
in Assyria 6 years.

NEBUCHADREZZAR I. takes possession of Mesopotamia.
Ashur-resh-ishi contemporary in Assyria. Reigned
— years.

BEL-NADIN-APLI. Mesopotamia lost to Assyria. Reigned
— years.

[1] King-list, Winckler, *U. zur. or. Gesch.* S. 146, gives 17.—*Craig.*

MARDUK-NADIN-AKHI. Wars with *Tiglathpileser I.* and
regains Mesopotamia. Reigned — years.

MARDUK-SHAPIK-ZER-MATI, a contemporary of *Ashur-bel-kala*, during whose reign he died. Reigned — years.

ADAD-APLU-IDDIN, "the son of a nobody," raised to the
throne. *Ashur-bel-kala* marries his daughter.

> If three Kings preceded Nebuchadrezzar I., Adad-aplu-iddin
> would occupy the seventh position. Reigned 22 years.

MARDUK-NADIN-SHUM reigned 1 year, 6 months.

MARDUK-ZIR[1] reigned 13 years.

The length of reigns appended above are taken
from the king-list "b," and nothing more than
this has come down to us with respect to the close
of the dynasty.

---

[1] The reading *zir* is more probable than *Mu*, otherwise we might
place here Marduk-nadin-shum. His name appears upon an orna-
ment from Babylon with the title *Shar kishshati*. He cannot,
therefore, be the Marduk-nadin-shum appointed by Shalmaneser II.,
but, doubtless, belongs to this dynasty.

CHAPTER XI

THE ELAMITES AS RULERS OF BABYLON, CIR. 1000

THE following years witnessed frequent changes in the ruling houses, but little information has come down to us of the progress of events in Babylonia and Assyria. The king-lists and a very brief chronicle furnish us with the following facts:

SHIBAR[1]-SHIKHU, "the son of Erba-Sin of the dynasty of Damiq-Marduk was murdered and buried in the palace of Sargon." Reigned 17 years.

EA-MUKIN-SHUM reigned 5 (or 3) months.

KASHSHU-NADIN-AKHE reigned 3 (or 6) years.

These three kings are assigned to the dynasty of *The Sea-Land,* that is, the land about the mouth of the two rivers on the Persian Gulf. We learn from a late document that they repaired the temple of the sun-god at Sippar which had been partly destroyed by the *Suti.* This is the same people whom we have already met with as nomad tribes

[1] It is more than doubtful that this is the correct reading. *Both* elements in the name as read here are Kassite names of deities. In both the king-list and chronicle the first sign in the name is *Nam* which is glossed in the texts as, *Sim* (si-im), and since Simmash is the Kassite for *lidanu*="child," the name should be read Simmash-shikhu=in Assyrian "child of Marduk."—*Craig.*

of the Syrian desert in the time of Kadashman-Kharbe I. (p. 90). They still continue to make inroads into Babylonia as they did shortly before, and to menace even the cities. We are confronted, as it appears, with a part of *a new immigration*. This is the most important fact which the record yields, and it is readily explained by the presence of foreign rulers in Babylon. As regards the nationality of these three kings it is to be observed that the first and third names reflect a lingering ray of the glory of the Kassite dominion, which accordingly must have maintained itself longest in the South.

THE DYNASTY OF BAZI, CIR. 985

The next three kings are designated in the king-lists and chronicle as the *Dynasty of Bazi*, a border district of Elam. Their names and the length of their reigns are given as follows:

E-DUBAR-SHUQAMUNA reigned 17 (or 15) years.
NINIB-KUDUR-UTSUR reigned 3 (or 2) years.
SHILANI-SHUQAMUNA reigned 3 months.

Following upon these *one* king appears in a dynasty by himself—and he is an Elamite.

We thus see that Babylonia was in a state of decline and the prey of every foreign invader. The Elamites were her most aggressive enemy when not held in check by Assyria. The period which these three dynasties lasted extends from about 1000 to 960. At the end of this time Assyria, that heretofore had been impotent to act, begins anew her conquests.

Who it was that wrested the power from Elam, or what was effected by a new dynasty, we have no means of knowing. The king-lists are broken off at this point and we are forced to revert to Assyrian sources for almost all that we can learn until *about 750*. From these, however, we can see distinctly what was the dominant force of the time even though the history of the separate reigns cannot be written.

CHAPTER XII

THE CHALDEANS

BABYLONIA, which had been the coveted spoil of the two great kingdoms of Assyria and Elam, is now overrun by a great tide of *immigration* similar to the hordes of Semites who had settled there previously, and in the course of centuries had become completely naturalized. These newcomers were compelled to struggle with varying fortunes for possession of the land. The progress of events may be best illustrated by comparing them with the occupation of Palestine by the Hebrews. From now on the Chaldeans press forward into Babylonia and seek to make themselves masters of the cities.

Later ages have much to say of the Chaldeans, and numerous details of information respecting their relation to Babylonia have come down to us. But, despite all this, it still remains impossible to draw for ourselves a satisfactory picture of their national life. All the Chaldeans who are known to us bear Babylonian names. No new element of speech seems to have been introduced into the Babylonian language by their arrival, so that we have no particular data by which we can determine their racial connections. Nevertheless, on

general grounds, since they undoubtedly issued
from the South and first settled in the regions
bordering on the Persian Gulf, we must look upon
them *as Semites who in the first instance came
from Eastern Arabia.* The previous migrations
had been from the West, and Mesopotamia and
North Babylonia were the first entered in their
line of movement. The Chaldean migration
would, accordingly, fall between the Aramaic and
Arabian, and in these two groups the Chaldean
would find its closest kin, or, perhaps, it is to be
connected with one or the other. If they were
Semites the rapidity with which they adapted
themselves to the Babylonian conditions would be
explained. The similarity of their languages
would facilitate intercourse, and, as we know,
Aramaic tribes had already poured into Babylonia. With this attempt to envisage the situation
the scant material which exists for a characteriza-
tion of the Chaldeans is in perfect accord. The
designation of Ur, the city of the moon-god, as
Καμαρινη, is probably to be traced to Berosus,
and this cannot be explained from any other language than Arabic in which *qamar* means moon.
The chiefs of the Chaldeans are called *ra'sāni*,
which is the Arabic for chiefs (Hebrew *rā'shîm*).
The only god whose cult may have been introduced by the Chaldeans is the war-god, designated
Girra, whom Nabopolassar, Nebuchadrezzar and

Neriglissar especially exalt. This would indicate that among the Chaldeans, or, at least, in the tribe of Nabopolassar, he was the chief god.

From this time forward we find in addition to a number of Aramaic tribes also a number of petty Chaldean kingdoms, or tribes, each of which is designated by the Babylonians and Assyrians as "house" (*bît*) of a princely family. Thus we have *Bit-Yakin*, the "*Sea-Land*," whose Kassite ruler, as we have just seen, occupied the throne of Babylon after he had been carried forward possibly by the new movement. *Bit-Sa'alli, Bit-Khilani, Bit-Amukkani, Bit-Adini, Bit-Dakuri*, in close proximity to Babylon and Borsippa, are among the most important of the others. The one aim of the princes of these "houses" was to get possession of the larger cities and, to crown their achievements, ascend the throne of Babylon. Chaldea enters now as the third contestant by the side of Assyria and Elam for Babylonian sovereignty, and the Babylonian people grew less and less able to assert their independence. An unstable condition of affairs was the natural outcome. In general the Chaldeans and Elamites were more closely united, whereas the Assyrian kings posed rather as the protectors of national independence, or of what they would have dignified by this phrase. The usual successes and reverses of war attended this struggle until, finally, with the fall

of Assyria, the Chaldeans reached their goal, and
Babylon once more, under a Chaldean dynasty,
rose to the rank of a powerful kingdom.

Our knowledge of the period before Assyria
regained control in Babylonia is limited, and
almost wholly confined to records of war between
the two states. The first king of the dynasty was,
perhaps,

NABU-KIN-APLI, CIR. 960,

who reigned, at least, twenty-six years. One document of his age appears to ascribe to him the
rule over Mesopotamia, about 960. He would, in
that case, be the last who was able to boast of this
supremacy. In that same period, and continuously from that time forward, the Assyrian kings
claimed the title to sovereignty there. The name
of Nabu-kin-apli's successor is missing on the
king-lists, but he is there said to have ruled
six months and twelve days. A gap in the lists
then follows until we reach the name of *Nabu-
natsir,* who began to reign in 747. There are
possibly two other royal names to be supplied
after Nabu-kin-apli, which we cannot discover
from other sources. The next king,

SHAMASH-MUDAMMIQ,

is known to us from his wars with Assyria in the
reign of *Adad-nirari II.* He died during the
conflict.

NABU-APLU-IDDIN, ?–854,

reigned at least thirty-one years, and died in 854. He came into conflict with *Ashurnatsirpal* and *Shalmaneser,* and sought during the reign of the former to advance along the Euphrates into Mesopotamia. In the year 879 he lent support to the princes of Sukhi, which was situated along the Euphrates and was under Babylonian influence, in their opposition to Assyria. But Ashurnatsirpal defeated the Babylonian contingent. From the manner in which he speaks of this victory it would appear that Nabu-aplu-iddin was a Chaldean. It is quite consonant with this that he seems especially desirous, in an inscription which relates to the restoration of the temple at Sippar, to put himself on record as a good Babylonian. During his reign Assyria refrained from overt acts against Babylonia. Ashurnatsirpal contented himself with Mesopotamia, but later he appears to have spread out toward North Babylonia and to have taken possession of the former "kingdom of the Four Quarters of the World."

MARDUK-NADIN-SHUM, 854–823.

In 854 Nabu-aplu-iddin died. Death, by the way, is one of the commonest occurrences in the Orient, and his was the occasion for a determined conflict between his sons *Marduk-nadin-shum* and

Marduk-bêl-usati for the throne. Babylonia was divided between them, probably in agreement with their father's disposition, so that North Babylonia and Babylon fell to the former, South Babylonia, and therewith the motherland of Chaldea, to the latter. War between the Chaldean princes and the Babylonian king, as might be expected, broke out immediately, and, as usual, the forces of the Chaldeans proved more than a match for those of the North. Marduk-nadin-shum then turned for assistance to *Shalmaneser II.,* king of Assyria, and thereby invoked the suzerainty of the latter. The *ultima thule* of Assyrian politics was the establishment of sovereignty over Babylonia and, naturally enough, Shalmaneser responded to Marduk-nadin-shum's invitation with foreboding alacrity. He poured his seasoned and disciplined troops into the country, and Marduk-bêl-usati's "Chaldean peasants" fled to the marshlands for refuge. Shalmaneser entered the Babylonian cities, offered up the sacrifices as lord-paramount over the country, and received the homage of the Chaldean princes. Marduk-nadin-shum reigned from 854 to *cir.* 823 *under Assyrian suzerainty.* North Babylonia, the "kingdom of the Four Quarters of the World," which from the time of Ashurnatsirpal had been under Assyrian domination, had, as a matter of course, been subject to Shalmaneser from the beginning. It appears,

indeed, that at the end of his reign, when he was
forced to flee Assyria, by the insurrection headed
by his son, Ashur-danin-pal, he turned for support to this part of his kingdom, and that his son,
Shamshi-Adad, used it and Mesopotamia as his
base in subjugating Assyria.

The impossibility during this time of making a
serious attack upon Babylonia must have given
the ever envious Chaldean another welcome opportunity to push northward. As soon, therefore, as
Shamshi-Adad was free from the assaults of more
pressing enemies he turned toward Babylonia.
Marduk-nadin-shum, who outlived the beginning
of the reign of Shamshi-Adad, as is witnessed by
a text in which their names appear together, died,
or was deposed, in 823. The next to ascend the
throne was

MARDUK-BALATSU-IQBI, 823–?,

a Chaldean prince, who was supported by the
Kaldi, Babylonian Aramæan tribes, Elam and
Median peoples, especially the *"Namri."* He
owed his throne, therefore, to Elamite assistance,
and consequently stood in the same relation to
Elam as Marduk-nadin-shum did to Assyria.
This is the first time that we discover clearly the
relations sustained by Babylonia to its neighbors, relations which we meet with again and
again—Ashur, or Elam as suzerain of Babylonia
with her king under their protection.

Shamshi-Adad's inscription does not record his success; but it informs us of expeditions undertaken in 813 and 812 against Chaldea and Babylon. The first of these presupposes the subjugation of the Chaldean king by Assyria, and, therewith, the restoration of Assyrian supremacy. The second took place during the first year of Adad-nirari III. It is possible, as so often happened, that the change of rulers offered to the Chaldeans, who were but partially conquered, an opportune moment for a forward movement.

BAU-AKHI-IDDIN, ?–785,

appears to have been king of Babylon at this time. He was besieged and taken prisoner by the Assyrians, and as Shalmaneser had previously offered up his sacrifices in the cities, so Adad-nirari did now as supreme lord. It is uncertain whether all this occurred in 812, or in the later expeditions of 796 and 795 against North Babylonia and that of 791 against Chaldea, the issues of which are unknown. This much, however, is established, *viz.*, that the characteristic note of the time is: *the attempts of Chaldean princes, with the assistance of Elam, to obtain the throne of Babylon, and the superiority of Assyria when not engaged in other quarters.* But with every change of rulers, or whenever Assyria was involved elsewhere, a fresh blow for independence was struck. The same acts in the historical drama are played upon every stage, and are best attested in the prophets of Judah and Israel: Two great parties at home turning for aid to two rival powers abroad and a constant vacillation between the two.

We cannot determine when Adad-nirari ascended the throne of Babylon, neither have we any information of the time which immediately followed. This is due to the reverse of Assyrian power after Adad-nirari's reign and the loss of influence upon Babylonia which accompanied it. But Assyria did not relinquish her claim to supremacy without a struggle, for several expeditions against Chaldea are attested, for example, immediately after in 783 and 782 with the accession of Shalmaneser III., and again under him in 777. So, also, his successor, Ashur-dan, immediately after he ascended the throne in 771 marched against North Babylonia and two years later against Chaldea. The explanation of this is to be found in the previous history, and we can picture the course of events in the light of the expeditions of Shalmaneser and Adad-nirari. But since we have no inscriptions of the Assyrian kings referred to, and only brief references in the "chronicles" none of the names of the Babylonian kings of this period are known. Three of them are probably lacking in our sources. One of them may have been ERBA-MARDUK, who is mentioned by Marduk-apal-iddin II. as his ancestor.[1]

In the tumultuous time which now succeeded Assyrian influence must have been utterly lost, and as a result Babylonia fell into the hands of the Chaldeans. From the Babylonian king-lists we learn that the next king who ruled in Babylonia was

NABU-SHUM-ISHK(UN?), ?–748.

He ruled until 748. If the restoration of the name is correct we have an inscription which furnishes us with a clear picture of prevailing Babylonian conditions. Nabu-shum-imbi, the governor of Borsippa, the sister city of Babylon, in an account of the building operations connected with the temple of Nebo relates as follows: "When there arose in Borsippa, the city of justice and order, tumult, devastation, riot and revolution, during the reign of Nabu-shum-ishkun of Bit-Dakuri, then the Babylonians, the people of Borsippa, and Dush-ulti from the shore of the Euphrates, all the Chaldeans, Aramæans, Dilbateans (from a Babylonian city) turned against one another in arms, smote one another and fought with the people of Borsippa over their boundary. And Nabu-shum-iddin (a high official of the temple of Nebo) worked up

---

[1] The name of the first of these kings appears from the traces to have begun with *Marduk*, and the second cannot have been *Erba-Marduk* on account of the shortness of the second reign, only 8 months and 12 days.

independently (a revolt) against Nabu-shum-imbi, the governor of Borsippa. At night, like a thief, enemy, bandit, etc., he collected them and led them into the temple of Nebo. . . . They raised a tumult. But the people of Borsippa and others who rendered assistance surrounded the house of the governor and defended it with bows and arrows.'' We have here revealed what was to be expected, the king of Babylon is a Chaldean of the Dakuri tribe, and the Chaldeans and Aramæans take possession of the regions about the cities which are divided by opposing factions within them. It was but natural that under these conditions the property-holding classes should greet the appearance of an Assyrian king as a deliverer, as they often did later on. Chaldean rule meant anarchy for Babylonia. The divisions of the Chaldeans among themselves, and the natural opposition of their ambitious projects to that of the city population in actual possession prevented the appearance of a strong Chaldean prince and settled conditions. To speak of an orderly, well-organized state constitution would be wide of the mark. The land again lay open for conquest as so often before and afterward.

NABU-NATSIR, 747–734,

or as the Ptolemaic Canon gives his name, Nabonassar, was the next king. He reigned from 747 to 734. The condition of affairs just described continued to exist under him. The lawless state that existed in Borsippa, as described by Nabu-shum-imbi, led to an attempt on the part of Borsippa during the reign of Nabu-natsir to cut loose from Babylon. This was met by determined opposition on the part of the king. Little more remains to be said of Nabu-natsir's deeds. Only one statement which rests upon Berosus, the Babylonian historiographer who lived in the Selucid age, affirms that he issued a decree for the *introduction of a new era.* And, in fact, the Ptolemaic Canon, and a Babylonian chronicle written in the time of Darius, begin with his reign in 747. It was the Ptolemaic Canon that made his name known. From that time on all astronomy, and therewith all scientific Assyriology of antiquity, reckoned a new era from the beginning of his reign. The occasion for the change was brought about by the entrance of the vernal equinox into the zodiacal sign *Aries,* whereas it had been from 3000 B.C. in *Taurus.* The ancients then began to count Aries first in the zodiacal signs, and we still continue to do so although the equinoctial point is now in *Pisces.* The change of the *era* necessitated a change in the calendar, and also in numberless doctrines connected therewith and based thereon. It is upon the introduction of this reform, by which scientific teaching was translated into practice, that the importance of Nabu-natsir's reign rests. His change of the calendar was an act of as great importance to antiquity as the introduction of Julian's Calendar was for Rome and the civilized world dependent upon her, or as the Gregorian for the modern world. But for the ancient Orient a reform of the calendar implied an infinitely greater effect upon the intellectual and religious life than it would with us.

For convenience of reference we add the following list of kings:

Broken off.   Reigned 13 years.[1]
Broken off.   Reigned 6 months, 12 days.
 ?   ?   or,
SHAMASH-MUDAMMIQ.
NABU-APLU-IDDIN, reigned at least 31 years, is mentioned by Ashurnatsirpal in 854.   Reigned 885(?)–854.
MARDUK-NADIN-SHUM reigned 853–829(?).
MARDUK-BALATSU-IQBI, opponent of *Shamshi-Adad*. Reigned 823–812(?).
BAU-AKHI-IDDIN, conquered by *Andad-nirari III*.   Reigned ?–785.
 . . .   Three other kings, ERBA-MARDUK one of them?
NABU-SHUM-(ISHKUN[2]? or iqisha?) reigned ?–748.
NABU-NATSIR, reigned 747–733.

[1] On p. 103 the author gives 26 years.   The 13 years given here is based on an early publication of a king-list.—*Craig*.

[2] Knudtson read *sha-ishkun*, and from the traces of the following sign he was the son of his predecessor.—*Craig*.

CHAPTER XIII

BABYLONIA UNDER THE NEW ASSYRIAN EMPIRE

NABU-NATSIR's third year, 745, was the beginning of a new period for Assyria under Tiglathpileser III., and Babylonia soon became aware of the change that took place. The first movement of the new king was into Babylonia where he chastized the Aramæans and the northernmost tribes of the Chaldeans, and, apparently, assumed a protectorship over Nabu-natsir. It is reasonable to conclude from this that the latter was a Babylonian and not a Chaldean. Tiglathpileser at once assumed the titles *"king of Sumer and Akkad"* and *"king of the Four Quarters of the World,"* and marched southward as far as Nippur. The Chaldeans, it is to be supposed, promptly submitted. Beyond this, however, he was unable to carry out his plans owing to threatening unrest in Armenia and Syria. Nabu-natsir thus exercised rule under the protection of Assyria. Though the insurrection of Borsippa shows that his power did not extend beyond the limits of Babylon, it must be remembered first, that it was not in the interest of Assyria to shield him from minor troubles, and, secondly, that Tiglathpileser was too busily engaged at first to give himself more concern for Babylon than the exigencies of the situation demanded. It is, nevertheless, an eloquent testimony to the wholesome respect in which he was held that for fourteen years no Chaldean attempted the reduction of Babylon. In the year 734 Nabu-natsir died. He was succeeded by his son,

NABU-NADIN-ZIR, 734–733,

or *Nadinu,* by abbreviation, whence the form Nadios of Ptolemy. Quite in keeping with the times, after he had reigned two years, 734–733, an insurrection broke out. The king was dethroned by a provincial governor,

NABU-SHUM-UKIN,

a Babylonian, and the leader of the party inimical to Assyria. He held the reins of government only two months, when he was forced to give place to the Chaldean,

UKIN-ZIR, 732–730,

the *"Chinzer"* of Ptolemy, the prince of Bit-Amukani The time had come for Assyria to interfere again, for a Chaldean upon the throne of Babylon could have no other ultimate aim than the conquest of the whole of Babylonia, which up to this had been under the control of *Tiglath-pileser III*. As soon, therefore, as the latter had squared accounts with Syria, and taken Damascus after a three-years' siege, during which the throne of Ukin-zir was free from attack, he led his troops into Babylonia. There he besieged Bit-Amukani, Ukin-zir's native land, together with some other Chaldean principalities, and took Ukin-zir prisoner. To put a stop to ceaseless disturbances, despite the onerous duty of being present every year at the New Year's ceremony in Babylon, and of residing there when possible to do so, he decided to take the crown of Marduk's kingdom himself. For the two following years of his life Tiglathpileser caused himself to be proclaimed king of Babylon. But the rights of the Babylonians had to be maintained. Tiglathpileser, and the other kings who adopted a like policy, ruled as kings in Babylon under other names. Shalmaneser was called in Babylonia *Ululai,* and Ashurbanipal received the name of *Kandalanu.* Tiglathpileser appears in the Babylonian lists as PULU, a name by which he is also known in the Old Testament.

Peace ruled during these two years, 729 and 728, and during the reign of his successor, Shalmaneser IV., who reigned in Babylon also, under the name of

ULULAI, 727–722.

But with his death, when the great revolution occurred which placed Sargon II. upon the throne of Assyria, a Chaldean prince,[1]

MARDUK-APLU-IDDIN II.,[2] 721–710,

king of the *"Sea-Land,"* used the opportunity to seize the Babylonian crown with the connivance of Khumbanigash, the king of Elam.

Sargon's troops were quickly turned against him, but the Elamite hastened to render assistance. A battle was fought at *Dur-ilu,* the outcome of which Sargon claims as a victory for himself and the Babylonians over Khumbanigash. Sargon, however, did not succeed in forcing Merodach-Baladan to withdraw from Babylon. He nevertheless established his authority over the most northerly part, the region known as *"The Four Quarters of the World,"* including Dur-ilu. Marduk-aplu-iddin calls himself *"king of Babylon, king of Sumer and Akkad."* He ruled as Marduk-aplu-iddin II., under Elamite protection, from 721 to 710, while Sargon was busily engaged in Syria-Palestine and Armenia, as Tiglathpileser had been shortly before.

[1] Of the Dynasty of Erba-Marduk, as he is called in an inscription of his reign.

[2] Or, as his name appears somewhat incorrectly in the Old Testament, Merodach-Baladan.

On the termination of these wars Sargon marched on Babylon, and put to flight Marduk-aplu-iddin, who after the loss of *Dur-Yakin,* his capital in the Sea-Land, sought refuge at the court of Susa. The Assyrian party in Babylon, especially the priesthood, welcomed the invader as savior and restorer of order. Sargon assumed the title of "governor of Babylon," that is, he undertook the post of royal representative, when in fact there was none in name. In this capacity he ruled Babylon and all Babylonia from 709 to 705, when his career was ended by death.

The following two years Babylon enjoyed peace, but at the end of this time an insurrection arose which placed

MARDUK-ZAKIR-SHUM, 702,

upon the throne for *one month.* Marduk-aplu-iddin immediately seized upon the opportunity presented and set out from Elam, with Elamite support, to recapture Babylon. But his triumph was of short duration. Sennacherib, more fortunate than his predecessor Sargon, had not his army on other fields and, therefore, appeared before Babylon nine months after Marduk-aplu-iddin's return. The armies met at *Kish* and the battle turned against Marduk-aplu-iddin and his Elamite allies. He fled again to Elam where he awaited a fresh opportunity. Sennacherib adopted a mild policy toward Babylon. It was not, indeed, the Babylonians who were the cause of the trouble, and only the possessions of Marduk-aplu-iddin and his supporters were confiscated. The Chaldeans were driven back into their own territory and the cities were given back the lands which formerly belonged to them. The Aramæan tribes, likewise, who under similar conditions always joined with the Chaldeans, were compelled to fall back to their old domain. Sennacherib now placed upon the throne of Babylon a scion of a noble family of Babylon who had grown up at the court of Nineveh, viz.,

BEL-IBNÎ, 702–700,

who reigned from 702 to 700. In the year 702 two provinces bordering on Elam were secured. The force of circumstances, however, ran counter to Bel-ibnî's loyalty to Assyria, even though he may have had the best of intentions. Sennacherib's policy of making Nineveh the first city of the Orient may have been apparent. In any case, Bel-ibnî was compelled during Sennacherib's engagement in Palestine to cut loose from Assyria and join forces with his own rival, Marduk-aplu-iddin, *Mushezib-Marduk*, another Chaldean prince, and Elam; in other words, acknowledge subjection to Elam. This step was, doubtless, not voluntarily taken. However, just as the Pales-

tinians miscalculated and took the field too late, so
now, the Babylonians and Elamites counted amiss.
Sennacherib abandoned the siege of Jerusalem
after he had conquered the entire land, turned
against his ambitious rivals and scattered the
hosts of the allied armies in confusion. Marduk-
aplu-iddin betook himself and his gods to Elam.
The Chaldean, Mushezib-Marduk, fell back upon
his desert swamps, and Bel-ibnî with his followers
had to return whence he came—to the court of
Nineveh. From this it appears that he joined
Elam and the Chaldeans under compulsion, otherwise he would certainly have suffered a severer
punishment.

ASHUR-NADIN-SHUM, 699–694,

a son of Sennacherib was enthroned in Babylon
and ruled from 699–694. Marduk-aplu-iddin must
have died soon after, for nothing more is heard
of him. Commotions in Elam were now rife, consequently peace prevailed for five years in Babylonia. In the year 694 Sennacherib advanced
against the inhabitants of *"The Sea-Land,"* who
had fled with Marduk-aplu-iddin to Elam. They
had settled in some of the coast cities and were
a constant menace to Babylonia, hence the determination of Sennacherib to drive them out. He
gives a detailed description of the work he undertook to effect his purpose—how he built ships and

brought them to Opis on the Tigris, thence over to the Euphrates and down to the Persian Gulf. He conquered the temptations which may have arisen within himself to dare the dangerous element, but he transported his army by ship to Elam. It proceeded a short distance up the river *Karun* (Ulai), devastated the Elamite provinces along the coast, and dispersed, or took prisoners the Chaldean settlers.

While the Assyrian army remained here in Elam *Khalludush,* the king of Elam, was not idle. Marching along the usual military highway he entered Northern Babylonia at *Dur-ilu,* conquered Sippar, took Ashur-nadin-shum prisoner and deported him to Elam. He appointed in his stead

NERGAL-USHEZIB, 694–693,

a Babylonian, king of Babylon. Sennacherib tells us only of the courageous face he presented to the threatening sea and of his success in Elam. The counter-stroke of the Elamite we know of only from the Babylonian chronicle. Neither is anything more heard of Sennacherib's deposed son, Ashur-nadin-shum. The new king at first had possession only of Northern Babylonia, but later he attempted to expel the Assyrians from the South also. He conquered Nippur; but Uruk, which appears to have gone over to him, was retaken by the Assyrians, and soon afterward the Assyrian forces appeared before Nippur. Nergal-ushezib marched out and met them in open battle which went against him. He was defeated and taken prisoner. He reigned only one and a half years, from 694–693.

While Sennacherib in the same year set out on a war of retaliation against Elam, the Chaldean,

MUSHEZIB-MARDUK, 692–689,

already mentioned,[1] seized the opportunity to establish himself in Babylon, where he continued to rule from 692 to 689. He put himself completely in the hands of Elam and even sacrificed the treasures of the temple of Marduk that he might pay *Umman-menanu,* the Elamite, his "presents," that is, the price exacted for assistance rendered. Here, again, it appears that the priestly party relied on Assyria. Sennacherib did not find it so easy this time to put Elam, the actual foe, to rout. In the year 691[2] a batttle was waged near *Khalule* in Northern Babylonia, with Umman-menanu, his vassal Mushezib-Marduk, the son of Marduk-aplu-iddin, and the rest of the Chaldeans. Sennacherib gives a glowing narrative of the engagement and naturally claims the

[1] *Cf.* p. 118.

[2] Not in 690! The Taylor-prism which gives the account of the battle was written in the *limmu* (archontat) of Bel-limuranni, *i.e.,* 691.

victory. The Babylonian chronicle ascribes it to Umman-menanu and, in so doing is, at least, virtually correct, for Sennacherib reaped no advantage from it: Babylon remained under Elamite protection. In 689 Umman-menanu died, and, in the same year, Babylon fell into the hands of Sennacherib, and Mushezib-Marduk was carried a prisoner to Assyria. We must infer that the Assyrian party in Babylon at this time was insignificant. It had apparently become clear that Sennacherib's policy aimed at the destruction of the city. Desperation led to a union with the Chaldeans. Sennacherib then hastened to effect his purpose by the quickest means: Babylon was completely demolished and her gods carried to Assyria. The possibility of reinhabiting the ancient city was, therewith, removed for some time.

After the destruction of Babylon Nineveh might have become the leading city in the Orient. But it is an easier matter to destroy the products of civilization than to charm them again into existence, and the economical conditions of thousands of years could not with impunity be ignored. For eight years there was "no king in Babylon," as the Babylonian chronicle sadly relates. There was indeed no Babylon. But, when Sennacherib was murdered, the first act of his son Esarhaddon, who succeeded him, and who appears to have previously been governor of Babylon,[1] was to issue a decree commanding the rebuilding of the city and the temple of Marduk.   The years that Babylon lay in ruins were naturally used by the Chaldeans of the neighboring Bit-Dakuri to transgress the Babylonian boundary.   Esarhaddon was obliged to expel them.   Descendants of Marduk-aplu-iddin sought alliances with Elam, in the hope of renewing the policy of their ancestor; but these attempts were also rendered abortive.[2]   Conditions, however, had changed after Sennacherib's death.   The latter stood for a purely Assyrian and, therefore, a strong military policy, but Esarhaddon was forced to depend on the priesthood as Sargon had been.   Thus the reconstruction of Babylon was exactly upon the old lines.   Evidently enough the military party did not disappear with the death of Sennacherib, but the condition of affairs in Assyria controlled it.   These two strenuous parties appear to have set their hopes for the future upon the two princes Ashurbanipal and Shamash-shum-ukin.   We shall see in the history of Assyria how the military party compelled Esarhaddon to crown their head, Ashurbanipal, king of Assyria, therewith securing control just as Babylon was ready and was again on the point

[1] It is quite likely that Sennacherib was forced by a Babylonian hierarchic party to give permission for the rebuilding of Babylon and also to appoint Esarhaddon as governor or royal representative.

[2] *Cf.* under Esarhaddon in Assyrian History.

of occupying the throne of Babylonia. Esarhaddon was able to secure only Babylon and
Southern Babylonia to

SHAMASH-SHUM-UKIN, 668–648.

In the year 668 the statue of Marduk was returned
to Babylon and the two princes proclaimed kings
of their respective realms while their father still
lived. But the old situation still continued—
Babylon stood under Assyrian Over-lordship, and
the new king of Assyria offered up sacrifices in
Babylon, Sippar and Kutha as the protector of
Babylonian deities.

Therewith the way was opened for the old
rivalries and the outbreak of hostilities was only
a question of time. For the first few years the
inscriptions of both of them abound with vain
expressions of good will and brotherly love, and
then the clang of weapons rings out anew. Shamash-shum-ukin sought for allies wherever the
enemies of Assyria were to be found, and these
were rarely lacking wherever her rule was felt
or feared. Elam, the Arabians, the lands along
the Mediterranean, Gutium (North Countries), he
incited to arms against Assyria. In the war which
followed the question to be decided was again:
Shall Babylon or Assyria dominate the Orient?
It was about the middle of the seventh century
that the war broke out owing to the refusal of

Shamash-shum-ukin to allow his brother Ashurbanipal to perform the sacrifices which, as protector of Babylonia, he was wont to offer. It
ended with a disastrous siege of Sippar, Kutha,
and Babylon, and the death of Shamash-shum-
ukin, who perished in the flames into which,
according to the account of Ashurbanipal, his
desperate subjects cast him. In 648 the war came
to a close, and Babylonia had suffered enough
from it to make peace seem desirable for some
time. From 647–626 the Assyrian king, Ashurbanipal, wore the crown of Babylon under the
name of

KANDALANU, 647–626.

His speech, delivered on the occasion of his accession, has come down to us. The successes which
he won over Elam prevented the latter from
further hostile movements against Babylonia. So
the land had rest until he died.

But as so often before, so it was now, change of
rulers gave opportunity to *a Chaldean* to grasp
the throne of Babylon. From 625 the lists
designate

NABU-APLU-UTSUR, 625–

or, as the name has come down to us through the
Greeks somewhat distorted, as other names and
facts delivered to us from the same source, Nabopolassar. He was a *Chaldean,* but we do not know

which was his native state. He is the first of the last dynasty of Babylon, which raised her again to the leading power of Western Asia and extended her dominion once more as far as the Mediterranean. In the uninterrupted struggle between Assyria and the Chaldeans over Babylon the latter were eventually victors, after their efforts were repeatedly thwarted for a couple of centuries. Babylonia was now Chaldean. The Chaldean migration had reached its goal and therewith also its end.

CHAPTER XIV

HISTORICAL RETROSPECT AND OUTLOOK

A. THE SOURCES

OUR knowledge of the ancient Orient is of recent date. The decipherment of the monuments which have supplied us with our information is the result of the last half century. Even from this brief period a large portion must be deducted when actual work is considered, so inadequate are the means with which science is compelled to labor. Even today it cannot be said that anything approaching a systematic exploration of these old culture lands has yet been undertaken. The monuments which thus far have been recovered and which have furnished us with the most reliable sources extant for the history of the times, constitute but an infinitely small part of that which we might recover and is lying in reserve for future excavators. Every attempt, therefore, to construct for ourselves *a connected history* of the development of ancient Oriental peoples is doomed to partial failure beforehand. We know the essential conditions of certain periods that are illuminated by abundant sources which accident has put into our hands, or, at least,

127

we can note the effect of certain forces that oper-
ate to produce results. But of other periods we
have only a few details from which far-reaching
conclusions must be drawn to derive from them
the most general knowledge of events. Of many
others—and they are many—we know nothing—
the most we can do is to insert the names of two
or three kings of whose deeds nothing has come
down to us.

It is further natural that the sources accessible
to us should relate rather to the political events
than to the active thought and dominant forces
controlling the inner life of the people. The
numerous inscriptions of the Assyrian kings were
the first to be discovered, and that part of the
history which is based upon them is as yet the
most complete. But these records relate almost
entirely to wars and territorial conquests, to battles waged and booty won; that which we would
more gladly learn of the people's life is to be
gathered from scanty suggestions.[1]

The consideration of the cultural achievements
and attainments of the ancient Orient remains,
therefore, in default of sufficient sources, unsatis-
factory. For some periods as, for example, the
time of the first dynasty of Babylon and, in
Assyria, the time from Tiglathpileser III. on-

[1] See, however, *Social Life and Customs of Babylonians and
Assyrians*, by Professor A. H. Sayce.—*Craig.*

ward, again, in Babylon, from Nebuchadrezzar to the Persian Conquest, and even for the age of the Seleucids, we have thousands of documents in our possession. They consist of contracts, judicial decisions, business documents of all kinds, and private letters and despatches. These supply a varied abundance of detailed facts touching the private life of the respective periods. But they have not yet been sufficiently studied to enable us to draw from the confusing mass of details the general characteristics of the cultural development—to sketch in clear and full lines the typical life of the times. The foundation for a thorough insight into the private life has as yet been laid only for the New-Babylonian period. Until this mass of material is mastered, and the numerous documents of the other periods have revealed their contents, there will be a demand for much studious toil and talent. And until the breaks between these periods, separated from each other by centuries and milleniums, are filled up by means of new inscriptions generations will have passed, and this notwithstanding the incomparably rapid strides which Assyriology has made. The civilization of three milleniums, forgotten for two thousand years, cannot be called forth again from the silence of buried cities, from a language unknown, and a script so complex in three or four decades.

But even if these numerous documents, for whose mastery the strength of the few workers in this field is inadequate, were forced to yield up their secrets they would still reveal, for the most part, only one side of the life of the Babylonians and Assyrians, *viz.*, that connected with business, and especially private business life. But so far as the popular and civic life of the people as a whole is concerned—in other words the social-economic conditions—less light is shed. Of much that remains of great importance to us in modern life we shall have to content ourselves for long with little or no knowledge. Business activities, and industrial life in the large, the conditions attaching to property ownership in lands and their effect upon the welfare of the state, governmental restraints, etc., are matters concerning which we receive little information from the royal inscriptions, and in a contract drawn up between A and B we naturally look in vain for such enlightenment.

As we have already seen we know as yet nothing concerning the beginnings of that civilization which was native to Babylonia. The Sumerians belong to the prehistoric age, as much so as the Babylonians and Assyrians did when history was supposed to begin with Greece. The long ages in which man was resident in the valley of the Euphrates and developed there a civilization, which, at the time of our earliest records, had stirred the conquering spirit of the foreigner, are still lost in the mists of antiquity. The time is yet distant when we shall be able to say from contemporary documents, or works of art, how the first inhabitants of the Euphrates valley, struggling against barbarous conditions and adapting themselves to the requirements of the country, raised themselves to the higher stages of civilization. When and how the more important achievements were made, how, for example, the greatest of intellectual feats, the development of writing, was accomplished, no sources have yet been discovered to tell us. The remotest antiquity of Babylonia, of which we have knowledge, had a fully developed system of writing as that of Egypt had in the valley of the Nile.

B. THE LAND IN ITS ORIGINAL STATE

The low land of the Euphrates now, for the most part barren and marshy, was once the most fruitful portion of the earth. The productiveness of the soil is described as remarkable in the records of every age. The land, through the rich alluvial deposits of the Euphrates, like the Nile, gave to the agriculturalist the richest return for the least labor. In the climate of the Orient, where rain falls seldom, the lands through which these rivers coursed were the only ones which in the initial stages of cultivation promised an adequate return to the tiller of the soil. On the other hand, in times of drouth, necessity compelled the Bedouin herdsmen to abandon the parched steppes with their flocks and herds and betake themselves to these fertile regions. Here bountiful nature provided them, at little cost of labor, with fodder sufficient to tide them over the dry season. The transition from nomadic to agricultural life thus finds its explanation in the nature of the soil.

The step from an agricultural state to life in fortified cities is not very great and is quickly taken in a land exposed on all sides to attack from nomad tribes. But even this stage of transitional activity in the Euphrates valley was completed long before the time where our sources begin. The ancient centres of civilization: *Eridu, Lagash, Ur, Uruk, Larsa,* have already an immemorial past when first they appear in history. Ages before they had reached the development which they maintained through all the varying changes of politics for three thousand years; they were the seats of old sanctuaries that had commanded reverence for unknown generations, the homes of city-bred populations that lived by business and industry.

Even at that time we must assume the existence of the regulations governing landed property and the various forms of professional activity borrowed from the Sumerians, just as they continued to reassert themselves through the long period of Babylonian culture. In contrast to Occidental civilizations, whose growth we can follow from their beginnings, we meet here with a perfected organization of society such as would correspond to that which European peoples arrived at in the Middle Ages. Through all the storm and stress of the following three thousand years it continued. Each new tide of immigrants that poured over the land quickly felt the power of the old culture and submitted to it. Certainly, even the less fortunate of the conquerors would get their share of the spoils, but an apportionment of the land among the peasantry has never been the custom. We cannot watch the progress of the people from the beginning. The leaders in the different conquests always took the place of the former kings. If they did not wish to destroy all the civilization they found they had to accept it with its temples and cities, its disposition of landed property, and its social classes. That is one reason why the different peoples were so quickly assimilated. They did not develop gradually, but leaped at one bound to a higher stage, beyond which they could not go.

We find consequently that a land system prevailed from the earliest times which we know onward which may best be described as clericofeudal. The deity was the landlord. He bestowed the land upon the priesthood and the king; hence there was temple property and state property. The king had control over the country lands, which he let out to his vassals. His authority did not extend over the territory which stood in the domain of the god: this belonged to the city in which the god dwelled, and there, naturally to the patricians and the temple. The land was tilled by dependent tenants who were required to deliver their share of produce to the owners— the temple, king, nobles, citizens. This organization which was ever adopted anew (with fresh arrivals) was never favorable under the circumstances to the development of a peasant class. If, in the case of a new immigration, a strip of added territory was divided among the conquerors this could not be long maintained against the greater power of the crown possessions, which reached out and appropriated it as vassal land. This did not necessarily result in bondage. These tenants were in most cases free—as free as a man can be who retains just so much of his products, won from the soil with the sweat of his brow, as may permit him to enjoy life in an Oriental fashion. Bondage rarely resulted from force or legal oppression. The necessary complement of slaves was furnished from prisoners of war. These, however, were employed more likely in the industries of the cities than in the cultivation of the lands. The frequently occurring cases of manumission met with in business life come from this class.

The disposition of the land was, therefore, rather into small tracts, which were cultivated by the tenants for the owners. With the simple means afforded by this petty farming, and all the strenuous industry and use of every foot of earth which this system enforced, it was more akin to gardening than to agriculture.

C. IRRIGATION

The most important requirement of a fruitful cultivation of the ground in the Orient, with its rainless summers, is a regular supply of water. Just as the lack of it led the Bedouins from the steppes to the river valley, so it is the task of the agriculturalist to irrigate as much of the land's surface as possible. On the other hand, the great rivers, Euphrates and Tigris, when the snows begin to melt in the mountains, flow down with such volumes of water that they submerge the most productive parts of the country. The river-beds become choked with the earthy deposits and the adjoining lands are turned into swamps, as is now the case with large tracts that once yielded bountiful harvests. Want of rain and spring floods combined to compel the inhabitants to cope with these unfavorable conditions. They were forced to collect the overflow for the rainless season. Self-preservation demanded the regulation of the water supply.

Thus it happened that the land from the earliest historical beginnings onward was intersected by a network of canals. This was a prime necessity in its development. By this means the overflowing waters at high flood were led off from the parts liable to inundation into the artificial channels, whence in time of drouth it returned to irrigate them. Some of these canals are constructed higher than the surrounding land so that the water can be let out upon it by means of sluices. Some of them are lower, and from these, as in Egypt, the water is raised by means of water-wheels, or, where less is required, by buckets. (The *Shadduf* of modern Egypt.)

Though the construction of these smaller means was the work of the individual who held the land, the building of the great canals was a national enterprise designed to regulate the water supply of the entire land. Thus we find among the meagre accounts which we have of royal measures for the national good accounts of the construction of canals. It is clear that they were fully aware of the economic value of these interior improvements. In the older times, when they dated not by the regular years but by important events, we find this entry: "In the year when such and such a war occurred" and following it: "When the king built such and such a canal." "After the conquest of Southern Babylonia," Khammurabi says, "when Anu and Bel intrusted me with the rule of Sumer and Akkad and placed the reins of government in my hands I dug the canal Nar-Khammurabi, the Blessing of Men, the bringer of abundance of water to the land of Sumer and Akkad. The land upon both sides thereof I restored to tillage; storehouses for the grain I built; water for ages to come I procured for the land of Sumer and Akkad." In similar speech Nabopolassar and Nebuchadrezzar tell of the waterways they built. These canals were also used for purposes of national defence as in Holland. We learn that Nebuchadrezzar in the last days of Babylonia built the "Median Wall," and Nabuna'id with its help converted his entire Babylonian empire into an island. Two famous canals traversed the whole of Babylonia; the one called *Palakuttu* (Palakottas),[1] the other *Nâr-sharri,* or Aramaic *Nahr-Malkâ, i.e.,* "the kings' canal," a name which is met with in Hellenistic times. The first runs almost parallel to the Euphrates on its

[1] Also Pallakopas, identified by Friedrich Delitzsch, Wo Lag das Paradies?, with an Assyrian word pisânu-canal which occurs in the vocabularies, and this again with the biblical *Pîshôn.—Craig.*

southern side; the other joins the Tigris[1] and Euphrates.

Great canals and smaller ones stretched in all directions through the land as well as rude irrigating ditches. Upon the maintenance of them depended the habitableness of the whole valley. Consequently the care of these internal waterways and works of irrigation occupied a prime place in the policy of the kings down to the destruction of the country by the Mongols. With the ruin of the canals a large part of the land was filled with pestilential swamps. The first task to be performed whenever the attempt is made to restore these waste regions to their former unparalleled prolific state[2] is the reopening and building of the canals, many of whose beds are still traceable.

While these numerous constructions were demanded by the nature of the Babylonian plain they were neither necessary nor possible in the higher lying regions, especially in the highlands of Assyria, where the climate is more temperate. But, on the other hand, we meet here with

---

[1] To the east of Babylon at *Kut-el-Amâra.* It is represented by the modern *Shatt-el-Hâi.—Craig.*

[2] Ashurbanipal in his annals records that during his reign the grain grew five cubits in height and that the heads thereof were five-sixths of a cubit. Apparently the grain (*sheam*) referred to is wheat and barley. The fact that such proportions are claimed would indicate that the actual growth was enormous. Some license must be allowed in the ancient "prosperity" speeches of the king as well as in those of the modern politician.—*Craig.*

instances in which the water supply of the city was brought from a distance. By means of canals Sennacherib conducted the waters from the mountainous regions of Bavian to the city of Nineveh, and Esarhaddon constructed a tunnel at Negub through which he brought the waters of the Zab to the city of Kalkhi as Ashurnatsirpal had done by other works. A relief from the palace of Ashurbanipal, now in the British Museum, represents a great Babylonian park which is supplied with water through an arched conduit which corresponds exactly to those of classical antiquity.[1]

D. THE ARTS

In architecture invention and style depend largely upon the material at the disposal of the builder. In Babylonia there was neither stone nor suitable wood. Date palms, fig, and olive

---

[1] Sennacherib gives an interesting account of his work in this connection in his rock inscription at Bavian. Unfortunately the text is slightly damaged and contains some words whose meanings are not quite clear. He tells us, however, that he connected eighteen cities, which he names, by canals with the river *Khosr*, and that from the region of the city of *Kisiri* he dug another canal to Nineveh and made "these waters" to flow into it. To this he gave the name "Sennacherib's Canal." The importance he attached to this work is evident from his mention of it in two other inscriptions. At the same time he "enlarged the reservoir" (?) of Nineveh which had fallen in so that the inhabitants, liable to a water famine, "turned their eyes to the rains of heaven" on which they were dependent. The construction of canals goes back to the earliest times, ante 4000 B.C., according to those who hold to the date given by Nabonidus for Narâm-sin, 3750 B.C. Urukagina constructed and dedicated one to his goddess Nina.—*Craig.*

trees, were practically alone in their *arboreta.*
Whereas in Egypt stone in abundance for their
large buildings was found on the Upper Nile, and
was easily transported down the river, the Babylonians were compelled to bring even those which
they used for their statues from afar, and for
the most part overland. Thus we find *Gudea*
bringing the diorite for his sculptures from
Magan (Arabia). The colossal statues of Egypt
were, therefore, utterly unknown in Babylonia,
and their buildings were constructed of the only
material at hand, *viz.,* clay. Babylonia was the
land *par excellence* of *brick buildings,* and the
influence of Babylon upon the Orient nowhere
appears more clearly than in the imitation of her
architecture by Elamites, Assyrians, and Syrians
in their art and use of brick, though they had stone
in abundance. In default of wood and stone for
pillars necessity led to the invention of pillars
built of brick, but, so far as our present knowledge reaches, these were not in general use. Cedars
from Mount Amanus, and from Lebanon, after
the former was denuded of its supply, were found
to be ready substitutes for the pillars and necessary beams. But these were only occasionally
employed in construction. Assyria copied Babylonia even in this.

The brick most largely used was sun-dried; but
for more substantial buildings kiln-dried were

employed, and these when used for veneering the walls were enamelled with vari-colored scenes and representations. Instead of mortar they used *asphaltum* with which the country abounds.[1]

One of the most characteristic products of Babylonian construction in brick is their stepped-pyramids (zikurrat) which were carried upward, story upon story, to the number of seven at times, the wall of each successive one receding several feet from the one below. These constituted the glory of the great temples, and the topmost story was no doubt regarded as the dwelling-place of the deity.

The story of the Tower of Babel is connected with the tower (or zikurrat) of *E-saggil,* the temple of Bel-Merodach in Babylon. E-saggil means "the temple with the lofty tower." Owing to the statements of classical writers the invention of the arch has hitherto been attributed to the Etruscans, but the Babylonians made use of it in their most ancient buildings in Lagash, or Telloh.[2] Their technical skill rested on scientific principles no less unattainable in modern architecture than the Grecian idea of beauty in the

---

[1] *Cf.* Genesis, Cap. 11. "They (the builders of the tower of Babel) had brick for stone and bitumen (asphaltum) for mortar."—*Craig.*

[2] Recent discoveries have proved that the principle of the arch was known and applied in Babylonia almost 3000 years prior to the construction of the *Cloaca maxima* in Rome, *cir.* 1000 B.C., the oldest trace of it on classic soil.—*Craig.*

plastic art. The buildings which they constructed with brick must have been built according to rules and laws unknown to modern architecture, which views many of these ancient works with the same astonishment as is evoked by the Pyramids of Egypt.

The temples are by far the most excellent examples of Babylonian architecture. To a greater degree than the churches and convents of the Middle Ages they united in themselves all that Babylonian culture had developed in spiritual and material ability. We have already seen that they were in possession of a large part of the land and we must look upon them as the centres of intellectual life. The influence of the priesthood was not confined to religion; the cultivation of science, and even the technical arts, no doubt, shared their attention. Such an organization with its temple forms a city with governing powers of its own, and the means is in our hands for obtaining full information respecting their administration of affairs. Countless clay tablets furnish data of importance, but, unfortunately, they have not yet received much attention from Assyriologists.

E. RELIGION AND SCIENCE

The nature of our sources makes it difficult for us to acquire a knowledge of the spiritual side of life. It was natural that education and instruction in religious matters should be assumed by the priests. They alone, in early times, understood the secret of writing and consequently were the protectors and patrons of all literature, sacred or profane, and the so-called practical sciences. Of the latter we have little documentary knowledge—only a few mathematical tablets being found in our collections.[1] Their astronomical observations on an extended scale are attested by hundreds of tablets. Babylonia is the motherland of astronomy, and of astrology, which in the Orient is inseparable from it. As late as Hellenistic-Roman times the "Chaldeans" were still the reputed masters of the science. The observation and record of the movements of the heavenly bodies were accurate. Omens were put forth and all manner of conjunctions were prophecies written upon the scroll of heaven. An eclipse of the sun is recorded even in the Assyrian-Eponym Canon as an event as noteworthy as a war. When Thales, the Ionic philosopher, astounded the Ionic-Greek world by foretelling a solar eclipse he borrowed his wisdom from the Babylonians, as Pythagoras

[1] The science of medicine had already begun to protest against the spell of the exorcist and rituals, and though the priestly M.D. was gruesome enough at times in the potions he administered to his patient, many of his concoctions were mild compared to the brews prepared for the "Ricket"-suffering New Englander two hundred years ago. Hippocrates and Galen were indebted to Babylon. The same *ideogram* was used for doctor and magician and the god Ea was accredited with the healing art.—*Craig.*

drew his philosophy, with its symbolism of numbers from the same Semitic source.[1] A vast number of these observations of the heavenly bodies have come down to us, and numerous are the omens of the commonest arts of the prognosticator which we would gladly exchange for other material. Just as the Babylonians have lately proved their title to honor over the Etruscans for the invention of the arch found in classical Italy, so, too, the knowledge of the Etruscans, the masters and teachers of Rome, was of old Babylonian origin. Etruscan hepatoscopy and divination has lately been traced to the same source through a most interesting tablet in the British Museum which represents the liver of an animal divided by lines into a number of sections for this purpose. The Babylonian omens are the precursors of the *old* Sibylline Books (not the pseudepigraphic writings that have come down to us).

The observation of the movements of the heavenly bodies was naturally accompanied by the determination of the times and seasons. Greece and Rome, significant as the fact is, borrowed their calendar from the Babylonians. Their year,

---

[1] Even the principle of organization in the Pythagorean Society is borrowed from the Orient. The *religious gild, or sect,* appears in opposition to tribal organization. The religious bond takes the place of racial relationship. Somewhat similar in its essence was Judaism before it became ossified, and also primitive Christianity and Mohammedanism. In Africa today societies exist which are founded on this principle.

month, and week we have still. The naming of
days of the week after the gods of the sun and
moon and the other five planets known to them has
descended to us from them. We still divide the
day into 12 *double* hours, as the faces of our
watches prove.

In connection and harmony with these divisions
stands their numeral system. This was the sexa-
gesimal system, with the subdivisions 5 and 12,
apparently founded upon astronomical observations and calculations. In conjunction with this,
however, the decimal system was also used. Our
sources do not reach back to the time when either
of these two systems was introduced nor to a
period when one of them was used exclusively.
The systems of weights and measures rests upon
the same method of computation. Ancient Babylonia had, therefore, a system of reckoning that
has only lately in modern times been carried out
in our decimal system, after the unity of that
original method of computation had, during thousands of years of development, been lost to science.
We can see now that some recollection of its
source continued down to our own days, as in the
case of our chronological divisions; and we can
also watch its effects upon the peoples of the Occident and elsewhere, in the new expressions of it
which continually appear, without, however, being
able to decide by what intermediaries it passed

over from the Orient. All such questions belong to fields of investigation scarcely touched upon, in which interesting discoveries relating to the pre-historic connections of our modern civilizations await the future.

We are confronted with serious difficulties when we attempt to sketch the service of the temple and priesthood, worship and religion. It would require an extensive treatise to set forth the mani-fold changes of ideas which took place in connec-tion with the *cultus* in the course of three thousand years. Our sources here are much more frag-mentary than in the field of political history, and we have scarcely begun to grasp the ideas in their origin and growth. So long as the primitive times of Babylonia and the beginning of its civilization are veiled from view it will scarcely be possible to reach a certainty of knowledge sufficient to throw a clear light upon the essential nature and origin of the multiplex pantheon revealed by the inscriptions. The fundamental character, how-ever, of the Babylonian religion is discernible at a glance. It is an *astral* religion; the moon, sun, and stars are the central objects around which it turns. But it would be a gross misunderstanding to suppose that Babylonian theology identified the gods with the heavenly bodies. To do so would be as incorrect as to describe the Christian religion as a worship of heaven (or the heavens). The stellar world was, on the contrary, according to Babylonian theology only the supremest revelation of divine power, that revelation in which the governance and purposes of the gods could be most plainly observed. Moreover, all that is, the visible and invisible, is but an expression or part of the divine being. There are, it is true, countless gods, but these are only the forms through which *the one divine Power* is revealed. Such are the moon, the sun, the earth, the water, etc., from the greatest of objects to the smallest. In these the deity reveals himself; they are the forms of the divine becoming in matter, but behind them lies the one great Power.[1]

[1] We must guard against misunderstanding. We have to do here not with a religion, or *doctrine of Being* intended for all, but merely with the fundamental concepts of a cosmic philosophy ("*Weltanschaung*") whose profounder truths were revealed only to the initiated. In the cultus, or in the form, so to speak, in which religion finds its confirmation, it does not appear. The people knew of it only as the doctrine of the learned. [And since in primitive times no esoteric doctrine such as this could have existed, prolonged reflection and observation being the necessary conditions of its attainment, we must further guard against the conclusion that the statements made above, *viz.*, that Babylonian *theology* did not identify the gods with the astral bodies, and that the countless gods were regarded only as the *forms* through which the one divine power was revealed, lend confirmation to the erroneous notion of a *primitive monotheism* as so often held by theologians and philosophers, *e.g.*, Kreuzer, *Symbolik;* or for ex., in the case of the Israelites, Baethgen, *Beitraege zur Sem. Religionsgeschichte*, who endeavors to prove in the last part of his book that the primitive faith of Israel was *monotheistic*. Complete failure must attend every attempt to maintain a theory so opposed to the history of the race as a whole and so irreconcilable with the ascertainable processes of human development. Ancient literatures, whether

The heavenly bodies are, consequently, only
the most important forms through which the
divine power is revealed. Whether this conception of things comes so near to the truth when
judged by modern thought is, perhaps, worthy of
reflection. The conception itself is unmistakably
uttered in an explanatory astronomical tablet.
This says of the planet Jupiter, the planet of
Marduk, the head of the Babylonian pantheon:
"When Jupiter stands some degrees above the
horizon he is the god of the planet Mercury; when
he stands higher he is the god of the planet Jupiter; when he reaches his culmination he is the god
of Mars." Jupiter always remains the same
planet independently of its position, but a different divine power reveals itself in it, is active in it,
according to the position reached: another aspect
of the divine activity appears with each succeeding change, just as others appear in the water, in
the earth, in the individual stone, tree, metal, fire,
man, etc. Therefore, among the Babylonians the
science of the stars, astronomy, was the science
of sciences. It pointed out to them the divine will
and taught them how this will revealed itself

Semitic or Indo-Germanic, point, in my judgment, to quite the
opposite—the heavenly bodies *were* regarded in the *primitive ages*
as supernatural beings, and that very naturally. Polytheism and
animism must have existed side by side. This Babylonian *esoteric*
theology did not spring up at once like Athena from the head of
Zeus.]—*Craig.*

everywhere in nature. The starry heavens is the open book in which the destiny of heaven and earth, and of all that is upon it, is recorded and in which it may be read. It is, consequently, no accident which made the Babylonians the world's teachers in astronomy. This conception of the universe *was* astronomy, and out of it alone could an astronomy be developed, just as our conception of the universe also grew out of astronomy.

In the stars, the Babylonian beheld the whole divine will and, therefore, all earthly things must be images of the heavenly. For that which exists above as archetype must find its counter type here below. The organized state must conform exactly to the heavenly prototype.

Times and seasons were determined by the greater heavenly bodies, as they were also by later Judaism in the post-exilic priestly code.[1] The conceptions of the Babylonians and the importance of their astronomy can, therefore, be most clearly perceived in the science of their calendar. For the calendar, based on the observation of the planetary movements, is the first requisite and, for practical daily life, the most important requisite for a conception of the world which concludes what its destiny is by observation of the courses of the stars. This calendrical-science stands in

---

[1] *Cf. e.g.* Gen. 1, 14.

the closest organic connection with the doctrine as to *all that is;* it reflects the entire system of the universe and forms its basis.[1]

A complete pantheon by itself appears in the inscriptions of the early rulers of Lagash (Telloh). It is possible that this still points back to the Sumerian influence of an early epoch which, nevertheless, was Semitic. This is suggested by the names and cults of certain gods. The period stands historically even almost by itself. It is nevertheless clear that peculiarities of the "Canaanite" inhabitants are discernible in it, and, on the other hand, that the broad general views as to God and the universe are specifically Babylonian. Here, as elsewhere, we are forced to recognize the fact that we are far from the beginning of civilization. But that which we meet with in the inscriptions of the *Southern Babylonian* dynasties helps us who have to study history backward. There the deities we meet with are the same deities that from then on constantly reappear. The simple explanation of that is found in the fact that these Southern Babylonian cities maintained their importance throughout the whole period of Babylonian civilization, whereas Lagash comes before us as the relic of a city of bygone times that was prematurely destroyed. But we are still too imperfectly informed to account for

---

[1] *Cf.* on the reform of Nabunatsir, p. 63.

the peculiar phenomena which we meet with here for the first time.

That which we do meet with is Semitic or Semitized, but how does it stand related to the past? The question cannot be answered until it is known how the old culture-cities—*Eridu, Ur, Larsa, Isin, Uruk*—stood in relation to the older culture. The names of the deities show at once what was the dominant cult: In Ur the moon-god, in Larsa the worship of the sun, in Uruk Nana or Ishtar, the female principle, in Nippur was the temple of Bêl, the "Lord of Lands," *i.e.*, the earth. But each one of these, and many another unknown centre, had developed in its temple during the centuries and milleniums a theology of its own. Mixed up with this, and matured by the effort to reconcile it with the teaching of other centres, was an independent view, as to the *causa rerum,* that grew up around the god. In addition the different immigrations left behind them a "deposit of faith." The newly introduced ideas and the old native *views* had always to be adjusted and adapted to one another. It is true that the *cultus,* so far as we can follow it historically, had already acquired considerable fixity. The Semitic immigrations of the three milleniums known to us introduced nothing very *essential*. Still, some important ideas appear even now for the first time as, for example, the change of the worship of the god of the

atmosphere, Adad or Ramman, by the "Canaanites." But, the less we are able to follow the
development of ideas, the more necessary it is to
seek for their origin in a time that as yet is
wrapped in obscurity. At best it would be a
herculean task to disentangle the various threads
that cross one another in the different traditions
of the temples and follow them back to their beginnings. It is very doubtful if this can ever be
done. At present, however, we are immeasurably
far from the beginning, for we know nothing of
the real object of the investigation, *viz.*, the temple traditions, with the exception of the little
that we know of the Marduk-cult in Babylon.

The farther *North* we go the purer appears the
Semitic in the period known to us; Sumerian is
no longer written here in the oldest discovered
inscriptions of the time of Naram-Sin. The dupli-
cation of the cultus shows that the country stood
divided into North and South. There was a South
Babylonian sun-god in Larsa, and a North Babylonian one in Sippar. The Ishtar of Uruk in the
South had a rival in the Northern city of Agade.
We know less of the North in the early times
than of the South. Later, after the first Babylonian dynasty, other cities appear; *Cutha* with its
cult of Nergal, the god of the under world.
Moon worship, which had its chief seat in Ur, had
not the same importance in the North; but in

Harran of Mesopotamia stood the most famous sanctuary of the moon-god.

Babylon has not yet come to light in the inscriptions of the oldest period. It is possible and probable that it owes its importance to political conditions of a comparatively late age. It may have been first founded by Sargon of Agade, if a much mutilated passage in the omens relating to his reign may be made to bear this interpretation. It became the most influential city of Babylonia, as we have seen, during the first dynasty. When it became the capital of the Babylonian empire, and thereby gained at the same time authority in economic life, there was developed in accordance with the Oriental way of thinking a *theologico-historico* justification of Babylon's greatness.[1] Just as Athens sought, when it reached the hegemony, through mythology and history to establish its antiquity, so the learned priests and scribes of Babylon tried to conjure forth witnesses and proofs to show that she was the seat of the oldest culture and the centre of the world, and they did it with greater success.

Marduk, the biblical Merodach, and former god of the city, becomes at once, by the priestly manipulation, the chief god in the work of creating the world. We have fragments of the creation-

---

[1] The Orient, everywhere, Babylon, Assyria, Israel, etc., knew the religious value of a " *Tendenz-Schrift.*"—*Craig.*

myth of Babylon which ascribe the leading rôle to Marduk. In Southern Babylonian temples there doubtless existed similar works of early origin which reflected the conditions of the most flourishing period of *their* respective cities. The creation-epic anticipates the predominance of Babylon which was first established by the dynasty of Sumuabi and Khammurabi. It is Marduk who is made to enter the lists in a world-struggle for the rule of the *dii superi* which is threatened by the chaotic *Tihamat*, and who, after cutting in two the monster, conceived of as a great serpent or dragon, creates the world and its firmament out of the two halves. In Nippur the hero was doubtless Bel, the god of that city. In the sanctuaries of the other cities the leading rôle of Shamash (sun), Sin (moon), Ishtar would be illuminated. The later the myth the greater the necessity for giving due consideration to those that preceded. Whether we shall ever become acquainted with the time in which the growth of these separate myths will appear clear to view we cannot say. At present we know chiefly some fragments of the latest which enable us to make out the connection. Of some of the others we have only insignificant remnants. Although we must assume that a copious literature of such epics and myths grew up during the thousands of years, we know, at present, not much beyond the fact that they received their final redaction in Babylon during the first dynasty. The Gilgamish epic, it is true, is for the most part known to us from the copies made for the library of Ashurbanipal. Some fragments of it, however, from copies made in the time of the First Dynasty, have lately been found. The deluge narrative had at that time been cast into the form in which it has come down to us; but this was by no means an ancient period in the life of Babylonia.

The creation-myths of Babylonia are the patterns after which the biblical are composed; just as Babylonia was the teacher of Western Asia in all intellectual matters. We have almost no other witnesses of this than the comparatively few fragments of Assyro-Babylonian literature which thus far have been recovered from the ruins (and for the most part from the library of Ashurbanipal) and the remnants of Jewish literature which have been saved for us through canonization in the Bible. The relation of each to the other is that existing between the focusing point of all culture and an insignificant, inferior state—that between origination and imitation. But so long as we have nothing more we must attempt to form from what we have our view of the religious life of the Orient.

Religion undoubtedly played a rôle in the life of this people which the modern man may only too easily underestimate. The priests were the fosterers of science. Consquently every doctrine, every attempt to penetrate into the essential nature of things, every confirmation and justification of that which is, and every attempt to introduce something new, had to be tested by reference to the hoary doctrine of "Beginnings," and, by that, justified or disapproved. The mental attitude of the Middle Ages which tested the rightness and righteousness of everything by the teachings of the Bible, as the reformers and their opponents appealed to the Bible in support of their religious and political demands, was exactly that of the ancient Orient. And more than this, these teachings whose power is still often more potent over the life of modern peoples than is clear to those not historically educated—these old Babylonian doctrines, carried forward in various forms by Jews and other peoples into the varied conditions of civilized life, remain in essence what they were—the expression of the Babylonian hierarchy as the *representative of all intellectual life in the most ancient civilization*. We may, perhaps, think we are justified in maintaining that the prayers and ideas of Judaism reveal *a different world of thought* from that presented by the polytheism of the rest of the Orient. But, the view, or pious belief in the development of Judaism, and in its later manifestations, takes on quite a different aspect in the light of universal history.

Proof of this in matters of *detail* cannot be adduced from the fragmentary literature; but it is evident to the simplest reflection on the nature and origin of human thoughts that the ideas which conquered the old civilized world did not spring up in some remote corner. In brief, where the exciting cause is present an idea may arise, and the same mental struggles which Israel and Judah had to pass through for the first time under the kings, or in the exile, Babylonia passed through frequently long before in the course of her prosperous periods. The fruits of such struggles had long since been acquired in the intellectual life of the Babylonians. It was thence that the "Prophet" of Israel got his spiritual weapons, his education, and his knowledge, and there Judaism must have received not only its impulse, but also its entire system.

In the life of a civilized people, such as the Babylonian, numerous occasions arise where discontent with existing conditions bring together large assemblies who frame their demands into a system, and, after the manner of the Orient, justify it. As all Oriental history teaches, life for many must also have assumed at such time the form of a sect, which grew out of social conditions, and which sought to establish its teachings especially on religious grounds. Many such sects must have arisen and have been favored by the force of circumstances; and from the ideas they promulgated Judaism must have drawn for its own. That the hidden courses of human thought and history which led to the development of these ideas shall be again made clear to view cannot be expected. This much, however, we may confidently conclude from what we know, and from the laws of human development, that the origins of the fundamental teachings of Judaism not yet discovered in cuneiform literature shall yet be found there. *The doctrine of a coming Deliverer* could arise only in the centre of culture where the prestige of power was no longer what it was in a greater past. The doctrine is genetically related to that view of the universe which inferred from the circuits of the planets the reoccurrence of everything else in the world, whether great or small, and which read by the light of the stars the future development of all things on the earth, and in the universe.[1]

Next to the teachings of religion and closely connected therewith mental activity finds expression in the development of mythology. In so far as this is a doctrine of gods and temples we have already seen how limited our knowledge is. We have to lament the same limitation with respect to the fragments of this literature which deals with mythological heroes and which always takes a prime place in the non-religious poetry. A great

---

[1] *Cf.* below the remarks on Sargon of Assyria.

number of fragments bear witness to the existence of a whole series of epics, but of very few
have we recovered enough to enable us to ascertain
their contents, or conjecture them. The best
known of all is the *Gilgamish*[1] *Epic.* The name
of the hero is written *Is-tu-bar,* and so he was
at first called; and, as he was supposed to be the
biblical Nimrod, the name Nimrod-epic became
general. Gilgamish is the Babylonian Heracles,
whose deeds are glorified in the poem which furnished the Hellenic Alexander-romance with the
legendary material it wove around the name of
the Macedonian conqueror. The form in which
the epic has come down to us it received in *Uruk.*
According to tradition the old Ishtar-Nana city
had been founded by Gilgamish, and the epic
reflects the conditions into which it had fallen
as the result of Elamite oppression. Gilgamish,
like Heracles, is essentially a *solar* mythological
figure. One of the episodes described in the epic
is the story of the Deluge which forms the basis
of the biblical account. The brief epic of *Ishtar's
descent into the under-world* to restore from the
world of spirits her dead brother and spouse,
Tammuz (Adonis), is preserved in its entirety.

[1] Formerly following Geo. Smith, who discovered the epic, the
name of the hero which is written ideographically was read phonetically *Izdubar* until Mr. Pinches discovered the true pronunciation
a few years ago. See for Smith's first account Trans. Soc. Bib.
Arch. ii., 213 ff., iii., 530 ff.—*Craig.*

Other epics, portions of which exist, are *Etana and the Eagle*, the legends of the *Plague Demon*, and of the *Storm-god, Zû*. But these are not yet perfectly understood.[1]

The *Fables of Animals*, so natural to the Oriental, were also complete in early times in Babylonia. We have fragments of the *"Ox and Horse*," the *Fox*, the *Serpent-god*, and others of which, however, we must be content to know even less than of the preceding until more has been discovered. Numerous unpublished fragments, too broken to be understood, as is the case with many similar compositions, create a hope that the future may reward us with a completer knowledge.

F. COMMERCE, BUSINESS, INDUSTRY

To present clearly the importance of *Babylonian industry* and *trade* would be one of the most worthy tasks and one accompanied by most satisfactory results. But we are by no means in a position to do this, though it is clear that during three thousand years the ups and downs of business were as great as the changes in political life. We can take it for granted that Babylonia's, and particularly Babylon's, importance and preponderance rested upon her industry and business. In the entire period through which we can follow

---

[1] Translations of the epics and myths are given by Jensen in Schrader's *Keilinschriftliche Bibliothek*, Bd. vi.—*Craig*.

Assyria's power, Babylon was as a political unity, powerless. It was compelled to purchase its independence from Assyria or, on the other hand, to win with gold the support of Elam against her. It lacked the men necessary to wage a war on its own account, as it could not otherwise be under the conditions which controlled landed property. This fact alone is sufficient to show that it was predominantly an industrial land. It was doubtless part of Sennacherib's intention in the destruction of Babylon to divert a part of its trade and industry to his own newly chosen capital, Nineveh.

We have previously seen that Babylonian politics from the time of the Kassite dynasty were bent on controlling the way through Mesopotamia to the Mediterranean, and that Kadashman-Kharbe then attempted to secure a road through the desert to Syria and the Phœnician harbors. In this effort there can be no doubt that he had Babylonian trade in mind. As to the conditions of trade in earlier times Gudea's inscriptions furnish us data for some conclusions. Gudea transported both stone and wood for his buildings from Phœnicia, Syria, and Arabia. The Tel-Amarna letters also throw some light on Babylonian industry.[1] Both Babylonians and the princes of Mitani demanded gold from Egypt. The *quid pro quo* was industrial products, especially lapis lazuli, so

[1] *Cf.* p. 78 ff.

highly prized by the Egyptians, or an imitation of it, one of the chief products of Babylonian exports. The Egyptians got weapons and battle chariots from Mitani and even from Assyria. When the Babylonians ordered inlaid work in ivory and ebony in Egypt they were dealing only in fashionable objects in Egyptian style such as have been found in Nineveh. These signified no more with them than Chinese porcelain or Japanese handiwork among ourselves.

Little is known as yet of the shipping trade on the Persian Gulf, and, consequently, the other question related to this, *viz.,* the commercial route to India, by which the eastern and western worlds communicated, cannot be answered. It is inconceivable that the oldest civilization of Babylonia which grew up in the South did not develop navigation on the "Sea of the Rising Sun." At the point at which our knowledge begins we find that it has already advanced inland toward the North. Naturally, in view of the contents, no mention of such matters is to be found in the oldest inscriptions, and there is little prospect that the near future will add to our knowledge. In later times the Chaldeans kept up navigation on the gulf. The country known as the "Sea-Land," which prospered for centuries, doubtless owed a part of its prosperity and its power to withstand Assyria to the wealth acquired through traffic with the East. Merodach-baladan possessed ships on which he fled across the "bitter-waters," or great Lagoon, to Elam. At that time there was no fleet in Babylonia. Sennacherib had to employ naval architects from Phœnicia to build ships for him in Assyria, and these were thence taken South by river.[1] Under these circumstances there could not have been any trade with the East. Dilmun, the island of Bahrein, including also the adjoining coast lands, which the early Babylonians regarded as a part of their territory, was in the time of Sargon II. a distant island from which he alone among the kings of the period collected tribute. None of his successors mention it. The traffic on the Persian Gulf was probably under the control of Elam.

Few products of Babylonian industry have come down to us. Only a very few and comparatively insignificant monumental remains of architure and sculpture, of which Assyria has furnished so many, have been recovered from the mounds of the mother-land. Those of Telloh have yielded the most and have supplied us with a goodly number of statues and sculptures of the kings and patesis of Lagash. Starting from the crude beginnings of the first kings, and rapidly progressing, the statues of Gudea and his age, the sculptures of Naram-Sin, show the highest

---

[1] Even the sailors who manned these ships were drawn from Tyre, Sidon, and Javan.—*Craig.*

attainment in technique. It appears as if we had here a sudden renaissance after a period of great decline. The careful and exquisite work on a monument of Merodach-baladan, in which he is represented in the act of clothing a vassal with the investiture of office, is one of the few known products of later art.[1] A great number of similar monuments, dating from the Kassite period onward, cannot compare with this in point of execution. Some few representations in clay from real life prove only that the future may yet reveal to us evidence of keen and humorous portrayal of private life.

The same limitations extend to our knowledge of the rules and form of the state constitution, the administration, and army. The Babylonian inscriptions, in contrast to the Assyrian, never deal with the wars and other deeds of the rulers. That which we are able to present on these points is rather to be inferred from the better attested methods of Assyria, which, since they sprang up under like conditions, manifest, in the main features, similar forms of development.

---

[1] It is now in the Royal Museum of Berlin. An excellent reproduction of it is to be found in Helmolt's *Weltgeschichte*, Bd. iii., S. 29. Notwithstanding its excellence the bano of Babylonian art, servile imitation, is nowhere better illustrated than on this monolith. The vassal, with the exception of cap and sandals, is simply a minor reproduction of the king. The robes they wear are identical and the lines in which they fall do not vary a hair's-breadth. A painful lack of freedom and spontaneity in conception is the result.—*Craig*.

II—ASSYRIA

ASSYRIA

CHAPTER I

THE MESOPOTAMIAN PERIOD

WE have already seen that the rise of Assyria took place in a time upon which the full light of history falls, or which can be illuminated without difficulty by the excavations. It has been further pointed out that its natural extension in the first place was toward Mesopotamia. This became a part of its undisputed territory, and the possession of it raised Assyria to a sovereign power as large and as important as Babylonia. Before we enter upon the history of Assyria it is, therefore, necessary to get a clear idea of the state of affairs in Mesopotamia.

We have assumed, and results, so far as they can be traced historically, confirm it, that the great Semitic immigrations within Babylonia followed, in the main, the direction from north to south. Mesopotamia was consequently exposed to them at a still earlier time. The first Semites that we meet with in Southern Babylonia, as representatives of historical times, must at one

167

time have been dwellers of Mesopotamia. What preceded them is yet still more a prehistoric question than life in Babylonia, inasmuch as no excavations whatever have been conducted there.

We have a large collection of omens which relate to conditions about 3000 B.C., the time of Sargon and Naram-Sin (although they also take account of later times and received their present form at a much later period). Their geographical boundary indicates clearly the extent of Babylonian influence and culture. This collection, beside mentioning the king of South Babylonia, and the one of North Babylonia, knows also of another king who bore the title *Shar Kishshati,* that is, *"king of the World."* (*Cf.* p. 47, "king of the Four Quarters of the World.") His kingdom can have had its centre only in Mesopotamia, at least northward from Babylonia. However that may be, we are certain not only that Mesopotamia stood under the influence of Babylonian culture, but also that it formed an integral part of it, and that it had its share in shaping the development of the Euphratean lands. That this was so is attested by the fact of the importance and honor ascribed to the chief sanctuary there, that of Sin, the moon-god of Harran. It is no accident when one of the biblical narratives makes Ur and the other Harran the scene of Abraham's early life. Both of them were in the eyes of all

Oriental peoples the ·places *par excellence* of
moon-worship, and *Sin,* on the other hand, was
the most important god of Babylonia. We meet
also with the worship of Ba'al-Harran, the god of
Harran, in Sendjirli in Northern Syria. A relief
from there consecrated to him is now in the
Berlin Museum.

In political history we can form a fair estimate
of the rôle which this country played. A development similar to that which we have traced in the
South must have taken place there. The kingdom
which grew up must have fought the like wars with
its rivals, as we find later to have been waged
by Assyria, who fell heir to it. "Kings of the
World" must have entered into rivalry with the
kings of Babylon for the dominion of Babylonia,
and, in turn, have fallen subject to them. As we
have already seen, Mesopotamia was, in ancient
times as now, the connecting link between Babylonia and the West. Our inscriptions furnish us
with no information of these wars in the time
prior to 1500 B.C., but the following period aids
us sufficiently in forming a general picture of
the times until the spade shall have won its honors
in these fields also. Sir Austen H. Layard once
began to dig in Arban, in the Khabur valley, and
secured antiquities from a palace of one of the
patesis (or priest-kings) by the name of *Mushesh-
Ninib.* These monuments indubitably belong to

the pre-Assyrian Mesopotamian period. In addition to these, antiquities have been found of a Hittite type, and of a crude age, similar to those found at Senjirli in Syria, at the ruin *Tel-Halaf,* near *Ras-al-cain* at the source of the Khabur. Moreover, the site of *Bit-Adini,* the outpost of the Mesopotamian Aramæan kingdom, and known to Ashur-natsir-pal and Shalmaneser II., has been fixed. Some remains exposed at Harran probably belong to Assyrian times, as Shalmaneser II. and Ashurbanipal both wrought on the temple of the moon-god.

We must assume that a kingdom that had its capital in Harran, or somewhere else northward from Babylonia, not only cast eager eyes toward the latter, but also, and at first, tried to acquire territory from less civilized peoples. As Mesopotamia was the intervening link in the connection between Babylonia and Syria and Palestine, so Mesopotamia, as an independent power was the natural conqueror of these lands, whether by peaceful methods or by force of arms. As an indication of the first side of this extension reference has already been made to the notices of Abraham's cult at Hebron and that of the moon-god in Sendjirli.[1] We shall see later how in historical times the successors of these Mesopotamian kings possessed the regions on the right

[1] P. 169.

bank of the Euphrates and the district of *Malatia* as far as Cappadocia and very probably as far as Cilicia beyond the Taurus. Harran furthermore ruled the roads which in the North led into Armenia. From this point we find the Assyrians at an early period under Adad-nirari I. and Shalmaneser I. pushing up between the two rivers, while still expanding toward Babylonia, and this immediately after they had taken possession of Mesopotamia. Clay tablets written in Babylonian very similar to the Tel-Amarna tablets, have been found in Cappadocia. They reveal the influence of Assyrian colonization in these regions, and consequently belong to the first period of Assyria's appearance there under Shalmaneser I., *cir.* 1300 B.C. The character of the language and writing show that they were not novelties in that region, but, on the contrary, that long practice in the art of writing antedated them.

CHAPTER II

THE KINGS OF MITANI

THE first records which we have show us Mesopotamia under foreign rule. Our sources are the Tel-Amarna Letters of King Dushratta of Mitani to Amenophis III. and Amenophis IV. The picture which they afford us of the intercourse between the two lands holds good also for the predecessors of the two Pharaohs, in so far as they advanced into Asia. *Naharina* is the name by which they generally speak of Mesopotamia. In this connection it is a matter of comparative indifference how much gold Dushratta begged for himself from Egypt, or how many letters he wrote to get the best of a bargain with his "brother" and son-in-law there. That which is of prime interest is to recognize that these *Mitani princes* are the represenatives of a *barbarian immigration* which took possession of Mesopotamia. The god *Teshub,* whom they worship, was also sacred to the Hittite people in the north of Asia Minor along the river Halys. This would seem to establish a relationship between them and the latter. The only letter in the native language, one from Dushratta to Amenophis III., is, therefore, a monument of "Hittite," or an allied language. Names similar to the Hittite and the Mitanian of this period we meet with again later in the people of Kummukh and their kindred under Tiglathpileser I. They belong then to the same family group. The deporting of Marduk's statue to the land of *Khani* as reported by Agu-Kakrime,[1] might lend support to the hypothesis of an earlier stage of this Hittite conquest. The Kassite occupation of Babylonia is a case in point, as it parallels the appearance of these Hittites or Mitani in the northern regions.

The residence of the Mitani kings is not disclosed by their letters; but the country known by them as Mitani must have lain approximately to the north of Harran, where at all events their national centre was. As we have already noted, it fell as an inheritance to the last old Mesopotamian kingdom and its extent can, therefore, be computed. In the direction of Babylonia it included Nineveh, which, accordingly, in the time of Dushratta, *cir.* 1430 B.C., had not become Assyrian as it must formerly have been Mesopotamian. As a matter of course the whole of Mesopotamia belonged to it, and Melitene (Khanigalbat) on the right bank of the Euphrates, and the adjoining part of Cappadocia as far as the Taurus, and possibly beyond as far as Cilicia. To this part of Cappadocia the Assyrians gave the name *Mutsri,*

[1] P. 73.

the Egyptians *Sanqara*. (In one of the Tel-Amarna letters from Alashia it is called Shank-har.) To the west and north of this portion of the kingdom were the Kheta (Hittites), the opponents of the Mitani but related by race to them. With them they waged wars and one of them is referred to in a letter of Dushratta to Amenophis III. The Kheta must either have pressed through the region of the Mitani when they got into Syria, or they only skirted the territory of Mitani and entered Cilicia through the Cilician gates.

Upon their profuse asseverations of friendship with Egypt there rests the same suspicion as upon those of the Babylonians. The kings of Mitani are also declared by Egyptian vassals in Phœnicia to be the natural enemies of a faithful servant of Pharaoh.

This kingdom must have existed a long time; for Dushratta, the writer of the letters, names his father, Sutarna, who sent his daughter, Gilukhipa, to the harem of Amenophis III. This is also attested by an Egyptian document. He also mentions his grandfather, Artatama, who had dealings with Thothmes IV., the predecessor of Amenophis III., and had concluded the same sort of a bargain with him. It usually turns on the question of dowry. The writer of the letter was himself at the court of Amenophis III.; he may have grown up there as a sort of hostage when his

father died. In one of his letters to Pharaoh he
informs him of an insurrection which broke out to
which his brother fell a victim, and how upon
his return he quelled it. In the same letter he
tells of the war with the Kheta, who wished to
make use of the opportunity against him.

In the midst of all the parley and pother about
presents there is one letter which contains an
important historical statement. Dushratta writes
to Amenophis III. that he would like to have him
return the statue of the goddess Ishtar of
Nineveh, which shortly before had been sent down
to Egypt, as she had been sent back with honor
during the days of his father when she had been
there. It is not quite clear what this journey of
Ishtar meant. One can hardly explain it otherwise than that Dushratta, as his father also, had
conquered Nineveh and did not dare to take the
goddess, the sign of victory, home with them,
but—presumably because of her anger, which
decided her to go into a strange land—sent her
to the Egyptian king whose over-lordship was
thereby acknowledged. With this the tribute
spoken of in the Egyptian inscriptions would well
agree. The question arises then: From whom
did Dushratta take Nineveh? Hardly from
Assyria, but rather from Babylonia; but the
answer cannot be given decisively. For us the
most important thing is the fact here attested that

Dushratta actually was lord of Nineveh, for this fact furnishes us with an assured starting-point from which to determine the advance of Assyria. Dushratta's date corresponds almost with the close of the brilliant period of his people. The next eighty or one hundred years saw Assyria mistress of Mesopotamia, and her kings take the title "king of the World" after they have driven out the Mitani, a title which they have to defend against Babylonia.

The rule of the kings of Mitani who are known to us coincides with the end of the epoch introduced with the advance of this group of peoples beyond the Euphrates. It may have passed in its first strength as far as Babylonia,[1] where at the time of the First Dynasty of Babylon, *cir.* 2000 B.C., it appears to have made itself felt. When during the Tel-Amarna period the Kassites of Babylonia and the Mitani of Mesopotamia appear as rivals, the most probable supposition would be that the Mitani or their predecessors were driven back.

[1] The origin of a clay-tablet containing a contract between "Hittite" or Mitani persons is not yet determined.

CHAPTER III

THE RISE OF THE LAND OF ASHUR

As was the case with "the kingdom of Babylon," the "land of Ashur" was originally limited. It comprised the territory belonging to the city of Ashur, the modern *Kalah Shergat*. In later times this lay almost outside of the limits of Assyria proper, that is to say, without the boundary formed by a line running from Nineveh to the mountain range, the Tigris, and the Lower Zab. It is certain, from the position of Ashur in the South, and at the same time on the east bank of the Tigris, that it could not be the capital of the later land of Ashur. It inclined rather in the direction of the south, toward Babylonia, than toward the north and west, in which direction it first began to expand. When we assume, therefore, that Ashur was once a city like so many in the Euphrates valley we are inclined to the opinion that its *patesis* ruled under the protection of Babylonia, at times under that of Mesopotamia. The territory between the Upper and Lower Zab formed almost a province by itself. It had its own capital, *Arbela* (Arba'il), which, in the time of Assyrian great-

ness, had an importance on the cultural side such
as Ashur had in the more limited Assyria, or Harran in Mesopotamia. After the fall of Assyria
this part of the country became again the real
seat of administrative power, or paramount in the
formation of states. Arbela must, therefore,
also have played the part of a capital in pre-
Assyrian times. The central point of the numerous forms of states which must have existed in
pre-Assyrian centuries and millenniums was also
at times to be found here, and excavations would
probably bring to light documents which would
reveal such a condition. On the east this region
was bounded by the mountain territory of the
Lulubî, one of whose kings, Anu-banini, left an
inscription in the Zagros mountains. It belongs
apparently to the period of Naram-Sin. In the
plain was the capital of the province, whose king,
Bukhia, son of Asiri, had his palace near Kerkuk,
east of the Lower Zab, and called himself "king
of the Land Khurshiti." The inscription is pre-
Assyrian and is written in ancient style. It was
the only one found, but, with a few more clay-
tablets from the same region and possibly from
the same place,[1] and also pre-Assyrian, it suggests

[1] The name of the mound is *Vyran-Shehii* near Kerkuk. Many
tablets were obtained from this place by Bagdad dealers in antiq
uities a few years ago, and 300 pieces of the collection are said to
have been sold in London. See Meissner, O. L. Z., 1902, S. 245.—
Craig.

what results might be anticipated if excavations were made.

Nineveh must have played in prehistoric times a similar rôle to that which we have assumed for Arbela. Nineveh and Assyria are almost identical names for us, but the city first rose to greatness under Sennacherib when it became the royal seat. But on the other hand, as the result of the rise of Assyria, it lost its original importance, a fact which is attested, as at Arbela, by the respect for its cult of Ishtar of Nineveh. In the period of the Tel-Amarna Letters it belonged as we saw to the Mitani. Naturally, as the former centre of worship in the country, it always maintained its influence under Assyrian rule—just as Arbela did—and the Assyrian kings shared in the building and restoring of its temples. But it was not until Sennacherib that it became the seat of government.

The city of Ashur was not the capital of a large kingdom in historical times, but was ruled by patesis. Sufficient evidence of this is at hand and also of the approximate time when the new power arose. Tiglathpileser I. lived about 1100 B.C. In one of his inscriptions he states that he restored a temple in Ashur and that this temple had been built six hundred and forty-one years before the time of his grandfather, who had repaired it sixty years previously. The original builder was Shamshi-Adad, *patesi* of Ashur, son of Ishmi-Dagan, *patesi* of Ashur. About 1800 B.C., at the time of the Second Dynasty of Babylon, there were accordingly patesis of Ashur who were dependent either upon Babylonia or Mesopotamia, more likely upon the former. The same situation may without hesitation be assumed for the time when the city of Ashur is first clearly mentioned. This occurs in a letter of the time of Khammurabi, when apparently it lay within his dominion. The names of four other patesis are known to us from their own inscriptions, *viz.*, Shamshi-Adad and his father, Igur-Kappapu, Irishu and his father.[1]

The first king of Assyria whose date can be approximately fixed is Ashur-rim-nishi-shu, the contemporary of Kara-indash of Babylon. Between 1800 and 1500 B.C. Ashur was, therefore, independent; its patesis call themselves kings, and, possibly under the influence of a new immigration, have begun to extend their borders. The cause and the conditions under which this was possible were akin to those which made the Kassites masters of Babylonia and gave Mesopotamia to the Mitani. Tumultuous times offered to vigorous rulers a favorable opportunity to found a kingdom for themselves. On the other hand, the

---

[1] The German excavations at Kalah-Shergat have lately brought to light the names of a large number of such Patesis, names which, for the most part, are to be found in later inscriptions that are not yet published.

separation which resulted between the two parts of
the formerly united land, through the rule of two
foreign peoples, made it possible for the intervening portion to found a state by itself. Before we
enter upon the history of this new kingdom it will
be of advantage to ask what it was in the general
breakdown of Semitism at this time that secured
the stability and power of the Semites of Ashur
which from that time forward gave success to its
arms, and what was the character of this future
ruler of the Orient?

The *Assyrian type* is markedly differentiated
from the Babylonian, which as we have seen is the
result of a mixture of races. The numerous
Assyrian representations show us a sharply
defined physiognomy, exactly that which it is customary to regard as Semitic; it is the type we call
"Jewish." Our designation is erroneous in so
far as this type is wholly different from the Arabic
in which we would naturally look for the purest
Semitic type, if, indeed, we are at all justified in
speaking of pure Semites. On the other hand, it
corresponds essentially to the modern Armenian,
whose language is Indo-Germanic. The explanation of this does not fall to the task of the historian; he has to do with the history of peoples
and takes language as a useful mark of differenti-
ation. The recognition of physical peculiarities
as a determining principle in matters of race is

quite a different thing, for racial connections and
linguistic divisions are matters entirely distinct.
How the Assyrians developed their type, and to
what larger group it is to be referred does not
concern us greatly here, and the answer is difficult owing to the lack of sufficient data. Starting with physical anthropological traits, it has
been suggested that a Mesopotamian Canaanite-
Armenian group may be differentiated, and this is
supported by facts of history. It is to be observed
that Assyria was as much affected by Canaanite
immigration as Babylonia was, if not more. The
fusion of races consequent thereon may, therefore, appear in the Assyrian type. Thus Canaanite ideas persisted longer in Assyria, which was,
moreover, in closer proximity to countries of
Canaanite population. The god Dagon, for example, was worshipped by the later Assyrians. It is,
however, sufficient for us to note the readily recognized Assyrian type.

The question then arises: Whence came the
remarkable superiority of this people over the
other nations of Western Asia? It must have
been due chiefly to two facts; national organization and social conditions. Assyria must have
possessed until the time of Shalmaneser II. and
Adad-nirari III., when it outrivalled Babylonia, a
free class of agriculturalists of its own, whereas
the more economically developed country, with

the oldest civilization, was under a feudal, ecclesi-
astical system on which its population was wholly
dependent. Hence the weakness of Babylonia. She
had no army of her own, but depended for her
defence upon allies whose intentions were often
doubtful. Assyria, on the other hand, as late as
Shalmaneser II., called out the militia when
important occasions arose. Tiglathpileser III.
attempted, as we shall see, to deliver the agricultural class from the chains of serfdom, which,
in the interim, had developed in Assyria, and the
reaction followed under Sargon. In the meantime Assyria had indeed attained to the height
of her power, the way for which had been prepared by Tiglathpileser; but she failed to reach
a true development. The brief success which
followed was without lasting influence and is
attributable to the other side of her national organization whose foundation was laid in freedom.

The growth of a *patesidom* into a kingdom, as
happened in the case of Assyria, was possible only
at a time when the city rulers could command a
force fit for combat. To what extent it may have
been connected with the entrance of a new population into Ashur and Assyria we know not. We
are, however, inclined to assume some connection.
Just as David with a trustworthy band was able
in a period of general disorganization to make
himself king over a state made up of several

tribes, so, to a greater extent did the patesis of Ashur. Assyria's strength as opposed to the industrially developed region of the lower Euphrates valley rested, in the first place, upon an army. This was the necessary condition of its rise and rule. It was thus possible for the land to produce a peasant or agricultural class. When at a later period this class was jeopardized, and the efforts of Tiglathpileser III. to save it proved fruitless, mercenaries from every land, subjugated and barbarian, were recruited, and with these Sargon and his successors waged their wars. With these it was possible to hold the Orient in subjection so long as money and booty were abundant; but after a heavy blow, and with the war chest exhausted, it was impossible to recover. Assyria's power, therefore, lay in her army and her people. When these changed her whole basis was changed. Whereas formerly she was always able to rise again after defeat, when she became Babylonianized and was ruled over by a military and priestly caste supported by mercenary troops, and without a national population, she was doomed to disappear.

The first accounts which we have of the kingdom of Assyria, which arose by conquest in the seventeenth or sixteenth century B.C., reveal the new state. A king of Babylon, whose name is not preserved, utters his maledictions in an in-

scription upon all of his successors who should
not show a proper regard for the work of restoration he had performed upon a certain building,
as follows: "That prince shall be accursed, never
shall he be glad of heart, so long as he reigns war
and battle shall not cease, during his reign brother
shall devour brother, the husband shall forsake his
wife, and the wife her husband, and the mother
shall bar the door against her daughter." Then
as a mark of the time he adds: "The treasures
of Babylon shall come to Suri and Assyria. The
king of Babylon shall bring [to the city of Ashur]
to the prince of Ashur the treasures of his palace." Here we find Suri and Assyria mentioned
together. Suri lay about the centre of Mesopotamia. Ashur has as yet no *king;* it is a "prince"
who appears as rival, and the evil which is here
predicted found frequent fulfilment in later times.

From another source which dates also from
that time we learn that Assyria was dependent
upon Babylonia. We have a remarkable letter
from an unnamed Babylonian king, perhaps Merodach-baladan I., to a patesi whose territory must
have lain in the neighborhood of Assyria,[1] and
who was a natural opponent of the Assyrian king.
He had made all manner of proposals to the king
of Babylonia, all of which were designed to aid

---

[1] *Arpach*, on the east, or Mitani, on the west, has the best
claim to consideration.

him in getting possession of Assyria. But the latter discovered his intentions and declined, refusing to extend to him recognition as king, and declaring himself to be thoroughly satisfied with things as they were. The condition of affairs was then as follows: During the life of the writer's father (Melishikhu?) the king of Assyria, Ninib-tukulti-Ashur, had fled to Babylon and found refuge there. He was "sent back to his own land," which means that the insurrection was quelled, and the *major domo,* who had fled with him, was appointed regent. The king was retained in Babylon, of course, only in accordance "with his own wish." Assyria appears here as a vassal state of Babylonia, and completely under her domination.

The original dependence of Ashur upon Babylon is further expressly declared in the claim of Burna-buriash. It is further supported by an inscription which the royal scribe Marduk-nadin-akhi, either a Babylonian or of Babylonian descent, inscribed in the reign of Ashur-uballit. He worshipped Marduk, the god of Babylon, as his lord and built his house under the protection of the temple of Marduk. The god of Babylon must, accordingly, have been regarded at this time as the patron god of Ashur, that is, Babylon must shortly before have held Assyria as a province. The relation was recognized down to the latest times in the cult. Again and again the god of Babylon is mentioned with the god of Ashur, and the efforts of Sargon, who delights to emphasize this relation between Marduk and Ashur, are clearly connected with such ancient traditions.

CHAPTER IV

THE OLD ASSYRIAN EMPIRE

A. ITS RISE

THE severance of the relation of dependence upon Babylonia was naturally the aim of the first period of Assyrian development. We are fortunately able to follow the progress of her relations to Babylon almost from the beginning by means of an important document. Under Adad-nirari III. all the compacts and wars between the two countries were tabulated in connection with a brief presentation of their mutual relationships. This document is commonly known by the somewhat inappropriate title *"Synchronous History."* It gives in brief the important contemporaneous events in the two kingdoms. The beginning of the clay tablet on which this history is preserved is broken off, and the first event which appears relates to the agreement between Karaindash and Ashur-rim-nishi-shu of the fifteenth century. The details of the compact are not given. It merely records that the two states concluded an agreement with reference to the delimitation of their respective territories. It is more than probable that the details of the compact were no longer

188

discoverable by the keepers of Adad-nirari's archives, nothing more being known than was found in the royal inscriptions. The same is true of a compact between the next named king of Assyria, Buzur-Ashur, and Burna-buriash (I.?) which brings us down to the time immediately preceding the Tel-Amarna period.

ASHUR-UBALLIT,

from whom we have a letter that was sent to Amenophis IV. of Egypt, lived in the Tel-Amarna age. By the help of this letter and other aids we can follow his career. In this letter he complains of preferences shown to the king of Mitani, and, as we have already seen, it was exactly this territory which, in the eyes of Assyria, was the first to be coveted. He mentions also letters which had been written by his "father," [1] Ashur-nadin-akhi, to Amenophis III. A letter of Burna-buriash to Amenophis IV. demands, at the same time, a refusal of the Assyrian request for support on the ground that Assyria was his vassal. And Ashur-uballit's great-grandson, Adad-nirari, calls attention to the fact that the royal salutation of his great-grandfather was recognized in distant lands, which means that Ashur-uballit's diplomatic efforts to secure alliances had met with

---

[1] He was his grandfather, for in a recently discovered inscription he calls himself " the son of Irba-Adad," who was the son of Ashur-nadin-akhi.

success despite all the letters of the Babylonian advising against it, and he was recognized by Egypt as independent king. He was also successful against the kings of Mitani. We have an account of a victory which he won over them, in which Nineveh, then, as we have seen, in the possession of Dushratta, must have fallen to Ashuruballit. He there undertook the restoration of the temple of the goddess Ishtar who was at one time carried down to Egypt. He appears to have been the first Assyrian who took the title "king of the World." This, however, may have been only temporarily. With respect to Babylonia under Burna-buriash, or his successor, Kara-indash II., he adopted the policy *tu felix Austria nube.* Kara-indash married his daughter and to them was born Kadashman-Kharbe, whose policy and relation to Assyria we have already learned.[1] We have also seen that the murder of Kadashman-Kharbe offered a welcome opportunity to Ashuruballit to interpose in Babylonian affairs. It is highly probable that during the remainder of his long life he was the power behind the throne of his great-grandson, Kurigalzu, who was still in his minority.

This relation of guardianship, however, necessarily gave rise to friction as soon as the young king reached his majority and was able to follow

[1] *Vid.* p. 83.

his own policy of state. It is recorded that a war was waged between *Bel-nirari,* Ashur-uballit's successor and Kurigalzu which resulted in the defeat of the Babylonians. The delimitation referred to was connected with the territory "from the border of Mitani (Shubari) as far as Babylonia."

Arak-dên-il,[1] the next king of Assyria, came into conflict only with Northern peoples: he held in check the Suti, the Bedouins of the steppe, and the Aramæan hordes who sprang up. His son was

ADAD-NIRARI I., CIR. 1300–1270.

Under him Assyria reaped the fruit of previous wars. He overthrew the kingdom of Mitani and became "king of the World" by the possession of Mesopotamia. This Babylon naturally enough could not view with equanimity. She was willing enough to leave the war with Mitani to Assyria— but the possession of the country, in view of its important position on the line of communication with the North and West she coveted for herself. War broke out under Nazi-Maruttash, the son of Kurigalzu. Assyria was victorious, and a boun- dary line between the territories was fixed which ran from the Sindjar range eastward across the Tigris to the mountains of the Lulumi. Assyria

---

[1] Inscriptions that were recently found at Kaleh-Shergat show that this is the name generally written *Pu-di-il.*

thus maintained the upper part of the territory between the rivers, the lower portion fell to Babylonia.

SHALMANESER I., CIR. 1270

completed the work of his father. He conquered the provinces of Mitani on the west of the Euphrates, *viz.*, Khanigalbat and Mutsri, and secured Mesopotamia by subduing the Aramæans, who were constantly reaching out in this direction, and by pushing forward between the rivers in the direction of Armenia where he planned for the settlement of Assyrian colonies. Assyria, it is evident, had a superfluous and vigorous population which needed an outlet—it was still a land of agriculturalists. Shalmaneser's colonies demonstrated their power to live. Notwithstanding the lack of support from the mother-land after they were founded they still existed after these regions had been twice wrested from Assyria, once after the reign of Tukulti-ninib I., and again after that of Tiglathpileser I. When Ashur-natsir-pal marched into Armenia about 860 B.C., he found these colonies still in existence through the Assyrian settlers had suffered greatly. Assyria's power of expansion is further attested by the cuneiform inscriptions from Cappadocia with their numerous Assyrian names. Their appearance there must also be connected with the successes of this period.

The old city, Ashur, was no longer suitable as a capital for the newly expanded empire. Shalmaneser, therefore, to meet the demands of the new conditions, moved his residence farther to the north, on the left bank of the Tigris. The name of the new capital was *Kalkhi,* on the site of the modern *Nimrud,* between the Tigris and the Upper Zab. The importance of this city to Assyria when in control of Mesopotamia is proved by the fact that when her power declined Ashur again became the capital, but when she rose again under Ashur-natsir-pal Kalkhi was chosen anew.

When Mitani was disposed of and the possession of Mesopotamia was assured the only question was whether Assyria should await attack by Babylonia or take the initiative herself. The latter policy had always prevailed in her previous history. War had already been waged under Shalmaneser I. with Kadashman-Buriash, and it was continued under his successor. During the reign of Kadashman-Kharbe, the second successor of Bit-ili-ashu, with whom he fought several engagements,

TUKULTI-NINIB

conquered Babylon, which at the time was seriously pressed by Elam. He thus made himself master of the whole of Babylonia. This was accomplished as the result of two expeditions. On the first one Bit-ili-ashu was conquered and taken prisoner. The second one had evidently as its object the suppression of a revolt under Adad-nadin-shum or Kadashman-Kharbe II. We have a copy of one of Tukulti-Ninib's seals that was made by Sennacherib from the original found during his reign in which the titles run: "Tukulti-Ninib, king of the World, son of Shalmaneser, conquerer of the land of Karduniash." A note adds that the original was made "600 years before Sennacherib"—a welcome remark which enables us to fix the time approximately at 1275 B.C.[1] Tukulti-Ninib did not assume the title "king of Babylon," but appointed Adad-shum-iddin to rule under his protection. This relation lasted for seven years, and during the rule of Adad-shum-iddin and his followers the statue of Marduk remained in Ashur whither it had been taken by Tukulti-Ninib. Then the Babylonian nobility arose, drove out the Assyrians and placed Adad-shum-utsur upon the throne. When we compare

[1] The "600" is in all probability only a round number, and it is possible that we ought to reduce the date to about 1255. 600, or the *sar*, plays about the same rôle in the Babylonian numerical system that 1000 does with us. Compare the Latin *sexcenties*. A *saros* would, therefore, have for the Assyrians about the same significance as a millennium has for us. [See, however, the definite number 641 + 60 given by Tlg. I., p. 179.] Nabuna'id tells us that he rebuilt the temple of Anomit in Sippar, which for "800 years," from the days of Shagashalti-buriash, the son of Kudur-Bel, had not been rebuilt; in another inscription that he rebuilt the Sun-temple in Larsa that Hammu-rabi had rebuilt "700 years" before Burna-buriash.—*Craig*.

the similar situation at the death of Sennacherib, and the uprising at the close of Esarhaddon's reign, we get the key to the understanding of that which the chronicle, from which these facts are gleaned, says in this connection: "Ashur-natsir-pal, his son, and the chiefs of Assyria revolted and deposed him from the throne. In Kar-Tukulti-Ninib they imprisoned him in a house and smote him with their weapons." From this we must conclude that Tukulti-Ninib, like later Assyrian kings similarly situated, allowed his politics to be shaped too much by Babylonian influence. This would naturally excite discontent in Assyria owing to her fear lest the superiority of the more highly developed Babylonians should deprive her of supremacy. *The insurrection was, therefore, an Assyrian-military one* called forth by the danger which threatened from the preponderance of Babylonian influence. It is possible that the Assyrian revolutionists acted in concert with the Babylonians.

One inscription records the building of "Kar-Tukulti-Ninib." From this it appears that it was a sort of new city added on to the old city of Ashur. It must have been here that the king had his palace within which he met his death. Apparently the construction of the city was connected with political plans which aroused opposition to him. Our suspicions are here aroused for the first time of the presence of Babylon's imperial politics in Assyria which was the natural consequence of its possession of Babylon and its claim to world-sovereignty.

If it was the aim of the insurrectionists to break away from Babylonia it was effectively attained, for now the war might begin afresh and Mesopotamia, especially, be defended against the enemy which had of late grown in strength. Of Ashur-natsir-pal I. nothing more is known. Assyria under him and his successors, the two brothers, *Ashur-nirari I.* and *Nabu-[dayan]*, who ruled together, appears to have been reduced to the position she occupied prior to her expansion under Ashur-uballit. The political schisms which ensued upon the insurrection, and the later occupancy of the throne by the two brothers was doubtless largely responsible for the decline. The tone assumed by the Babylonian king in a letter addressed to them is in marked contrast to the usual courteous manner of speech. They are no longer addressed as "brothers," but sharply reprimanded as inferiors. In consonance with this change of tone the Babylonian assumes the title "king of the World." Assyria was evidently reduced again to the "land of Ashur," and was as before a feudality of Babylonia.

From this point the connection of events is difficult to follow on account of the fragmentary state of the tablets. But it is most probable that this condition continued and that an effort was made in Ashur to throw off the Babylonian yoke, which resulted in placing *Bel-kudur-utsur* on the throne. He fell in battle with the king of Babylon, who, it is to be supposed, was Merodach-baladan from whom the account comes. *Ninib-apal-ekur* succeeded him and the length of his rule did not exceed the twelve remaining years of Merodach-baladan, inasmuch as it was *Ashur-dan* who was involved in war with his successor, Zamama-shum-iddin, who reigned only one year. The details are uncertain, but it is apparent that Ashur and Babylon were both actuated in these wars by a desire of predominance.

B. THE SECOND ADVANCE OF ASSYRIA

Babylonia continued to assert her superior strength under Marduk-bal-iddin I., for he boasts of a victory over Assyria, under Ninib-apal-ekur, or his son Ashur-dan, and calls himself "king of the World." But under his successor, Zamama-shum-iddin, a victory on Babylonian territory east of the Lower Zab, was won by Assyria under

ASHUR-DAN, CIR. 1200 B.C.

This victory, however, did not mean the reconquest of Mesopotamia. We have already seen that even the first kings of the Pashe dynasty still held it: Nebuchadrezzar I. advanced again as far as Palestine. Ashur-dan was succeeded by *Mutakkil-Nusku.* His son was

ASHUR-RISH-ISHI,

the contemporary and rival of Nebuchadrezzar I. According to the "Synchronous History" the Assyrian came off triumphant in repeated battles. *He reconquered Mesopotamia,* and one of his inscriptions speaks also of his chastisement of the Aramæan hordes, and of successful undertakings against the Lulumi in the Western Zagros range, and of others against the Kutians in the North. The work which he accomplished for Assyria in this renewed extension of her power resembled that which had formerly been done by Adad-nirari I. But in the reign of his successor,

TIGLATHPILESER I. (CIR. 1100 B.C.)

there was a repetition of the successes and subsequent collapse of Assyria under Shalmaneser I. and Tukulti-Ninib. The first step was to secure Mesopotamia again by renewed expeditions to the North and by the reconquest of Khanigalbat and Mutsri on the west of the Euphrates. At this time there was in this region another of those great migrations taking place which can be followed so instructively especially in the Orient. It was that of the peoples of Kummukh, Muski,

and Kaska, who, as we have already seen, were
connected with the Hittites. When our information from Egyptian sources ceases we hear almost
nothing of the Hittite kingdom in Asia Minor.
In the Tel-Amarna period it exists beside the
kingdom of Mitani, to which it is ethnically
related and with which it is at war. In the succeeding period, when the Egyptian power was on
the decline, it extended itself over Syria and
almost all of Northern Palestine, into which Hittite bands may have entered in earlier times. In
the twelfth century Egyptian kings fought with
the Hittites for the possession of Canaan, and
Ramses II. concluded a defensive alliance with
the Hittite king, Kheta-sar. The dominating force
in this treaty was clearly the Hittite, and notwithstanding the pretentious claims of the Egyptian
king he virtually played the rôle of a dependent
although formally recognized as an ally on equal
terms. It was an alliance common enough everywhere in the Orient and in antiquity, and such as
must always result where unequal powers combine.
The actual relation appears also very clearly in
the delimitation of their provincial boundaries.
Egypt acknowledged as Hittite territory everything to the north of *Nahr-el-Kelb* (Dog River)
near Beirut, if not also all the country to the
north of Mount Carmel, that is, all of Northern
Phœnicia and Syria.

The migrations of the people of Kummukh and Muski thus show that the Hittite territory along the river Halys must have been overrun by new peoples in the time of Tiglathpileser I. As was usually the case, these peoples soon established homes for themselves in the land. If then a powerful state continued to exist on the Halys it must of necessity come into conflict with Tiglathpileser. For, on the one hand, the latter, through his victories along the Euphrates, had become neighbor to the Hittites and, on the other, he had taken possession of territory in Khanigalbat and Mutsri which the Hittites were bound to contest, and which separated them from the southern part of Asia Minor and Phœnicia. As in the case of Dushratta, it was necessary for him as ruler of Mesopotamia to repel the Hittites before he could take the next step and crown his ambition by an advance to the Phœnician coast. The account which tells of his victory over the Hittite king, . . . *Teshub,* is only fragmentarily preserved.[1]

We have a large inscription of Tiglathpileser which recounts his wars in this region during his first five years. He began by purging the territory to the north of Mesopotamia, by repelling the tribes that had forced their way in, or by compelling their submission, and he advanced in the direction of Armenia. He sought to establish

---

[1] See p. 172.   The first part of the name is not known.

Assyrian control over the same region that Shalmaneser had formerly settled with Assyrian colonists. He further subjugated the Nairi Lands,
the mountainous country to the south of Lake
Van which separates Armenia from Mesopotamia. On one of these expeditions he erected
at the source of the Subnat, the fountain head of
the Tigris, his image which is still preserved with
a brief inscription that tells of three such expeditions to the Nairi Lands. He also, like Shalmaneser, checked the Aramæan hordes who had
spread out over the Mesopotamian steppes, and
drove a portion of them across the Euphrates
into the territory about Carchemish. He crossed
the river himself and took six of their fortified
towns ''in the region of Mount Bishri.'' This
region corresponds to that part of *Bit-Adini* on
the right of the Euphrates, which in the time of
Shalmaneser II. appears with *Til-Basheri*. During the Crusades it was the feudal-tenure of Josce-
lin of Tell-Bashir, who held it in fief from the
District of Edessa. He also occupied *Pitru* at the
junction of the Euphrates and Sagur, the Pethor
of the Old Testament (erroneously said to have
been the home of Balaam), and peopled it with
colonists from Assyria. Following further in the
path of Shalmaneser I. he subjugated Melitene
(*Khanigalbat*) and further extended his conquests
over Mutsri, which was then in possession of the

Kumani. He thus *restored the boundaries of the old Mesopotamian kingdom.*

Nothing now stood in the way of his occupation of Northern Phœnicia, and we read consequently of his setting sail at Arvad upon an ocean trip as a mighty huntsman of the denizens of the deep. As landlubbers the Assyrians always regarded themselves as heroes whenever they ventured upon the mysteries of the high seas. Tiglathpileser mentions on this occasion an exchange of presents with the king of Egypt who, among other gifts, presented him with a crocodile (*namsuch*). Who this king of Egypt was we are not informed. We see, however, from this notice that the intercourse between the civilized countries was always the same as it appears from the detailed information of the Tel-Amarna Letters, and that the Egyptian kings, though they exerted little influence in Palestine at this time, when the kingdoms of Saul and David were shaping, had, nevertheless, not allowed it to drop wholly out of sight. The correspondence between the kings has not been preserved for us. When, however, we remember that shortly prior to this time Nebuchadrezzar asserted his authority over Northern Phœnicia the inference is natural that weightier matters were discussed in connection with this courteous exchange of royal gifts and that an understanding was arrived at as to the boundaries

of their respective spheres of influence or interest
in Palestine. The sending of presents to the new
ruler of the region which Ramses acknowledged
as Hittite indicates the formal recognition of
Assyria as the rightful successor to Hittite claims.
If formerly Burna-buriash complained of Pharaoh's too great willingness to recognize Assyrian
claims, Tiglathpileser, now that he held equal
title, perhaps assumed the same attitude toward
the Egyptian king as Kheta-sar had toward
Ramses.[1]

When now the West had been secured attention was naturally next given to the East. With
this we come to that part of Tiglathpileser's reign
which corresponds to the rôle of Tukulti-Ninib.
The Synchronous History speaks of two successful wars against Marduk-nadin-akhe of Babylon
in which the North Babylonian cities and Babylon were taken, and a fragment of Tiglathpileser's
annuals tells of his entrance into the capital itself.
This rapid advance, however, was followed by
an equally rapid turn of fortune. When Sennacherib conquered Babylon in 689 he found statues
of gods which had been carried away from the
city of *Ekallati,* by Marduk-nadin-akhi, "418 years
before, in the time of Tiglathpileser." Marduk-
nadin-akhi in one of his inscriptions bears the
titles "king of Sumer and Akkad," and "king of

[1] P. 199.

the World." He, therefore, not only ruled the whole of Babylonia but had also re-established Babylonian rule in Mesopotamia. Consequently, Tiglathpileser must at one stroke have lost all which he had previously won. Assyria then stood exactly where it did after the overthrow of Tukulti-Ninib.

ASHUR-BEL-KALA AND SHAMSHI-ADAD I.,

Tiglathpileser's sons, occupied the throne after him. During this period Mesopotamia must have been chiefly under Babylonian influence. The spread of the Aramæans nevertheless proves that Babylon did not vigorously assert her authority. Assyria was reduced again to the "Land of Ashur" and was, therefore, compelled to begin anew. But Babylonia was not now a formidable opponent, and peace existed between the two states. Ashur-bel-kala and Marduk-shapik-zer-mati of Babylon, who held the title "king of the World," and, therefore, like his predecessor, was in possession of Mesopotamia, entered into terms of peace. When the latter died and Adad-aplu-iddin ascended the throne the Assyrian king married his daughter, and, according to the Syn-chronous History, received with her "a large dowry. Thereafter the two peoples lived peace-ably with one another." Nothing is known to us of Ashur-bel-kala's brother, Shamshi-Adad. And of his son, Ashur-natsir-pal II., we know only the name from a hymn that has been preserved. Tradition is now practically silent for one hundred years,[1] during which we hear little or nothing of either Assyria or Babylonia.

We learn from the later records of Shalmaneser II. that *Ashur-irbi* must have been king of Assyria at this time. He seems to have taken the initial step toward the recovery of the lost territory, for Shalmaneser discovered a statue of his son on the shore of the sea. This can only have been Lake Van or the Mediterranean Sea, and from the connection the latter is more probable.[2] Ashur-irbi then, like Tiglathpileser I., advanced as far as the Phœnician coast. Whether his image was found among those to the north of Beirut on the Nahr-el-kelb, or still farther to the north, cannot be determined. At all events the statue seems to have been alone, for Shalmaneser says: "My statue (tsalmu) with his statue I set up." As we learn from another source during his reign Pitru, which had been taken by

[1] Few royal names, however, can be lacking, since six are known to us of the time between Tiglathpileser, 1100 and later, and 911, with which the Eponym-Lists begin, *viz.:* the two sons of Tiglathpileser I., Ashur-natsir-pal II., lacuna?, Ashur-irbi (lacuna), Tiglathpileser II., Ashur-dan II. (p. 209).

[2] See monolith-inscription col. ii., l. 10. Shalmaneser says that the statue of Ashur-irbi was "in the land of *Atalur.*" In K. 4415, a geographical list, Atalur follows immediately upon Lebanon (Lib-na-nu).—*Craig.*

Tiglathpileser I., fell into the hands of the Aramæans. This brings us to the most important
movement of these times.

C. THE ARAMÆAN IMMIGRATION

In addition to the immigrations of the Kassites
from the east, and the Hittites (Mitani) from the
northwest, the third Semitic immigration poured
into Mesopotamia and Babylonia at this time.
This was the *Aramæan*. We have already frequently noted that the Assyrian kings (Arak-
dên-il, Shalmaneser I., Ashur-rish-ishi, Tiglathpileser I.), when they entered Mesopotamia,
sought to hold in check, or repel beyond the
Euphrates, the "Aramæan hordes" who were in
possession. These nomadic Aramæans, as they
are expressly called by Tiglathpileser I., had,
therefore, overrun the country, as early as 1300
B.C., in the same manner as the other two great
immigrations had previously.

Invited by the great steppes of Mesopotamia
this was at first their natural halting place, and
thence they moved southward toward Babylonia
which, like the "Canaanites" and "Babylonian
Semites" who moved in the same direction, they
later occupied. And here wo meet them frequently as Aramæan tribes when Babylon was
under Assyrian domination, that is, under Tig
lathpileser III. and his successors. There they

met with opposition in their movements from the Chaldeans who were pressing upward from the South. They were still further hindered from spreading over the country by the tribes which had preceded them and which were most closely related to them, the relation between them being exactly similar to that between the Hebrews and Canaanites. These advance tribes were those known as the Suti, who, as we have already seen, were in possession of the Syrian desert during the reigns of Ashur-uballit and Kadashman-Kharbe. They were driven thence by the Aramæans into Babylonia, and, in the twelfth century, they were described by the kings of the Sea-Lands as a destructive race. They were finally forced into the mountainous region on the east of the Tigris, and were still resident in Yamutbal in the time of Sargon II. At the close of the eighth century we can thus clearly see in Babylonia, as the result of these migrations, the successive layers of population which rose from the Suti and Aramæans. As these tribes first entered the land when the Kassites, owing to the weakness of Babylonia, were able to establish their power, so they were able to spread out undisturbed after 1100, when neither Assyria nor Babylonia was in a position to offer an effective resistance. It is to this time then that we must refer the recorded devastation of Babylonia by the Suti, who were driven for-

ward by the Aramæan tribes that were then entering into possession of Northern Babylonia and
later settled in the South.

At the same time also they took possession of
Mesopotamia which lay more exposed, and there
events developed as usual in the course of all these
immigrations. While in Babylonia they were prevented by the Chaldeans from entering the cities
and were confined to the country regions, it was
otherwise in Mesopotamia. There they took possession of the entire land. When the silence of
Assyrian records is again broken we find Aramæan cities and an Aramæan population in full
control. Now the language of the *Land of Suri*
has changed to *Aramæan*, and the words Syrians
and Aramæans, which originally connoted wholly
different ideas, began to be synonymous. A clear
instance of this is observable in the occupation
of Pitru.[1] Numerous similar occurrences must
have been witnessed in Mesopotamia in the century following Tiglathpileser. But how did the
Assyrian kings regard all this? Evidently they
did not remain inactive, and we have already tried
to show that a movement was directed against
them under Ashur-irbî. The war which was waged
was doubtless one of varying fortunes, and perhaps we can best picture the progress of events
by recalling the course of the Chaldeans in
Babylonia.

[1] P. 201.

CHAPTER V

ALTHOUGH Babylon and Assyria were powerless to protect Mesopotamia against the Aramæan migration they were able to dispute its possession with one another. We have already seen that Babylon was superior to Assyria after the reign of Tiglathpileser, and this state of affairs appears to have continued until the beginning of the "Chaldean dynasty." But as soon as the Assyrian records speak again the question of relative strength is settled beyond dispute. Henceforward *all the kings of Assyria* until the fall of the kingdom call themselves "kings of the World."

The first of these kings whose succession we can now follow uninterruptedly are:

> ASHUR-RISH-ISHI, *cir.* 970.
> TIGLATHPILESER II., *cir.* 950.
> ASHUR-DAN II., *cir.* 930.
> ADAD-NIRARI II.

Of these the first is known to us only from a genealogy of his grandson in which Ashur-dan's name is also given. Of the last we have a brief inscription, and it is with his reign that the

Eponym Canon begins which enumerates the Assyrian Eponyms in whose names the successive years were dated. From this point on to the end of the kingdom each year of Assyrian history can at least be determined by its *limmu*, or archon.

Each of these three kings bore the titles "king of the world, king of Ashur," which henceforth were constantly assumed. *Harran* and *Ashur* are the chief cities of the two parts of the land. But the one part is held entirely by an Aramæan population who in the old cities caused the old population the same troubles that the Chaldeans prepared for the Babylonians, and it contained beside a number of Aramæan cities whose princes seized every opportunity to strike for independence or even the reins of government. Near to Harran there stood an Aramæan state, *Bit-Adini*, a counterpart to the dukedom Edessa during the Crusades, just as the Chaldean Bit-Dakuri existed near Babylon. Others still we shall have to note in the time of Ashur-natsir-pal.[1]

The subjugation of these states and tribes was, therefore, the first aim of Assyria, which refused to be made the sport of their desire for conquest as Babylonia was by the Chaldeans.

---

[1] *Cf.* also Bît-Agusi (or Bît-Gusi) and its relation to Arpad during the reigns of Shalmaneser II., Ashur-nirari II., and especially Tiglath-pileser III.

TUKULTI-NINIB II., 890–885,

succeeded Adad-nirari II. On one of his expeditions to the "Nairi-Lands" he cut an inscription
by the side of one of Tiglathpileser I. in the rock
at the source of the Subnat. His son, Ashur-
natsir-pal, and his grandson, Shalmaneser II.,
followed his example in this respect. The object
of these expeditions of Tukulti-Ninib to the north
was to secure the regions of Assyria that had been
colonized by Shalmaneser I. and retaken by Tiglathpileser. Their possession is, therefore, also
presupposed under his son,

ASHUR-NATSIR-PAL, 885–860,

with whom our sources begin again to be more
abundant. Detailed accounts of his expeditions
have come down to us in several lengthy inscriptions. He is the most conspicuous figure in the
work of establishing order in Mesopotamia and
putting an end to the independence of the Aramæan princes. He did away with the feudal system and established the country on a provincial
basis. In the narrative of his deeds we gain considerable knowledge of the conditions which prevailed. In the very first year of his reign, 884,
an insurrection broke out in the Aramæan state,
Bit-Khadippi, on the lower Khabur. The rebels
put to death their prince who had previously been

subjugated to Assyria and was loyal to his oath of allegiance, and placed in his stead a prince from the neighboring Bît-Adini near Harran, one of the arch-enemies of Assyria. Ashur-natsir-pal was in Kummukh on the Euphrates at the time and he advanced in all haste to Bît-Khadippi. The Aramæan princes of Shadikanna (or Gardi-kanna) and Shuna hastened to meet him on the way with their tribute as assurance of their sub-mission. Sura, the chief city of Bît-Khadippi, submitted on his arrival and delivered over their prince, Akhi-Yababa, but were made to pay the penalty of their temerity in the destruction of the city. Azil, a native sheikh, was appointed governor.

The course of this revolt is typical of the most of the wars Assyria was forced to wage against the Aramæans as well as with all other tribes similarly situated. Whenever a favorable oppor-tunity arose they sought to effect a union with others and then refused the allotted tribute, but offered little resistance to the Assyrian army. On the right bank of the Euphrates and lying between Syria and Babylonia, as the result of the Aramæan influx, Ashur-natsir-pal found three of these half-nomadic states, *viz.*, Laki, Khindanu (at the mouth of the Khabur), and Sukhi. These were subjugated as the result of several expedi-tions. We have previously seen in the history of

Babylonia that she also played a part in the war with the Sukhi. Generally speaking, all such insurrections sprang up not as a chance venture but with the encouragement of larger powers, in other words, Babylonia. In this way Babylon tried to regain her influence over Mesopotamia and abandoned the effort only when Assyria had established over it a provincial government.

The worst enemy of Assyria was Akhuni, the prince of Bît-Adini, the Aramæan state adjoining the region of Harran and dominating Northern Mesopotamia. He was the prime mover of most of the revolts among the small states on the river Khabur. As soon, therefore, as Ashur-natsir-pal had brought the peoples along the Khabur and Euphrates to submission he turned against this fomenter of trouble. Akhuni, and also one of his allies, Khabini of Tel-abnaya, promptly submitted. On his expedition against Syria in the following year, 877, these regions were again traversed and tribute collected. Akhuni was even compelled to join the Assyrian army. Aramæan tribes in the northernmost part of Syria, beyond the Euphrates, were likewise forced to pay tribute. These invasions of the Aramæans were more of the nature of military skirmishes than of serious wars; the restless Bedouins had already become settled in the land and readily submitted on the approach of a large army.

The most of Ashur-natsir-pal's expeditions were to the Nairi-Lands of the North, which either had to be reconquered or Assyrian authority reinforced within them. The Assyrians who had been settled in the regions to the west and south of Mount Masius had been severely dealt with by the surrounding population and forced to fly for refuge to the mountains. These were restored to their place, and the province with its capital, *Tuskha,* in which Ashur-natsir-pal erected a palace, was established anew. At the same time, Tela, another rebel stronghold guarded by a triple wall and settled with Assyrians, was razed to the ground. Three thousand of its warriors fell in its defence, many were taken alive and mutilated and young women were burnt in the flames. A similar lot overtook the rebellious city of Kinabu whose governor, Khulai, was flayed and his skin nailed upon the walls of Damdamusa which he had attempted to take. In other expeditions Ashur-natsir-pal crossed the Tigris and penetrated farther into the Nairi-Lands. He likewise crossed over beyond Arbela and up to the Urumia Sea where, among other conquests, he reduced Khubuskia, Zamua and Gilzan.

When this work in the North was accomplished Ashur-natsir-pal, like Tiglathpileser I., marched toward Phœnicia. Setting out from the conquered state, Bît-Adini, he crossed the Euphrates

by means of rafts buoyed up by inflated sheep-
skins—a means still in vogue—and advanced
along the left bank to Carchemish, the Hittite
capital. Sangara, the king of the "land of
Khatti," paid tribute and added his contingent
to the Assyrian army. The Syrian state Patin,
now in the hands of the Aramæans, lay to the
west of the territory of Carchemish and beyond
the Sagur and included the region north of the
sea of Antiochia, known as the Amq, and extended southward as far as the Orontes. Azaz
was first conquered; and when the Assyrian
army had crossed the Afrin and stood before the
capital, Kunalua, King Lubarna (or Liburna)
paid tribute and joined his troops to the Assyrian
army. Gusi, the prince of the Aramæan state
Yakham, near Arpad, found it expedient to do
likewise.

Leaving Kunalua the army marched across the
Kara-su, in the western portion of the Amq, and
then turned southward and crossed the Orontes
to the south of the lake of Antioch. Here in the
northernmost highlands of the Phœnician coast,
which had belonged to Patin and was named by
Ashur-natsir-pal "Lukhuti," he founded an
Assyrian colony, Aribua, thus following the example of Shalmaneser I. in Nairi. The march
was continued southward along the Mediterranean, where offerings were made to the gods. The

place where this occurred must have been on the Nahr-el-Kelb, where one of the weather-beaten Assyrian reliefs probably represents the monument of victory which the king caused to be sculptured in the rock. The cities of Arvad, Gebal, Sidon, Tyre and several in the highlands, sent their tribute. Another detachment of the army was sent northward to Mount Amanus to cut cedars for the buildings in Nineveh. Tyre is the most southerly of the Phœnician cities that is mentioned in his narrative. The dynasty of Omri was then ruling over Israel, and there the movements of the Assyrian army must have been followed with some anxiety. Ashur-natsir-pal did not, however, venture the march farther southward, for the southern regions were tributary to or even under the protection of Damascus, which at that time controlled Syria. With her Ashur-natsir-pal ventured nothing. In fact this state of which he was in dread is not once referred to in his inscriptions. He exacted tribute of those states only which were not under the influence of Damascus. In other respects the expedition of Ashur-natsir-pal was almost a repetition of the one by Tiglathpileser I. The latter seems to have been his great exemplar. His undertakings seem to have followed in the same course and to have had similar results. In one of his inscriptions he follows closely the deeds of Tiglathpileser and repeats a large section of one of his inscriptions. The events of the last years of his reign and his less successful undertakings are wanting also in his inscriptions. If, as we have previously seen, the success of Tiglathpileser's expeditions to the West was to be judged by his victory over the Hittite king it is interesting to note what attitude this great power of Asia Minor now maintained toward the advancing Assyrians. In the eighth century it reappears again as Muski (Phrygia). In the annals of Ashur-natsir-pal a brief account is given of successes won over the Muski. Apparently he felt the necessity of putting on record some statements which would imply a success there corresponding to that of his great predecessor. Although we must assume that his victories were unimportant this reference to the Asia Minor power is nevertheless significant for the larger connection of the history of Asia Minor.

The most important work of Ashur-natsir-pal's reign was the establishment of Assyrian supremacy in Mesopotamia. As Shalmaneser I. had previously done, he moved the capital from Ashur to *Kalkhi* as better suited to the new requirements of government. It was here that Layard unearthed the "North-West" palace of this king. Evidence of his efforts to improve the city is found in his laying a conduit which connected the city with the river Zab. His successor was

SHALMANESER II., 860-825 B.C.,

who carried on the work of his father from the point where he was obliged to lay it down. We have already learned of his success in Babylonia.[1] In Mesopotamia he brought the subjugated Aramæan vassal princes under Assyrian rule. The regions to the north which his father had reduced he held in subjection and added others to the realm. He completed the work which had been left undone by his predecessor in Syria and waged a successful war against Damascus.

During the first years of his reign Shalmaneser II. devoted his attention to Mesopotamia. In three expeditions, 859, 858, 857, Akhuni of Bit-Adini, who had again revolted, was compelled to submit, and his territory finally annexed as an Assyrian province and in part settled by Assyrians. In 854 the same fate overtook another Aramæan prince, Giammu, in the valley of the Balikh. Gradually Aramæan independence in Mesopotamia was crushed and the inhabitants forced to become citizens of Assyria.

Syria and Palestine were the next in order, as in the case of Ashur-natsir-pal, to invite the conquering ambition of Shalmaneser. Patin, the northern part of Syria, had yielded to his father, and now that it was out of the way it remained to

[1] P. 104 ff.

subdue the state that ruled over the whole of Coele-Syria and Palestine. In the year 854 he crossed the Euphrates near Til-Barsip, which not long before was Akhuni's capital but was now under an Assyrian governor. He descended to Pitru, which also had been taken from the Aramæans and was now under Assyrian rule. At this point he received the *tribute of the Syrian princes,* who willingly submitted or had previously been subjected. These were Sangar of Carchemish, who in 877 had bowed before Ashur-natsir-pal, Kundaspi of Kummukh, Arame of Gusi, Lalli of Melitene, who also had paid tribute to Ashur-natsir-pal, Khayna[1] of Gabar (Sam'al), Kalparunda of Patin, and Gurgum. The last two ruled over parts of the former kingdom of Patin in the region of Senjirli. From this point he marched toward Khalman (Aleppo), which immediately yielded, and Shalmaneser offered up a sacrifice to the god of the city, Adad or Ramman.

Proceeding southward he came to the regions bordering on Hamath that stood under the influence of Damascus. Irkhulini, the prince of Hamath, was either an ally of, or under tribute to *Bir-idri*[2] of Damascus. The latter advanced

---

[1] In a Canaanite inscription from Senjirli in Sam'al Kalummû, his son is called *Bar-Khaya.* [Kalummû speaks Aramaic (*bar*), though he writes in Canaanite.]

[2] *i.e.* Benhadad of the O. T. This Hebrew form (בֶּן הֲדַד) appears to have arisen through the mistake of a scribe who con-

against the Assyrians and the opposing armies met at *Karkar* near Hamath. Shalmaneser mentions the following vassal kings and princes of Syria who were compelled to join her ranks, *viz.*, Irkhulina of Hamath, Ahab of Israel, the princes of Kue (Southeastern Cilicia), Mutsri, Irqana, Matinbaal of Arvad, the North Phœnician princes of Usana and Siana, Gindibu the Arabian (this is the first mention of Arabians) and Ba'sa (Baasha) of Ammon. Shalmaneser claims a great victory over the allied forces.[1] But when he returned to Assyria Damascus remained in all its extent as before. Owing to the developments in Babylonia in 852 and 851 it was not until 849 that he again crossed to the west and then with no

founded the name of the divinity Bir with *bar*, the Aramaic for son (Hebr. בֵּן, ben), and the final letter *d* was wrongly read *r*, which it closely resembles both in the earlier and later script. The LXX. reads Ἀδερ and the Assyrian *'idri.—Craig.*

[1] Mon. II., 88, gives a detailed account of the victory. "I approached the cities of Irkhulini . . . his capital I took, his booty, possessions, the property of his palace I brought out, and burned his palaces. . . . Karkar his royal city I devastated, destroyed and burnt with fire. 1200 chariots, 1200 horses, 20,000 warriors of Bir-'idri of Damascus; 700 chariots, 700 horses, 10,000 warriors of Irkhulini of Hamath, 2000 chariots, 10,000 warriors of Ahab of *Israel*, 500 of the Kueans, 1000 warriors of Mutsri, 10,000 of the Irqanateans, 200 of the Arvadites, . . . 10,000 of the Sianean Adoni-baal, 1000 camels of the Arabian Gindibu, 1000 warriors of the Ammonite Ba'sa, . . . 14,000 (of the united forces of those 12 kings) I slew with the weapons, like the storm-god Ramman. I reigned (destruction) upon them." According to this there fell in battle 14,000 of the combined infantry, which amounted to 62,900 (Israel provided more than half of the war chariots), of which only 20,000 belonged to Bir-'idri.—*Craig.*

more decisive results. The same is true of his descent upon Hamath from Mount Amanus, in the tributary state of Patin, in the following year, 848. Victory is recorded in the monuments but results prove that in this, as in many another case ancient and modern, the scribe was mightier than the Tartan. Thus it appears that Damascus proved her ability to defend herself successfully. The Assyrian army found itself confronted by well organized troops, not by a militia force of uncivilized tribes. Shalmaneser felt, therefore, that the necessity was all the greater that this foe who blocked his way to the control of Syria and Palestine should be conquered. Three years later, in 845, he collected the army "of the land" and set out on another expedition. Again his opponent took the field with an unusually strong army, and Shalmaneser won the same kind of a "victory" as before.

It was not until 842, when a change of rulers took place in Damascus, that he achieved success by winning over some of the vassals. Bir-idri died and Hazael ascended the throne of Damascus. An insurrection in Israel placed Jehu upon the throne and he sought aid from Assyria. The Old Testament narratives indicate that the prophets of Israel (Elisha) had an important hand in this crisis and in the overthrow of the family of Ahab, which was allied to Tyre. Elisha was also apparently connected with the elevation of Hazael to the throne (2 Ki. viii.), and we must assume that a similar state of things existed in Damascus, for Hazael was not the son of his predecessor. The same movement which overthrew the dynasty of Omri in Israel must have, as is hinted in the Old Testament, been opposed to the throne of Damascus. Assyria, doubtless, incited the opposition or, at least, covertly abetted it, although the new king of Damascus disappointed the hopes of the diplomats at Kalkhi. We have often previously seen how vassals were wont to throw off their allegiance on the death of the king, and so it happened now. Damascus was deserted by her former allies and Hazael stood alone. Shalmaneser marched from the north along the coast, and then past Beirut, where he sculptured an image of himself on the rocks of the Nahr-el-Kelb, toward Damascus. Hazael attempted to block his way between Mount Hermon and Anti-Lebanon and failing in this he was compelled to fall back behind the walls of Damascus. Shalmaneser laid siege to the city for a time, but this proved ineffectual. His battering rams met more serious hindrance than the clay walls of provincial towns. He was consequently compelled to satisfy himself with the devastation of the land as far as the Hauran, and, after receiving from Tyre and Sidon the price they always paid for peace, and exacting of Jehu of Israel the oath of allegiance, he returned to Nineveh. A sixth attempt was made in 839 with no better results. *Damascus asserted its independence.* Thus the state that proved the barrier to Assyria's advance on Palestine remained. The whole course of Israelitish history was determined by this fact. The next one hundred years Israel and Judah stood under the influence of Damascus, and it was not until she had fallen (731) that the fate of Israel was sealed.

After 839 Shalmaneser desisted from further attacks on Damascus. Israel and the rest of Palestine were left free to manage their own affairs with Damascus. If for the present Coele-Syria and Palestine had evaded the grasp of Assyria nothing remained for the latter but a further subjugation of Northern Syria and further expansion in the direction of Asia Minor. Melitene (Khanigalbat), Patin, and the Amq had acknowledged Assyrian sovereignty. Shalmaneser had, therefore, driven northward the old Hittite state, or as it was then called, Muski, to its own territory on the river Halys. Now he reached out from the south over the Amanus and into the region of the Taurus. Kue at the beginning was tributary to Damascus, but now in the years 840, 835 and 834 it was conquered and Kirri was appointed king in Tarsus instead of his brother Kate. On the north of the Taurus Tabal, with its independent chiefs, was put under tribute. Thus the work of establishing a series of Assyrian vassal states from Cilicia across the Taurus as far as Mitylene was completed.

The region of Malatia (Melitene, Khanigalbat) belonged to the *Armenian* highlands and was naturally the next to be overrun by a conquering army sent in that direction. It was assured to Assyria in the reigns of Shalmaneser I., Tiglathpileser, and Ashur-natsir-pal, who conducted expeditions as far as Lake Van. Inasmuch as there were evident signs of a united, independent state springing up here in the North in Urartu, with its centre on Lake Van, Shalmaneser waged war on its kings. In 857 he had traversed the regions on the south of the Upper Euphrates, *viz.*, Alzi, Zamani, Anzitene, and beyond the Arsanias those of the Sukhme and Dayaeni who had been subjugated by Shalmaneser I. and Tiglathpileser. From this point he penetrated Urartu and King Arame fled to the interior. Shalmaneser set up his image on Lake Van and then continued his march through the eastern passes into Gilzan and Khupushkia to Arbael. Fresh expeditions set out again in 850 and 845, and probably during the last he carved his inscription on the Subnat.[1]

In the meantime a change must have taken place in the ruling power in Armenia which had placed

[1] *Vid.* p. 201.

on the throne the strong dynasty that had its
seat in Thuruspa, on Lake Van, whence it founded
the powerful kingdom of Urartu. In later times
it was a source of much trouble to Assyria and
disputed with her the sovereignty over Syria. A
trace of the ambitious designs of these kings is
probably to be sought in the revolt of Lallas of
Malatia in the year 837. Four years later, in 833,
an Assyrian army was despatched to the Arsanias
apparently to retake Sukhmi and Dayaeni, which
lay on its right bank. Sarduri I., the new king of
Urartu, was, therefore, apparently advancing. In
829 another expedition set out from the other side
through the passes of Gilzan and Khupushkia.
Mutsatsir, a state lying south of Lake Van, was
plundered, and a part of Urartu was also spoiled.
But no permanent results were effected here by
the Assyrians. On the contrary, the strength of
the new state continually grew, and from the time
of Adad-nirari onward Assyria was more and
more driven out of these regions. The kings of
Urartu reached out toward Mesopotamia and
Syria until under Tiglathpileser III. they were
forced back to their highlands.

While on the south and southeast the Zab
formed the boundary under Ashur-natsir-pal,
Shalmaneser advanced against the countries lying
between the Urumia Sea and the valley of the
Tigris. These had frequently before been under

Assyrian supremacy, as the Lulumi, but now, as often happened in other cases, they had fallen under Babylonian influence. In 860 an expedition was made into the passes of Holvan, in 844 another into the land of Namri, Southwestern Media, and in 836 Shalmaneser marched against the princes which had been raised to rule there in Bit-Khamban. Thence the army moved northward toward Parsua to the east of the Urumia Sea. Median chiefs, which now first appear in the rôle of Assyrian history, brought their tribute and then the march continued southward to Kharkhar to the east of Holvan. Kirkhi and Khupushkia south of Lake Van and the Urumia Sea, which Ashur-natsir-pal had overrun, were again subjected. Man, which lay on the west shore of the Urumia Sea, and Gilzan to the north of it were likewise scourged.

Shalmaneser's successes in Babylon have already been discussed in the history of Babylonia. The close connection with Babylonia and the influence which it exerted doubtless occasioned the revolt which arose toward the close of Shalmaneser's reign. The agricultural class of Assyria must have suffered by the wars—Babylonia was the seat of the hierarchy: in this insurrection these antitheses must have had their effect. Almost all of Assyria and her provinces, and first among them the former capital, Ashur, which had

greatly suffered by the change of residence, withdrew. The capital Kalkhi and the Mesopotamian
royal seat, Harran, in which Shalmaneser had
rebuilt the temple of the sun-god, were the only
important cities which remained steadfast. Shalmaneser, as it appears, found refuge himself in
North Babylonia which then belonged to him. The
leader of the insurrection was Shalmaneser's son,

ASHUR-DANIN-PAL, 829–824,

who held the throne for at least six years, and
certainly bore the title "king of Ashur," as the old
capital was in his possession. In 825 Shalmaneser
died, and his son,

SHAMSHI-ADAD, 825–812,

although at first in possession of Mesopotamia
only, and, therefore, only "king of the World,"
reconquered Assyria. The only inscription of his
that we have brings us to his fourth expedition,
which was directed against Babylonia. The first
one was to the Nairi-Lands, and connected therewith he secured obeisance from the entire Assyrian kingdom from its northermost to its southern
boundary and from its eastern line to the Euphrates. As yet there were no Assyrian provinces in Syria. The second of his expeditions was
also toward the Nairi-Lands, and this time he
passed through the region between Lake Van and

the Urumia Sea, and devastated also a part of Urartu, whose king, Ispuinis, the son of Sarduris I., Shamshi-Adad calls Ushpina. Thither the third expedition went also, and, advancing as far as Man, circled the Urumia Sea and reached Parsua. Thence proceeding toward the southeast through Media it arrived probably at Holvan. Numerous Median districts are enumerated which he placed under tribute. In the stronghold Sibara, of the land of Gizilbunda, he set up a monolith statue[1] of himself on which he inscribed an account of his victories in the Nairi-Lands. His fourth expedition was the one against Babylon and the narrative of it ends with his victory over Marduk-balatsu-iqbi.

From the reign of Shamshi-Adad onward we have another document which is an invaluable guide for the later period. One fragment of it refers to the beginning and end of the reign of Shalmaneser II. This is the Eponym Canon, a *limmu-list*,[2] with a brief statement of some important event or events, generally with an expedition of each year added. It is especially valuable for the period following Tiglathpileser III., of which we possess few inscriptions. We have short inscriptions of

---

[1] Other inscriptions have recently been discovered by the German expedition at Kalah Shergat, but they await publication. One contains extended information of the first two years of the king.

[2] *Vid.* p. 210.

ADAD-NIRARI III., 812–783,

which give a brief general survey of his enterprises, and those we can supplement with the aid
of the Eponym Canon.   In general the work
undertaken was a continuation of the conquests
of his predecessors or the restoration of dis-
affected territories.   It seems improbable that he
made any important conquests.   In the East he
subjugated Ellipi, bordering on Elam, and Kharkhar and Araziash as far as Parsua, which are
known to us from Shalmaneser's wars.   Andia,
on the northeast of Parsua, he conquered for the
first time.   Median chiefs were also compelled to
pay tribute.   Three expeditions were made to
Khupuskia and the Nairi-Lands and two to Man.
Urartu, however, continued to grow in power and
he did not venture an attack upon her territory.
In Syria, on the other hand, he won successes.
In 806 and 805 he marched against Arpad and
Azaz, and in 797 against the Syrian city Man-
zuate.   It was probably in connection with this
that Mari of Damascus paid tribute—possibly the
result of a change of rulers.   Tyre, Sidon, and
Israel are also named among the tributary states,
and Edom and Philistia were added by him to
the number.   This gives evidence of a dominant
Assyrian influence and a consequent loss of prestige and power by Damascus in Palestine.   But

so long as she retained her independence she remained a bulwark of defence for the southern countries. Adad-nirari's relations to Babylonia have already been discussed under Babylonia.

We are but meagerly informed as to the inner movements of Oriental states, especially where we draw our information from royal, that is, official reports. In these the king does everything, even when he is no more than a puppet in the hands of his officials. The insurrections show clearly enough that other forces as well as the will and wisdom of the ruler determine the popular life, and that occasionally they culminate in volcanic eruptions. Tukulti-Ninib I. and Shalmaneser II. illustrate this fact instructively.

Besides the army, the leading rôle is played in the Orient by the priesthood, which often controls not only the minds of the people, but also a large part, often the largest part, of the landed property, and appears especially, in the rôle of the modern citizen, in trade and industry. Great movements from within whose deeper causes lead to social conflicts are, consequently, constantly bound up with similar ones in the priesthood. Every revolution receives a religious expression, for all thought and all law is religious; every party fights for the law, that is, for the true and uncorrupted will of the deity. The best known, and also the most instructive example up to the present is the reform, or revolution, of Amenophis IV.,[1] which rested on the worship of the sun-god as the only form in which the deity was revealed, and which sought to establish accordingly a *monotheistic* religion. Every inner movement must express itself in corresponding forms, and when we shall have gained a clearer view of the historical development of ancient Oriental civilizations these facts will be everywhere discoverable.

We can now point to only one such case in Assyria during the reign of Adad-nirari. We have a remarkable inscription upon statues of the god Nebo. These statues and the inscriptions, strange to say, were not dedicated by the king, but by one of his governors, Bel-tartsi-ilu-ma,[2] whose authority extended over many provinces. He presented them "for the life of the king." With the king he also mentions his spouse, *Sammuramat*. Ever since this inscription was discovered efforts have been made to identify it with the legendary *Semiramis*. It may be that story has to do with a woman who played a leading part in a political revolution and, therefore, her name became adorned with legendary material—that is all that can be said of it. Of vastly more importance is the fact that Bel-tartsi-ilu-ma, who acts

---

[1] On the religious revolution of Amenophis (Ikhnaton) see Breasted's History of Egypt, Chap. xviii.—*Craig*.

[2] He was *limmu* in 798.   One of his official seals is in our possession.

here the part of a *major domus,* plainly preaches
in this text a religion quite different from the
prevailing state religion, and a monotheistic one
in the same sense as that of Amenophis IV. "Put
thy trust in Nebo; trust not in another God" is the
"essential" truth with which he closes his inscription, just as the Protestant reformers declared
their fundamental position: "The word of God
endureth forever." [1] But this is a complete break
with the old religion, and when Nebo is regarded
as the only true manifestation of deity we appear
to have a development of doctrine from the Assyrian point of view which corresponds to the theological position reached in the West—in Palestine.
As the reform of Amenophis IV. found its echo
in Palestine—in Jerusalem and Tyre—so also in
name at least, if not in effectiveness, did this
one undertaken during the reign of Adad-nirari.
Adad-nirari was the king who rescued Israel from
her oppressor, Damascus,[2] and whom Jonah found
at Nineveh when he went there and found royal
sympathy with his teaching.[3]

We have no inscriptions of the following period
and are consequently compelled to draw entirely

---

[1] Following I. Peter 1, 24 f., which quotes from Isa. 40, 7 f., where,
however, "the word of our God" is not "the word of God" of the
Reformation.—*Craig.*

[2] *Vid.* 2 Ki. 13, 5.

[3] This is not meant to confirm the *historic* character of the story
of Jonah.—*Craig.*

from the Eponym Canon. The absence of inscriptions is evidence in itself of a time of weakness, and this is confirmed by the few established facts. In general, it may be said that the next forty years were spent in maintaining that which had been won previously, and this effort was not always crowned with success. We shall see when we come to the rise of power under Tiglathpileser that much had been lost and had to be regained. This was particularly true of the regions that lay within the sphere of interest of the new kingdom of Urartu. When Assyria ceased to attack she was herself attacked. This was the case from now on in Armenia, whose kings extended their sway southward and deprived Assyria of the Nairi-Lands and her control in North Syria. The successor of Adad-nirari III.,

SHALMANESER III., 783–773,

was principally engaged in defensive wars against Urartu. Six out of his ten expeditions were against this new and advancing power. On the East, in the lands along the Median frontier, less loss seems to have been sustained; but there the states were in the main semi-barbarian and defectively organized. Two expeditions were sent thither to the land of Namri, in 749 and 748, and one advanced against the Medes in 766. The next king was

He marched several times into Syria, the first time against Damascus, and the second against Khatarikka to the north of it. Twice he advanced into Babylonia, in 771 and 767, where he sought to oppose the Chaldeans. The second half of his reign witnessed a weakening of his kingdom which compelled concentration of effort upon the maintenance of that which had been slowly accomplished in the tributary states. In 763 an insurrection broke out which, in the years that followed, was repeated in different quarters until by degrees a large part of the kingdom was involved. The Eponym Canon puts a division line before this year (the year which it tells us the eclipse of the sun occurred—a valuable notice for the determination of the old chronology) as it does before the beginning of a new reign; for, since the insurrection took place in Ashur, a rival king must have been called forth. What the deeper underlying cause may have been we are not informed, but it is not difficult to discover it, for the insurrection originated in the old capital. When we consider that Tiglathpileser then chose Kalkhi again, and, on the other hand, that Sargon II. restored to Ashur its privileges, we may infer that it was connected with a movement of the injured priesthood of Babylon who suffered by a removal of the royal residence. The Eponym Canon does not name the king who was raised to the throne by the insurrection, but from various statements it is clear that he was recognized as king. He was

ADAD-NIRARI IV., 763–755,

whose filial relation to his predecessor did not necessarily prevent opposition to his father. He in turn experienced the same treatment from his son, who rebelled against him. According to the view of the Eponym Canon, which is that of the capital Ashur, the latter, it is true, is only a repression of the insurrection by

ASHUR-NIRARI II., 754–746,

who was clearly influenced by the ancient capital, for the first act of his reign was to make Ashur his residence. This means that the *hierarchy triumphed over the army* on which Assyria's strength rested. Therewith, the kingdom, in giving up its only support, acted fatally for itself. Ashur-nirari ruled eight years, during which, with one exception, according to the Eponym Canon, he was "in the land," that is, there was no war. But from the same source we learn that in 746 there was an "insurrection in Kalkhi," and the following year Tiglathpileser III. ascended the throne. We know from his inscriptions that he resided in Kalkhi and that he was not of the royal line. It thus appears that he ascended the throne as the result of a military insurrection. Ashur-nirari II., who ruled in Ashur under the influence of the priests, was the last of his house.[1] As in the case of his predecessors none of his inscriptions have been discovered. But we have a valuable document which presents an agreement made between him and Mati-il of *Arpad* (Arvad), wherein the latter acknowledges Assyrian sovereignty. It was probably drawn up during the expedition to the West in 754. The wars of Tiglathpileser III. show how much value this agreement had. It is one of the numerous examples of prevailing conditions at this and other times in Western Asia, and is an instructive illustration of Palestinian conditions ten years later.

[1] From sources not yet authentically published it seems, nevertheless, that Tiglathpileser may have been the son of Adad-nirari IV. That would harmonize perfectly with the view of Assyria's internal politics presented above.

CHAPTER VI

THE NEW ASSYRIAN KINGDOM: ASSYRIA THE PARA-MOUNT POWER IN WESTERN ASIA

A NEW period of Assyrian history begins with

TIGLATHPILESER III., 745–728.

With him there came an advance in power which made Assyria the ruling power of Western Asia. It was he who laid the foundations of Assyria's fame. This is the period when Assyria subjugated Damascus and Palestine. Thus she entered into the history of that little people whose literary remains were for so long the best known of antiquity, and which for two thousand years preserved the name of Assyria while her own monumental records lay beneath the earth and no man knew what language she had spoken.

Tiglathpileser's wars fall under three geographical heads: viz., in Babylonia, the North, and Syria-Palestine with Damascus. His successes in Babylonia have already been described. In the North he had to fight against Urartu, now vigorous grown. In the West tribute was withheld since the last war, 773, and, owing to the weakness of Assyria, Damascus had risen again to strength.

After the Babylonian expedition during the

first year, 745, and one against Western Media
in the second year, war broke out two years later,
in 742, with Sarduris II. of Armenia. The latter
had in the meantime gone forth to conquer without reserve. Melitene, Commagene (Kummukh),
the northern part of Patin, and Gurgum, he subjugated and compelled their kings to pay tribute
to him instead of to Assyria. Then he entered
into an agreement with Mati-il of Agusi who
resided in Arpad, the centre of his little kingdom.
On the advance of Sarduri Mati-il joined forces
with him, whether voluntarily, with the hope of
winning advantages, or under compulsion, it matters not—it is the old story of the small state
ground between the upper and the nether mill-
stones of the larger powers. According to the
Eponym Chronicle Tiglathpileser appeared in
743 before Arpad, doubtless against Mati-il, when
an Armenian army led by Sarduris fell upon
Mesopotamia. Sarduris was worsted in the
region of Kummukh and pursued to the "Bridge
of the Euphrates, the boundary of his land," and
thus an end was put to his inroads into Mesopotamia. Further measures against him had to be
postponed. The following three years were spent
in expeditions "against Arpad." Mati-il must,
therefore, have offered an energetic resistance.
After his fall the majority of the Syrian princes
paid tribute, among them Kustaspi of Kum-

mukh, and Tarkhulara of Gurgum which, therefore, seceded from Urartu, further Rezon of
Damascus, Hiram of Tyre, the prince of Kue,
and Pisiris of Carchemish. Assyria's rule in
Syria was consequently restored during these
three years and Urartu driven out. Only a
part of Patin, Unqi (that is, the Amq) joined
the capital city Kinalia, or Kunalua, in opposition
for which its prince Tutammu lost his throne and
this part of the land was made into an Assyrian
province.

In the following year, 739, Ulluba, one of the
Nairi-Lands, was brought under Assyrian rule.
This was, of course, a blow at Armenia, from
which this region was taken. It was fortified so
that it might be able to withstand her attacks and
bore the name "Fortress-land." It formed,
therefore, a kind of military borderland, and the
Assyrian precaution in constructing a line of forts
shows what a dangerous enemy Urartu had become. Azriya'u,[1] the prince of Ya'udi, bordering
on Samal-Sendjirli revolted and his city, *Kullani,*
was conquered. This event cast its shadow down
to Israel and Judah, and Isaiah, the prophet,
pointed to Calno as an example of warning.[2] A
number of North Phœnician districts—where
Ashur-natsir-pal had founded his Assyrian colony,

[1] Formerly falsely identified with Azariah (Uzziah) of Judah.
[2] Isa. 10, 9.

Aribua, and which now belonged to Hamath—
also joined Azriya'u and shared his fate. Out of
these the Assyrian province Tsimirra, stretching
from the Orontes to Gebal, was formed, but it did
not include Gebal or Arvad which remained independent. This new Phœnician province, which
was enlarged in 733, was given by Tiglathpileser
to his son Shalmaneser as governor. Thus a part
of the frontier lands of Damascus passed over to
Assyria. Damascus itself as well as the other
Syrian and Phœnician states, Kummukh, Carchemish, Sam'al, and Gurgum in the Amq,[1] Hamath,
Kue, Gebal, Tyre, and Menahem of Israel paid
tribute, and from the biblical account it appears
that the latter paid only when part of his territory
had been taken. So, too, the larger circle of states
which once had been subject to Shalmaneser again
paid tribute: Melitene, Kasku, Tabal, and principalities in Cappadocia and Cilicia. Now that the
Assyrian king was feudal lord of Damascus he
received presents also from the Arab king, Zabibi.

Expeditions were sent against Media and Nairi
in 737 and 736, the principal object being to
break the power of Urartu in these quarters. The
following year the war was carried into the
enemy's country; Urartu was traversed and Tiglathpileser besieged the citadel Thuruspa (Van),
but in vain. He was obliged to withdraw after

[1] P. 239.

setting up his royal image before the eyes of the besieged. He, however, incorporated the southern part of Urartu with the province of Nairi, and this was a serious blow to the kingdom. The border provinces were also fortified and the possibilities of advance were thereby lessened. This put an end to the rule of Urartu over Syria and Nairi, but her plans for conquest were not abandoned until her strength was broken by Sargon and the Gimmirai[1] (Cimmerians) appeared a threatening foe on the western side.

Up to this time Damascus had paid its tribute; but nothing was so certain as the uncertainty of the tributary states to Assyria. On the one hand the demands were so high that the tribute could only be wrung out of them by feudal princes; on the other, this state of affairs was a constant temptation to revolt whenever there was the slightest hope. Moreover, tributary states may have been provoked to revolt in order to furnish an excuse for incorporating them as provinces: compare the dealings of the Romans with their Socii. In 734 an expedition was made to Philistia and Askalon was put under Assyrian control. It was evident that all Palestine must yield with Damascus. But soon afterward Damascus broke loose. Rezon and his vassal, Pekah of Israel, had

---

[1] Gen. x., 2, "Gomer." The word survives also in the modern Crimea.—*Craig*.

shut up Ahaz of Judah in Jerusalem in order to compel him to join with them and Tyre in a coalition against Assyria in which help was expected from Egypt. Ahaz appealed for help, and in 733 Tiglathpileser's troops stood before Damascus.[1] On the approach of the Assyrian army the pro-Assyrian party of Israel revolted and deposed Pekah and appointed Hosea, their own leader, king in his stead. This well-timed revolt robbed Tiglathpileser of a pretext for interference. A brief respite of ten to twelve years was thus purchased, but Israel's fate was only postponed. As previously, Damascus offered successful resistance; but at last, in the year 732, she became an Assyrian province. Israel, already weakened by loss of territory, stood now in immediate contact with an Assyrian province: the state which had before dominated her politically and was her guide in cultural development was now under the rule of an Assyrian governor! Tyre also, the rich mercantile city, which could most easily pay its tribute, made her peace on the approach of the Assyrian army.

The next years were devoted to the conquest of Babylonia and Babylon.[2] For two years Tiglathpileser ruled as king of Babylon, and in 728 he died. He was succeeded by his son,

[1] *Cf.* 2 Ki. xvi., 5 ff., Isa. vii., 1 ff.
[2] P. 114 f.

SHALMANESER IV., 727–722.

His reign is only an appendage to that of his father's, whose policy he appears to have closely followed. None of his own inscriptions have come down to us. During his reign Samaria was again forced to withhold her tribute, but the help that was hoped for from Egypt failed, and, after a siege of three years, the city was taken and an Assyrian governor appointed. Thus the Assyrian boundary was extended southward almost to Jerusalem. Before the fall of Samaria Shalmaneser died, and the conquest is, therefore, attributed to

SARGON II., 722–705.

This Sargon,[1] like Tiglathpileser, was the founder of a new dynasty, and he became king as the result of a reaction against the same movement which placed Tiglathpileser upon the throne. His statements about his predecessor's acts which he nullified reveal the nature of this inner movement that had already manifested itself in the insurrections of Ashur-danin-apli and of the year 763.

Tiglathpileser, therefore, strove to limit the *powerful influence of the priesthood* and the *larger cities' privileges* which were also of *priestly* origin. They were in possession of unlimited rights and exempt from almost every bur-

[1] His name appears in the O. T. only in the brief reference to the conquest of Ashdod. Isa. 20, 1.—*Craig.*

den. When we consider that the largest part of the landed property also belonged to them it is clear the income of the state grew constantly less, and clear also why the Assyrian kingdom became at the last so powerless—it was priest-ridden. This also determined the attitude of Assyrian kings toward Babylon. Tiglathpileser, Shalmaneser, Sennacherib, Ashurbanipal, all took energetic measures against her, Sargon and Esarhaddon favored her. It was here that the freedom enjoyed by the priesthood and the cities and that induced the national weakness was most insisted upon. Tiglathpileser and Shalmaneser sought to put an end to the system, and in their effort must have looked to the agricultural class, such as still existed, for support, not because the kings were particularly interested in the plight of the "poor man," but rather with a view to conditions that would yield more taxes and provide subjects more fit for service. They were aware, however, that a kingdom which depended upon the cities and the hierarchy could maintain itself only so long as it had advantages to offer them.

From this point on we are able to follow the active opposition of the two contending parties in Assyria—the violent changes of rulers reveal it clearly. It is self-evident that a drawing together of the privileged cities and temples resulted in no good to the country population, which at best only furnished the masses for a movement. In reality, indeed, it turned on the antithesis between land and city, but the land was actually *represented by the nobility* who *partly controlled the army.* Consequently, Tiglath-pileser and Shalmaneser were under their influence. Sargon, who was raised to the throne by the opposite party, favored the cities and temples and restored to them their former privileges. Sennacherib again represented the nobility and army as is clear even in his conduct toward Babylon. He was murdered, and with Esarhaddon the Babylonian hierarchical party triumphed. Then when he tried to secure the throne for his son Shamash-shum-ukin, who was similarly disposed, an insurrection broke out, and, by the enthronement of Ashurbanipal, the Assyrian nobility was victorious. These are the two political factors which from now on determine Assyrian history. When Tiglathpileser ascended the throne a well defined and conscious opposition between them was developed.

Thus in the year 722 when Shalmaneser IV. died Sargon, who was not of royal descent, was suddenly placed upon the throne, but despite his descent he became the head of the royal house under which Assyria witnessed the climax of its power and its rapid fall. His reign, which in internal affairs was the opposite of Tiglathpileser's, was externally a continuation and completion of that which had been begun by the latter. That he effected it with other means than his predecessor we have already seen. From now on the Assyrian army was composed of *mercenary troops*, gathered from all lands and provinces, wholly at command of the king so long as he was able to provide them with money and plunder, but instantly recalcitrant when these failed. Henceforth it was the "royal" army that held the Orient in check. Assyrian rule thereby devolved upon a government (according to Oriental custom—plundering) by the nobility and hierarchy. An Assyrian people, to whom Shalmaneser I. and Ashur-natsir-pal had assigned land in conquered provinces, no longer existed. Now when the king wishes to settle a conquered region with new settlers he must resort to an exchange of peoples from different quarters of his kingdom. The agricultural class in Assyria was destroyed: there remained only large estates of the nobility or the temple cultivated by slaves or homeless hirelings.

The wars of Sargon are, in the main, only a continuation of his predecessors on the old battle-grounds—in Babylonia with the Chaldeans and Elam, in the North with Urartu, and in Palestine where he sought further conquests.

His successes in Babylonia we know already (p. 117). In Palestine, as we have just mentioned,

Samaria was incorporated and "the ten tribes carried into captivity," a fact which gives importance to the name of Sargon for the student of the Old Testament, though it was clearly the result of the siege by Shalmaneser IV. Up to this time Hamath, north of Damascus in Syria, had warded off the blow by prompt payment of tribute, but it had evidence in 738 of Assyria's altruism in the way of "benevolent assimilation" when the rebellious Hamathite cities were taken and incorporated in the province of *Tsimirra.* Hamath's hopes must have been quickened by a change of rulers in Assyria, and so in 720 we find the subservient king, Eni-il, dethroned and a "rustic" *Ya-u-bi-'di* in his stead in open opposition to Assyria. Hanno of Gaza, who was compelled to submit to Tiglathpileser, united with him. Evidently both of them had put their trust in Egypt.[1] They were also supported by the peoples of North Arabia whose marts were in Gaza, and who consequently paid tribute to Assyria. The newly established provinces of Arpad, Tsimmirra, Damascus, and Samaria also joined them, incited thereto by Ya-u-bi-'di. Thus the greater part of Syria and Palestine tried to rid itself of Assyrian dominion or tribute. But the effort of the

---

[1] A few years later the Assyrian commander of Sennacherib's army, when he parleyed with Hezekiah's officers at Jerusalem, aptly described Egypt as "a staff of a broken reed, which if leaned upon will pierce the hand." Isa. 36, 6.—*Craig.*

allies failed to bring about concerted action—a common defect of petty states in such undertakings. Hamath was conquered and placed under tribute and Ya-u-bi-'di flayed. Hanno, who with the help of an Arabian force was trying to conquer Gaza, not as yet in his hands apparently, was repulsed at Raphia, on the southern border of Gaza's territory. The rebellious provinces were easily subdued. Peace reigned again in Syria and Palestine.

Sargon was now at liberty to confront his third enemy, *Urartu*. There Rusas I. had again sought to bring North Syria and the bordering Median states on the east under his influence, and apparently his project found approval. Sargon saw the immediate necessity, as Tiglathpileser did during his reign, of subjecting this faithless vassal. In 719 two cities of Man (on the west coast of the Urumia Sea), whose king held to Assyria despite the influence of Urartu, were overrun and plundered because they had gone over to the Indo-Germanic tribe, *Zigirtu,* which favored Urartu. The same fate befell a couple more cities that revolted to Urartu. In 718 Kiakki, one of the princes of Tabal in Cappadocia, who had thrown off the Assyrian yoke, was carried captive with 7,350 of his troops and his capital delivered over to a neighboring loyalist, Mattî of Atun.[1] The in-

[1] Or Tunnu *Keilinschriftliche Bibliothek*, II., 56, 1.

habitants of these regions were separated in the main by the Taurus, from Syria the particular field of interest to Assyria. They naturally belonged to Asia Minor. They entered their territory during the last Hittite immigration which, as we have seen, occurred in the time of Tiglathpileser I. The relation they occupied to the old Hittite kingdom on the Halys and to the west of it corresponded to that sustained to Assyria by the petty Syrian states which she was forced to subdue in the period following Shalmaneser II. One of these peoples which meets us most frequently at that time is the *Muski.* They had taken possession of the land of the *Khatti,* the old Kheta kingdom, and there played a part similar to that played, as we have often seen, in the countries of the Euphrates by the different immigrants, the Kassites, Chaldeans, etc. Just as the Old Testament spoke of the Babylon of Nebuchadrezzar and its rulers as Chaldean, so the people who occupied the seat of the old kingdom of Khatti could be designated Muski. After the eleventh century new immigrations arrived in these regions; and after Sargon's time, in the seventh century, we witness the intrusion of the Indo-Germanic tribes. A new population arose, or the old was greatly modified by the new, and thus a new name might be given to the regions as happened in the case of the Muski.

A glance at the historical development of these peoples and states readily explains why a well known figure of classical tradition comes before us under a different name in the inscriptions of Sargon. The ruler in Asia Minor who attempted to oppose the advance of Sargon in the direction of Armenia and in Cilicia (Kue), and who represented the strongest of the powers of Asia Minor is Mita of Muski, that is, *Midas,* king of Phrygia, with whom the earliest Greek traditions of Asia Minor begin. In his opposition to Sargon he shows that the mantle of the old kings of Khatti had fallen upon him.

Karchemish, that had paid tribute from the time of Ashur-natsir-pal, fell in 717. Assyrian oppressions had exhausted the patience even of this wealthy city and goaded her to hopeless war. Here again the consciousness of the old historical connection appears to view. Karchemish had always been the advance post of the Khatti power in Syria; her kings were sometimes briefly called kings of Khatti. Now again she turned for support against Assyria to the master of the old Khatti kingdom on the Halys. But the Asiatic power of Muski-Phrygia was no match for Assyria. The protection of Midas (Mita) availed no more in bringing help to the vassal against Assyria than Egypt, or earlier Mutsri, did in warding off Sennacherib from Judah. Pisiris was the last king of Karchemish—and the last remnant of the Khatti kingdom in Syria now became an Assyrian province.

In 716 and 715 war was again waged in the east of Urartu where Rusas, having abandoned Syria and turned eastward, had attempted in the meantime to take Man by force. By exciting certain tribes to insurrection and regicide he succeeded in placing on the throne Ullusunu, son of the murdered king. But before the party friendly to Urartu had time to establish themselves Sargon appeared with his troops and forced their appointee to do homage. His little kingdom had been overrun, fifty-five of Rusas' walled cities had been burned, and he had sought refuge in the mountains; but a timely supplication to the conqueror saved him his life and with it his partly ruined kingdom and capital. In his palace Sargon set up his stele with his royal image and "the might of Ashur" engraved thereon as a reminder for future days. The prince of Nairi and other chiefs of these regions followed Ullusunu's example.

In 714 the war was continued in Urartu. Proceeding from Man through Mutsatsir, whose conquest he represented in the sculptures of his palace, Sargon advanced toward Lake Van, devastating the land. Rusas, when he heard of the havoc wrought in Mutsatsir and of the capture of the prince's family and gods, ended his life with his girdle dagger, although Sargon failed to effect a complete conquest of his land. From now on, however, the power of Urartu as a rival of Assyria was broken. It was now compelled to contend for its existence with the Kimmerians, the new enemy already mentioned, upon its northern border. But, while Assyria had disposed of an enemy she had thereby weakened the natural barrier against the imminent danger of being overrun by the Indo-Germanic hordes. She had already come into conflict with the van of this movement in the above mentioned Zigirtu. The Assyrian army officers in the border provinces of the North were thereafter compelled to keep a close watch upon the struggles between Urartu and the Kimmerians and other related tribes. In the reign of Esarhaddon, the latter, as we shall see, have already begun to threaten Assyrian territory.

Of the earlier land of Patin many districts were already incorporated in Syria. Under Sargon the remainder, *viz.*, Gurgum, with its capital Marqasi (Mar'ash), was included. Kue and other Cappadocian districts, among which was Kammanu, which represented the earlier Mutsri in Anti-Taurus, Melitene, and Kummukh, were reduced to Assyrian provinces as the result of futile attempts to win their liberty. Therewith the limit of Assyria's extension on her northwest border was attained. Near the close of Sargon's reign the governor of Kue attempted to push across beyond the Taurus to curb the predatory desires of Mita of Muski, who was trying to advance there as well as against the northwest of Assyria.

When the occupation of Babylon was effected by Sargon he received presents from seven Greek "kings." This is the earliest attested contact with "Ionians." The princes who offered their homage were on the west of the island, and they sought assistance from Assyria in their efforts to dislodge the Phœnicians of Tyre from the East. Here again, as in the case of Midas, we see connections with Greek history long before there is any connected Greek tradition.

Ashdod alone, in Southern Palestine, relying upon Arab support, refused her tribute. It is noteworthy because of the mention of Ashdod's capture in Isaiah XX., 1.[1] This revolt in the immediate neighborhood must have been followed with hope and anxiety in Judah. According to Sargon Judah was also plotting with Moab and Ammon against Assyria, though it never came to open revolt, when an Assyrian army fell upon Ashdod and there founded an Assyrian colony.

In the East Elam was unable to accomplish any-

---

[1] The gods of Ashdod most of the inhabitants, and the treasures of the city were carried off to Assyria.

thing in Babylonia after the expulsion of Mero-dach-baladan. But the opposition of the two rivals found expression over a struggle for the throne of the borderland Ellipi. There two brothers contested each other's claims, the one seeking the support of Elam, the other that of Sargon. Nibe, the protégé of Elam, won at first in the conflict over his brother Ispabara, but the latter finally triumphed with the help of Sargon.

Near the end of Sargon's rule the great palace which he had been building at Khorsabad, north of Nineveh, at the foot of the mountain, was completed, and in 707 it was entered with all the pomp of religion and magnificence of state. The capital was thus removed from Kalkhi, although Sargon ascended the throne by the aid of the party which there found its chief support. But, on account of its location, it was no longer suitable as the seat of government. Therefore the new capital was founded, to which Sargon gave the name *Dur-Sharrukin* (Sargon's City), following the example of his somewhat legendary ideal whose name he assumed at the time of his accession. "Sargon II." was the name given him by his faithful scribes who were prepared to furnish scientific evidence—always on hand for the successful conqueror—that he, by divine decree and the natural course of events, was the one ordained to introduce a new era and fulfil the expectations of the nation.[1]

The inscriptions and the sculptures of the palace of Dur-Sharrukin, the first of all to be excavated,[2] are the main source for the history of his reign. He died in 705. The details of his death are wanting. According to a statement of Sennacherib he met with a violent death and "was not buried in his house," that is, he did not receive a customary burial. The only explanation of this is that he *fell in battle with barbarians* as Cyrus did. These were to be found almost alone on the northern border of Assyria in the Indo-Germanic tribes, the Kimmerians, and "Scythians." We naturally think first of the Scythians. The exultant pæan of Isa. 14, 4–21, was composed, in all probability, on the occasion of the unexpected death of Sargon and afterward applied to a king of Babylon. The hopes which it aimed to arouse were not wanting: Palestine and Phœnicia attempted a widespread revolt.

SENNACHERIB, 704–681.

Sennacherib was at first engaged in Babylonia, and his second expedition was directed toward the Zagros, where he chastised the Kashshu, a

[1] Apocalyptic calculations, such as are met with in the Book of Daniel, form one of the persistent factors in pre-Christian historiography.

[2] By Botta, 1842–45.

remnant of the old Kassites, and also the Yasu-bigalli. Then, in 701, he turned toward Palestine.

Here the moving spirits in the insurrection were *Luli of Tyre,* and Hezekiah of Judah. Luli was "king of the Sidonians." He possessed Tyre and Sidon and a territory that reached from the south of Beirut to Philistia. Moreover, the eastern part of Cyprus was his with the most important city, Kition, or Carthage. We have already seen[1] the western part was held by the "Ionians" and friendly to Assyria because of its opposition to the Phœnicians. Hope of help from Mero-dach-baladan was also entertained, but he was quickly driven off. Promises had come like-wise from the Arab princes, and later on Arabian auxiliaries arrived. That Hezekiah was the leader of the insurrection is clear from the fact that the party opposed to Assyria in Ekron delivered into his hands Padi, its king, who favored Assyria. This was the development of events between 705 and 702.

When in 701 Sennacherib set out and marched along the coast of Phœnicia, leaving behind a rock-hewn image of himself on the *Nahr-el-Kelb,* it was again evident that each power expected the others to destroy the much feared tyrant—concerted action was wanting The Phœnician cities, Arvad and Gebal, the southern kingdoms, those of

[1] P. 253.

Philistia, and Judah's neighbors, Ammon, Moab and Edom paid tribute. Luli abandoned Sidon and fled to Cyprus where he soon afterward died. Tyre alone resisted and held out against the siege of Sennacherib. In Sidon a new king, Ithobal, was appointed, thus rending the "kingdom of Sidon" in twain. He then advanced southward against Judah, where Hezekiah held out, trusting to the help coming from Arabia. He conquered Ekron, beat the relief army made up of Arab troops belonging to the princes of Mutsri and the king of Melukha, and gradually reduced 46 fortified cities. He then besieged the capital on all sides. The defenders held out, trusting that disturbances would break out in Babylon, and, in fact, Sennacherib was compelled to withdraw without the surrender of Jerusalem. Judah's independence—for the present—was saved. Hezekiah had, it is true, lost the greater part of his territory, for the conquered cities were apportioned to his neighbors, and he made haste to regain them.

After the destruction of Babylon in 689, Sennacherib was again free to act in the West. Meantime some minor wars were waged in Cappadocia (Khilakku), and in Kammanu, the province founded by Sargon. Attempts of the "Ionians" to land in Cilicia were also frustrated. No more great conquests were made here and the territorial limits were not enlarged by the erection of new provinces. In 701 Tyre had successfully defended herself against siege and maintained her independence. The Arabs who came to the help of Hezekiah were repulsed, but Sennacherib was unable to mete out chastisement upon them. It appears as if he now undertook an expedition into Northwestern Arabia (Melukha) and Egypt. Jerusalem also anticipated attack, but fortune was again favorable. The Assyrian army did not even touch the land. Possibly on the march to Egypt it may have been overtaken in Arabia by plague or have succumbed to the unfavorable climate. Sennacherib was compelled with the loss of his army to return to Nineveh. There the fate of so many Oriental kings overtook him; in an insurrection he was put to death by one of his sons.

CHAPTER VII

THE DECLINE

SENNACHERIB's reign was nowhere successful. He made an energetic attempt to solve the Babylonian problem, and, apparently, not without success. But even in Babylonia he got as many blows from Elam as he gave. In 694, while his army was plundering Elam, the Elamites laid waste Northern Babylonia and took captive his son, Ashur-nadin-shum. Compared with Tiglath-pileser and Sargon he failed in the West, being powerless to take either Tyre or Jerusalem. Neither in the East toward Media, nor in the West in Asia Minor, where his predecessors had made important conquests, did he succeed in making any noteworthy additions to the provincial territory. When we look to the North we discover no evidences that he made any effort to check the threatened danger from that quarter, where, both in Urartu and Man, the Indo-Germanic tribes were constantly spreading.

His failures explain his end. He owed his ascent to the throne to the military party, and, when he lost his army, he fell a victim of the rival faction, the "Babylonian." Within the latter

there must, nevertheless, have been different tendencies.   The   actual   and   natural   leader   was
clearly

ESARHADDON, 680–669,

under whose administrative authority Babylonia
was at the time.   But one of his brothers[1] must
have attempted to anticipate Esarhaddon's accession to the throne of Assyria, and it was, doubtless, he who instigated the insurrection in which
Sennacherib was murdered while "he was wor-
shipping in the house of Nisroch, his god."[2]
Esarhaddon advanced against his foe and defeated the insurrectionists in Melitene, whither
they had fled in hope of help from Armenia, the
implacable enemy of Assyria.   Therewith, Esarhaddon became king of Assyria and Babylonia.

In internal affairs Esarhaddon's policy was
opposed to that of his predecessors, his most abid-
ing work being the rebuilding of Babylon.[3]   The
natural results followed: Babylonian culture
revived, and the dominion over Western Asia was
assured.   For Assyria herself, the master of the

---

[1] The Babylonian Chronicle and Berossus speak of only *one*
son of Sennacherib as the murderer.   The Old Testament gives the
names of Adrammelech and Sharezer, the result, probably, of a
corrupt text.   This Sharezer may be the same as Shar-etir-(mati)-
ashur, *Shar kishshâti shar matâti* to whom the letter, of which we
have a fragment, was addressed containing a report of affairs in
Northern Mesopotamia and mentioning the city Bît-Zamani.   *Vid.*
Winckler, *Altor. Forsch.* II. s.

[2] *Cf.* II. Kings, 19, 37;   Isa. 37, 38.

[3] *Cf.* p. 122 f.

hour, it proved fatal. In other respects Esarhaddon appeals to us as one of the most sympathetic figures in Assyrian history. He showed unwonted clemency to political offenders. Above all, his court must have been the centre of literary activities which evidently drew their inspiration from the monarch whose inclinations were strongly Babylonian. Ashurbanipal, his son, boasts of the literary education he received and to it we owe the priceless collection of his library.

Apart from the useless conquest of Egypt the Assyrian kingdom was not materially enlarged under Esarhaddon, as it had not been under his father, and was not later. His military undertakings resulted in general only in the maintenance and defence of the conquered territory. This, it is true, is in noteworthy contradiction to the idea, due to the influence of old Babylonian traditions, of a Babylonian world-power realized by him. At the very beginning of his reign, as the result of the expeditions against Arabia by Sennacherib, Esarhaddon proclaims himself master of a territory which corresponds to that of Naram-Sin. Even the old Babylonian designations are used in order to make his time appear as a renaissance of that age of Babylonia's highest achievements—"king of Suri (Mesopotamia and Western Asia Minor), Gutium, Amurru, Khatti-land, king of the kings of Dilmun, Magan and Melukha."

These are the titles he assumes even prior to his expeditions against Arabia and the one connected therewith in which Egypt was conquered. His rule was to re-establish the old Babylonian world-power and Babylon was to be the capital. Attempts at revolt by the Chaldeans were not wanting in Babylonia, but they never resulted in the recognition of a prince. In the "Sea-Land," Nabu-zer-kitti-lishir, a grandson of Merodach-baladan's, attempted the conquest of South Babylonia, advancing as far as Ur, but was compelled by an Assyrian army to flee to Elam. There, contrary to precedent, instead of meeting with a friendly reception, he was put to death. His brother, Na'id-Marduk, concluded that refuge in Elam was more dangerous than to be in the den of the lion, and, returning to Nineveh, received both pardon and the premiership of the Sea-Land.

The conditions that resulted from the destruction of Babylon and the character of the Chaldeans are alike illustrated by the treatment of *Bit-Dakuri*. This tribe had quickly taken possession of the exposed territory of Babylon and that of the neighboring Borsippa. The restoration of Babylon made it necessary to deprive them by force of their unlawfully seized possessions. Their "king," Shamash-ibni, was deposed, the lands returned, and Nabûsallim of another family was appointed to rule. At a later period, under

Shamash-shum-ukin, he appears again, in a transaction relating to the property and legal rights of certain towns in the territory of Bit-Dakuri.

Khumba-khaldash of Elam, as we have seen, offered no refuge to the grandson of Merodach-baladan. But, in the year 674, he wrought serious havoc in Northern Babylonia, which he plundered as far as Sippar. Esarhaddon was no more able than Sargon and Sennacherib to carry the war into the inaccessible territory of this dangerous enemy. On the contrary, he limited his efforts to securing the obedience of the *Gambuli,* on the Elamite border at the mouth of the Tigris, whose chief, Shapi-Bel, he intrusted with the protection of the boundary after he had strengthened his stronghold for that purpose. In this he followed an age-long policy of Oriental states. With the successor of Khumba-khaldash, his brother Urtaki, the relations with Esarhaddon became more friendly. The gods which had been carried off from Sippar in the spring he sent back and received aid in return from Esarhaddon in view of a famine that had in the meantime broken out in Elam. The famine made for friendship.[1]

In the West Tyre had maintained her resistance from 701 on; and, moreover, from about 694 she

[1] The Elamites doubtless attributed their ill-fortune to the wrath of the gods who were avenging themselves upon their enemies and captors, just as the Philistines attributed the "tumours" to the ark of the God of Israel. *Vid.* I. Sam., 5, 1 ff.—*Craig.*

was backed by Egypt under the ambitious Kushite, Taharqu. Sidon, too, that was separated from Tyre by Sennacherib, revolted in 678 under the new king, Abd-milkot, Ithobal's successor. She was conquered and the old city that was situated, like Tyre and Arvad, upon an island was destroyed with the national sanctuary of all the "Sidonians." A new city was built upon the mainland, which the conqueror named *Kar-Esarhaddon* and an Assyrian governor was stationed within it. Sidon thereafter remained a province and, probably, was not ruled by her own kings until the Persian period. *Esarhaddon-burg,* which probably bore the name of Sidon also, formed the nucleus of the later city. A Cilician prince, Sanduarri of Kundi[1] and Sizu, were in alliance with Abd-milkot. After three years' opposition their citadels fell before the Assyrians, and the heads of Sanduarri and Sizu were carried to Nineveh almost at the same time as that of Abd-milkot.

The resistance of Tyre was more stubbornly maintained. The "island" Sidon must have lain close to land, but the island Tyre offered greater difficulty to the besieger, and was first taken by Alexander by means of his famous dam which thereafter united it with the mainland. On his way to Egypt Esarhaddon attempted the reduc-

---

[1] Perhaps the old name of the stronghold Kyìnda, the later Anchiäle; Sizu the Sîs of Islamitic time.

tion of Tyre, and besieged it on the land side by taking possession of Usu, that lay close by, and cutting off the islanders' access to the water by the erection of earthworks. But the island being open to the sea held out, until the news arrived from Egypt in 670 that Taharqu was defeated. Ba'al, the king, then concluded that further resistance would be fruitless and submitted to tribute, accepting, at the same time, the condition usually imposed, namely, that the territorial *status quo* should remain unchanged. In other words, he was to hold the island-city, Tyre, while the territory on the mainland that had been seized by the Assyrians was made into an Assyrian province.

In the same year, 670, the monolith of Esarhaddon which represents Taharqu and Ba'al kneeling as captives at his feet was erected at Senjirli, in Northern Syria. The royal images had been sculptured and all that remained to do was to add the inscription. Suddenly, however, Taharqu returned to Egypt, and Ba'al, who had nothing more to lose, again revolted. It is better, therefore, to ignore the close of the inscription, which goes on to tell of Ba'al's subjection.[1]

[1] The correctness of this view cannot yet be determined, inasmuch as we are not sufficiently informed of the events connected with Esarhaddon's first attack on Egypt in 674. The sculptures on the obverse may refer to the results of that expedition while the inscription may relate to the second. Another account relating to the year 674 reports the capture of the "king of Melukha." Is it possible that Taharqu is meant, or some Arabian prince? It would

When, however, in 668 Taharqu was driven back the second time, and Tyre had endured the siege five years, from 673 to 678, probably without interruption, Ba'al again submitted. Tyre, since she was not conquered, kept her independence though reduced to the island. But her possessions on the mainland remained under Assyrian control.

The possession of all the trading towns on the Syrian coast, and especially of Gaza, the terminus of the caravan road, as well as of Edom, through which this road passed, connecting Syria and Yemen, brought Assyria into close touch with the Arab tribes who conducted the overland trade. They had previously offered their homage to Tiglathpileser and Sargon. Sennacherib afterward attempted the subjugation of the Arabs of the steppes. On one expedition which ended in the destruction of his army[1] he reduced the "kingdom" of Aribi, took its capital and deported its queen and gods to Assyria. The latter were returned by Esarhaddon after he had bound the land by an oath of fealty. His army further went on exploiting expeditions, which are recounted with certain embellishments, far into West Arabia (Melukha) as well as toward the East, into Yemama. Probably they penetrated farther into

seem, moreover, that South Arabia was then under Kushite rule, so that Esarhaddon and Taharqu may have contended for supremacy there.

[1] *Vid.* p. 258.

the interior of Arabia than any other armies except possibly those of Sargon I. and Naram-Sin in their conquests in Magan and Melukha.

The murmurs of discontent were naturally always to be heard on the borders of Cilicia and Cappadocia. Esarhaddon tells of an excursion he made into the region of Du'a, in the Taurus range adjoining Tabal. Melid (that is, Malatia) was conquered by Mukallu, who was possibly a chief of Tabal, or of some related tribe, and he with Ishkallu of Tabal threatened the Assyrian possessions. But concerning this the scribes of Esarhaddon remained silent. We know of it only from the questions addressed to the oracle of Shamash, the sun-god, questions which show that Assyrian possessions in Asia Minor were on the wane. What contributed to this change in the former Khatti-land we know not. The Kimmerians no doubt even then participated in the disturbances. The death of Midas of Phrygia is attributed to them.

From the same oracles we are best informed as to the Indo-Germanic movements in Armenia. The governors of the border provinces no longer report defeats suffered by Urartu at the hands of the Kimmerians as they did in the time of Sennacherib. Now the oracle of the sun-god is anxiously asked whether the Kimmerians, Saparda, Ashkuza, Medes, who are devastating the neighboring regions, will spare the Assyrian provinces; or, whether the Assyrian troops will succeed in relieving besieged places, or in retaking others that have been lost. The triumphant notes of Sargon's reports are no longer heard. Though Esarhaddon tells of victories over Kimmerians and Ashkuza he chronicles no permanent results. The conclusion is justified that, at the best, these victories were confined to outposts, if, indeed, they were not merely successful rear-guard actions. On the whole the decline of Assyrian power in this quarter is evident. A stage is reached where Assyrians and barbarians begin to meet on equal footing. In view of the danger which threatened from the Kimmerians, Esarhaddon sought and found an ally in the Ashkuza, to whose king, Bartatua, he gave his daughter in marriage. This same tribe, as we shall see, was in alliance with Assyria in her last days.

The expeditions in the direction of Media were also ineffectual. There Indo-Germanic activity witnessed an increase after the disappearance of Namri and Parsua. It was certainly not difficult for a trained Assyrian army to annihilate, here and there, individual hordes and districts and bring back their captives and plunder. But the expeditions to the "Salt deserts," on the southeast of the Caspian Sea, and as far as Demavend, secured nothing of permanence. Fresh tribes immediately came to the front, and when one wave of the rising flood had spent itself it was quickly succeeded by another. The doom of the ancient civilization of the Orient, despite all the boasted victories, was here irresistibly sealed. It is, however, no reflection upon the Assyrian king that he failed to see the greatness of the danger and acquire new resources by the conquest of other lands. One success he won which none of his predecessors had achieved—and the question whether it was achieved by a Babylonian monarch prior to the year 2000 remains to be answered by new discoveries—he conquered Egypt. In doing so he but followed the dictates of necessity. Conquest was imperative. Assyria's mercenary army, whose spears were still her only support, needed both employment and booty. Considerations of state were, however, not wholly wanting.

Egypt as well as the countries of the Euphrates looked toward Palestine. If the use of the havens on the Mediterranean were necessary to the latter Palestine, nevertheless, lay contiguous to Egypt and was richer in promise in case she desired to expand. The history of these lands, accordingly, as far as we know it, shows Egypt either in possession of Palestine or struggling to regain it. In every revolt against Assyria Egypt was involved, though the help she promised was rarely given. "The broken reed that pierced the hand

of him who leaned thereon" is the descriptive
phrase Isaiah coined with reference to Egypt and
her false promises of assistance. The uninterrupted disturbances in Palestine counselled a
repression of the fomenter of discord. Sennacherib had attempted that on his last expedition
when he lost his army.

Esarhaddon took up the task the more eagerly
as the Ethiopian, Taharqu, against whom Sennacherib's expedition was directed, had reunited
Egypt and was more ambitious of conquest than
the last of the Pharaohs. We have already seen
that he participated in the revolt of Tyre in 673.
In that year, according to the Babylonian Chronicle, the Assyrians were defeated in Egypt. The
first attempt, therefore, to carry the war into the
enemy's country was repelled. But in 671 a fresh
army invaded Egypt and this time Taharqu was
unable to resist. From Ishupri, where the first
battle was fought, to Memphis, the Assyrian army
advanced irresistibly in fifteen days. On five
occasions Taharqu attempted to stay their march
but was wounded in battle. He then fled to
Thebes. The advance continued, and in "a half
day" Memphis was taken. The family of
Taharqu, his son Urana-Hor, and much treasure
fell into the hands of the Assyrians. Fifty-five
royal statues were taken to Assyria. Taharqu
appears also to have failed to establish himself

in Thebes. His army was scattered and he, a
stranger in Egypt, received no support. Consequently he withdrew from Thebes and fled back
to "Kush," that is, to Nubia.

Over the separate districts of Egypt Esarhaddon appointed twenty-two "kings," whose names
all appear in an inscription of his son Ashur-
bani-pal. But with each one an Assyrian officer
was appointed as overseer as well as a host of
Assyrian officials. The most southerly district
was Thebes, from which it appears how limited
the Assyrian rule was and also how exaggerated
Esarhaddon's claims are when, on the basis of
his achievement, he described himself as *"king
of the kings of Mutsur,"* or Lower Egypt,
"Paturisi," or Upper Egypt, and "Kush." The
Senjirli monolith also, as well as the inscription
on the rock at *Nahr-el-Kelb,* near Beirut, states
rather what was wished than what was accomplished, when Taharqu is represented on his knees
before Esarhaddon, with a ring in his lips, im-
ploring mercy. This glory lasted only a few
months, when Taharqu took up his designs afresh.
The Ethiopian was no Egyptian, and his flight
was only for the purpose of gathering a new
army. In the meantime Esarhaddon had been in
Assyria where an insurrection, in which the moving spirit was his son, Ashur-bani-pal, called for
his attention. Taharqu, doubtless, was aware of

this. At this juncture a "courier" arrived in Nineveh with intelligence that Taharqu had retaken the whole land, was ruling as "king" in Memphis, and had either put to flight or slaughtered the Assyrian soldiery. The Egyptians who, for two thousand years, had been accustomed to submit to exploitation, no doubt looked upon this "restoration of orderly conditions" with as much equanimity as they displayed in their acceptance of the numerous masters of earlier as well as of later times. After the internal affairs of Assyria were settled, and Ashur-bani-pal and his brother, Shamash-shum-ukin, crowned in 668, the army was again available for Egypt. Esarhaddon himself set out thither—his presence in Assyria was no longer desired, and he was sufficiently familiar with the character of an Oriental kingdom to see that nothing remained for him but to die. This he did on the way, the same year, 668. The expedition, therefore, was carried through in the reign of Ashur-bani-pal, whose annals give to him the glory. The Orient, with its ancestor and family worship, has little reverence for the memory of the dead when once one is "buried in his house."

ASHUR-BANI-PAL, 668–626.

The causes which led to the crowning of Ashur-bani-pal have already been touched upon.[1] When

[1] P. 70.

Esarhaddon was prepared for the crowning act of his work, *viz.,* to announce his own ascent to the throne of Babylon which he had raised from her ruins, or that of his son Shamash-shum-ukin, whose mother was a Babylonian, the Assyrian party's time for action was ripe. In 669 "the king caused many nobles to be slain in Assyria" says the Babylonian (!) Chronicle; but Ashur-bani-pal says that when he was called to the throne and made co-regent in the beginning of 668 he "interceded" for the nobles. It was clearly Esar-haddon's purpose first to make Shamash-shum-ukin king of Babylon in order to insure for him, after his own death, the undivided sovereignty. But this was prevented. With the elevation of Ashur-bani-pal the Assyrian military and noble party triumphed over the Babylonian priests and commoners. During the long reign of Ashur-bani-pal, from 668 to 626, the military power of Assyria, with its mercenaries gathered from all lands, celebrated its final triumphs.

The expedition to Egypt on which Esarhaddon died terminated quickly and favorably. The army with which Taharqu attempted to defend Lower Egypt was speedily worsted. Memphis was abandoned and Taharqu fell back upon Thebes. In "one month and ten days" the Assyrian army stood before the walls of Thebes. Taharqu, not having confidence in the population of the capital, withdrew from the city and threw up fortifications on both sides of the river higher up, apparently to block the valley of the river. The Assyrian army advanced only to Thebes, and Ashur-bani-pal, like his father, was compelled to confine his appointment of provincial, or district governors, to the regions north of that city.

Taharqu died that year, or shortly after, in possession of his fortifications. His successor in Napata was Tanut-Ammon, his sister's son. He immediately took the field. The Assyrian army had apparently already withdrawn from Thebes, and the rest of Egypt fell easily into Tanut-Ammon's hands. In Memphis alone did the Assyrian garrison offer resistance. Tanut-Ammon besieged them and took up a position in On (Heliopolis), which lay to the north. Again a courier appeared in Nineveh, and the Assyrian army hastened by forced marches to the relief of the besieged garrison. Tanut-Ammon abandoned the siege and retired upon Thebes, which he attempted to hold. But the city was conquered in 667 or 666 and the Ethiopians driven out of Egypt. Ashur-bani-pal was able to reappoint his provincial governors. Again, however, what was done was quickly undone. Naturally enough the Egyptians looked upon Assyrian rule only as a means to get rid of the Kushites. When that was done the next thing to be considered was deliverance from those who had helped them. A couple of years had barely passed before Psammetik, the son of Necho, to whom Ashur-bani-pal had given the districts of Memphis and Sais, declared his independence. Assyria's army was elsewhere engaged and Psammetik's *coup d'état* succeeded. With the help of the Assyrians they had expelled the Kushites, and then they chose the proper moment to repudiate their debt.

The unselfish Ashur-bani-pal complained of similar base ingratitude on the part of Gyges of Lydia. About the beginning of his reign the Kimmerians were advancing to attack Lydia. They had crossed the Halys and pushed on westward. Since the Assyrians were united with the Ashkuza against the Kimmerians Gyges asked assistance of Ashur-bani-pal, whose Cilician and Cappadocian possessions on the Lydian border were likewise liable to attack. Ashur-bani-pal accordingly offered help—he prayed to Ashur, and so effectually that Gyges actually won over the much feared enemy. He sent two chieftain captives in chains to Nineveh, where the inhabitants gazed in astonishment at the barbarians "whose language no interpreter understood." Therewith the thankless Lydian felt that he had sufficiently acknowledged his obligations. He ceased to send his messenger and "gifts" and supported the rebellious Psammetik—not with prayers, but with troops. Ashur-bani-pal again lifted his hands in prayer to Ashur and Ishtar that "his corpse might be cast before his enemy and his bones carried away." The prayer was answered and the insolent offence expiated. The Kimmerians returned to the attack and Gyges was impotent before them. The land was overrun and Gyges fell in battle. His son, unnamed by Ashur-bani-pal, but called Ardys by Herodotus, succeeded him on the throne. Profiting by the fate of his father he sent to Ashur-bani-pal saying: "Thou art a king acknowledged of God. Thou cursedst my father and evil befell him. Me, thy humble servant, accept, and let me bear thy yoke." But Ashur-bani-pal, by his silence as to assistance, appears, for the time being at least, to have left the Lydians to their own resources. The Kimmerian storm first broke over Cilicia on the Assyrian border, although it is unlikely that Assyria was at all responsible for that. All this occurred in the year 668 and later.

In the same year Ba'al of Tyre finally submitted after Taharqu had abandoned Thebes. He had, as we have seen, to content himself with his island. The king of Arvad, Yakinlu, whose hopes were also in Taharqu, now paid tribute and sent his sons as hostages and pages to Assyria. In these earliest years of Ashur-bani-pal's reign an expedition was also made against the rebellious people of Man, on the Urumia Sea, where the Assyrian ally, Ashkuza, had become emboldened. The causes that led King Akhsheri to withhold his tribute are not far to seek. With the Ashkuza, the king's own allies, in the country the resources must have been seriously affected. Nevertheless, an Assyrian army advanced, an insurrection arose, and Akhsheri fell. His son Ualli submitted to the Assyrians.

About the same time expeditions were made against one or two Median chieftains, but Ashurbani-pal did not advance as far in this direction as Sargon and Esarhaddon had gone. The East was already in the grip of the advancing multitude.

In 660, or a little later, there was again war with Elam, and this time Elam was the aggressor. Since the time of Esarhaddon peace had prevailed with Urtaki. But now he was trying, in connivance with certain Babylonian tribal chiefs, especially with the Gambuli, to establish himself in Babylonia and for that purpose he despatched an army. Ashur-bani-pal does not appear to have had his army in readiness; the Elamites had reached almost to Babylon before he appeared and drove them back over the border. There he halted. It is clear, therefore, that Assyria remained on the defensive as regards Elam ever since Sennacherib's ill-fated venture.[1] Urtaki died soon after. The complications which fol-

[1] *Vid.* p. 259.

lowed the change of kings led to war with Teumman, his successor, who marched against North Babylonia, but was forced to retreat at Dur-ilu. Now, for the first time, the Assyrian army marched through the Zagros passes and appeared before the walls of Susa. The successes of Kurigalzu II. and Nebuchadrezzar I.[1] were in this instance repeated. With this war, about 655, Ashur-bani-pal's undertakings during the first half of his reign come to a close.

All the succeeding wars of Ashur-bani-pal are bound up with the great insurrection of Shamash-shum-ukin which broke out in 652.[2] The superiority of the Assyrian army was manifest in his overthrow, but the encouragement that Shamash-shum-ukin everywhere met with, and the hopes connected with his project in all parts of the kingdom, showed at the same time that the kingdom was held together by force only and that without its army of mercenaries it could not last. His treatment of Babylon was different from Sennacherib's; nevertheless, as representative of the "Assyrian" policy, he certainly dealt with her in much the same way as Tiglathpileser and Shalmaneser had. Tangible evidence of this is seen in the fact that he, following their example, assumed the crown of Babylon and ruled there as King *Kandalanu* from 647 to 626.

----

[1] Pp. 87, 94.   [2] P. 124.

Babylon's strongest support during the revolt came from Elam. The result was that a series of wars were waged against her which culminated in the conquest of Susa and the complete destruction of the Elamite kingdom. But all that Assyria attained by this was that she, having made no effort to hold the conquered territory, played into the hands of the advancing Indo-Germanic tribes on the border. Just as in Urartu, so it was here; she had destroyed the buffer-state between herself and the enemy. The events connected with the overthrow of Elam reveal the lasting confusion which followed, but a narrative of these belongs properly to the history of Elam. Within Babylonia the different tribes were likewise won over from Shamash-shum-ukin. The Gambuli and Puqudi and some of the Chaldean states were severely chastised. The submission of the great grandson of Merodach-baladan in the Sea-Land also followed, and this contributed in its way to Elam's distress.

Furthermore, the Babylonian revolt paved the way for a punitive expedition into Arabia. The Bedouins, ever eager for plunder, had sent an auxiliary force to Babylon, and, naturally enough, it was completely annihilated; but this was not enough. Since the land of "Aribi" was under Assyrian protection the defection must needs be punished. An Assyrian army marched through

the Syrian desert, plundering as it went, in a
semicircle from Assyria to Damascus. This was
soon after 648. Quiet, however, did not long
endure. Abiyate, the king who had been placed
on the throne in place of Uaiti' soon "forgot the
name of the great gods" and had to learn his
lesson anew. Ashur-bani-pal's reports of these
expeditions to Arabia are particularly oratorical
and correspondingly obscure. "No bird of the
heaven flies in the land of Mash" into which his
army penetrated, "no wild-ass nor gazelle feeds
there."

In Phœnicia, Ushu, a city on the mainland opposite Tyre, and Akko were both visited and the
revolters deported or killed. The "province
Tyre," we see, had tried to become independent—
that seems to have been the only practical result
wrought in the West by the instigations of
Shamash-shum-ukin.

The king of Urartu, Sarduris III., compelled by
the pressure of the Indo-Germanic tribes, now
voluntarily submitted to Assyrian sovereignty.
From now on we hear nothing more of Urartu.
The new immigrants changed the old order of
affairs, and a people now developed which afterward is known as Armenian. Ashur-bani-pal
closes the political account of his reign with
Sarduris' salutation: *"Lu shulmu ana sharri
bêliya"*—"Peace be to the king, *my lord.*"

CHAPTER VIII

THE FALL

WE have no information covering the last part of Ashur-bani-pal's reign—a comparatively long period, possibly of ten or fifteen years. In view of his victories we may assume that in general he maintained the glory of Assyria. This conclusion is justified by the fact that until his death he remained king of Babylon. The extent to which this glory rested upon one man and his army is witnessed by the rapid dissolution which set in after him.

Ashur-bani-pal's chief interest for us centres in his literary proclivities, rather than in his victories on the field of battle, although it was in connection with the latter that the name of "Sardanapalus" became famous through the semimythical figure of classical tradition. In his palace in Nineveh he collected a library of cuneiform tablets containing copies of all the Babylonian literary works and old inscriptions that were accessible. To the scanty remnant that has been recovered by excavation we owe almost all our knowledge of Babylonian literature, and of many other important documents whose originals have perished.　If through his victories Ashur-bani-pal is not distinguished from other Assyrian rulers he, nevertheless, is distinguished by his zeal in causing these documents to be written, and also as a student, a zeal for which we can almost forgive him that he was an Assyrian.

Two kings ruled in Assyria after Ashur-bani-pal, the brothers

ASHUR-ETIL-ILI AND SIN-SHAR-ISHKUN.

We know very little of the period during which they reigned.　With the death of Ashur-bani-pal Babylon was lost, but not Babylonia, portions of which were held until the end.　How long each of these kings reigned we cannot say.

We are somewhat better instructed concerning the last days of the kingdom.　The Chaldean Nabopolassar could no longer look to Elam, as his predecessors had done, for support on the throne of Babylon, for Elam was no more.　He found instead a strong ally in Elam's successor, the Medes.　From the time of Esarhaddon Assyria was in alliance with the Ashkuza who, as the neighbors of the Medes, were their natural enemies.　In 609 Nabopolassar was in possession of Mesopotamia.　He called himself "king of the World," and boasted of his victory over Shubari, the ancient name of Mesopotamia.　Accordingly, the strength of Assyria must have been already broken. Soon afterward we find Cyaxares, the Mede, before Nineveh. The Ashkuza despatched a force of auxiliaries under the command of Madyas, the son of Bartatua, Esarhaddon's son-in-law, but these were defeated by Cyaxares. The fate of Nineveh was therewith sealed. The city fell about the year 607.

SIN-SHAR-ISHKUN,

the last king, is said to have destroyed himself in the flames—the fate which mythical tradition ascribes to Sardanapalus.[1]

The Median hosts carried out the work of plundering and destroying more thoroughly than was agreeable to their ally, for not only was Nineveh destroyed but also all the cities of Assyria, as well as those of Babylonia that remained loyal to Assyria, were completely despoiled. Harran, likewise, with its famous temple, suffered the same fate. And it was not until 54 years later—in the third year of Nabunaʿid, when these "Umman-manda" under Astyages were driven off by Cyrus, that the city and temple reverted to the Babylonians, despite the "friendship" with Nabopolassar and Nebuchadrezzar. Nabunaʿid gives an interesting description of his restoration of the temple and re-establishment of its cult.

---

[1] Abydenos relates, Müller-Didot, *Frag. Hist. Gr.*, iv., 282 f., that Saracos (Sin-shar-ishkun) so perished.—*Craig.*

Nineveh never arose again from her ruins, and fortunately so for us, for the mound has safely guarded the remains which otherwise would have been used for building material by a later age.

Nabopolassar watched the procedure of his allies with little satisfaction now that his own lands were not spared. But, strange to say, the barbarians appear to have actually kept to their agreement. They retired from the conquered territory and observed the compact whereby the Tigris was to be the boundary between the respective provinces. Whether this action is to be attributed to their undeveloped diplomacy, or whether, as one is led to suspect, there lay behind the apparent good faith an unethical compulsion from without cannot be definitely determined. At present, however, nothing is known in support of the latter assumption. In any case the new disposition of territory was effected. All the country to the north of the river region from Elam to Asia Minor fell to the Medes. Elam itself appears, as in the earliest times, to have fallen to Babylonia. On the other hand, the relation of both to Harran for the present remains doubtful. Again there were kings of "Anzan and Suri" of which the oldest Babylonian inscriptions speak. Babylonia, Mesopotamia, Syria, and Palestine remained to Babylon; Assyria to the Medes.

The Assyrian kingdom had therewith disappeared from history. We have already frequently intimated why no effort to recover herself was possible—the country was in the hands of an army of mercenaries and a tribe of officials. There was no longer an Assyrian people. It was a matter of complete indifference in the provinces whether the governor exacted his extortions in the name of the king of Assyria, or in that of the king of Babylon. All interest languished except that which ever looked longingly for a change of masters in the false hope that a change of rule would bring an improvement of conditions. In the provinces of Syria and Palestine action had been long since paralyzed. It was only in isolated cases, as in Judah, that life was manifested in a resistance that was easily overcome by a superior army.

CHAPTER IX

THE CIVILIZATION OF ASSYRIA

THE country of Mesopotamia and Assyria, lying to the north on the Euphrates and Tigris, has an essentially different character from Babylonia with its warm climate. The proximity of the mountain range moderates the heat of the great plain, and an abundant waterfall, with snow in the winter season, makes it not unlike the milder countries of Europe. The two great rivers lie far apart and their banks are for the most part rock-bound, rendering the extensive system of canals that was maintained in Babylonia impossible. Smaller streams, especially the Khabur and Balikh in Mesopotamia traverse the plains, fertilizing large regions of the country. Between these lie broad steppes. There the nomads have always found a stamping ground, and thence they could sally forth on predatory excursions into the cultivated lands.

Until some worthy discoveries of material reaching back to pre-Assyrian times have been made in Mesopotamia it will be impossible to say what the essential features of Mesopotamian civilization were which distinguished it from the

Babylonian. It is only the comparatively brief period of Assyria's predominance that comes within our range of observation. We have already seen that the earliest history of Assyria is guessed only dimly through the enveloping clouds, and the internal life and conditions are naturally less illuminated. The clearer light breaks first only when Assyria begins her conquests and extension over Western Asia, and then she appears in the peculiar character which made her master of West Asiatic civilization. But the process of development from the beginning up to this point still awaits new documents for its determination. All that we are now able to do, in a measure, is to set forth the dominant features of Assyria as a ruling power. The region to the left of the Euphrates above the Lower Zab did not develop an independent culture. It was in every respect dependent upon the civilization of Babylonia and Mesopotamia. Its dominance when the great rôle of leadership in the world's civilization was nearing its end was purely political and won by might of arms. It is of prime importance, therefore, that we first look at the essential character of this dominion.

We must assume that Assyria, when it began to expand in the fourteenth and thirteenth centuries, had still a fresh, vigorous population, and this presupposes a large peasant class. How it

developed we do not know, but the fact is attested
by the ability of the country at that time to establish colonies, which is possible only where there
is an abundant peasant population. On the other
hand, colonial enterprises imply agricultural unrest; a surplus population has arisen, or, more
properly expressed, the existing allotment of
lands no longer permit of a further peaceful
development.

Assyria, consequently, in the later period of
Ashur-natsir-pal and Shalmaneser II., had a very
different population, modified, in part, also by
the Aramæan immigrants. It is true that Ashur-
natsir-pal still sent out colonies to newly conquered or reconquered lands. But we can hardly
suppose that these colonists were a surplus mass;
they were in all probability rather portions of a
population that had lost their property which is
indispensable to any true development of a people. We have already seen that only once, in
a special emergency, did Shalmaneser II. call ''the
land'' to service. In the ninth century, therefore,
Assyria's wars of conquest were already waged
with a standing army, that is, with an army of
mercenaries. This proves a complete change of
the basis on which Assyria's power rested. Here-
after there is no Assyrian people who by their
self-won victories expand, but only a military
robber-state that, with an army recruited from all

lands, oppresses the peoples and compels them to furnish the means for their oppression. The people of Assyria, so far as it still existed, disappeared, on the one hand, behind the priesthood, which had come to power here also, and, on the other, behind the throne with its feudal attachments. We noticed in the policy of Tiglathpileser III. an attempt to put the state upon a broader basis, but the attempt did not succeed. The powerful reaction of Sargon restored again the character of Assyria, and sealed her doom.

Assyria's power rested, therefore, upon her army. This was a composite mercenary force made up of parts drawn from all quarters. Their support devolved upon the king, who had to provide their pay. Hence the motive was always present for fresh expeditions of conquest or plunder. On the one hand, an army so constituted demands occupation and booty, on the other, experience showed that the means for its support never sufficed in the Orient unless it were forced from conquered lands. The greater part of the land was in the possession of the temples and the feudal-lords; the larger cities were exempt from taxation, and the comparatively small and oppressed peasantry naturally could not furnish the necessary means. Thus the very basis of the state organization gave rise to a constantly recurring incentive to fresh conquest. Assyria might have abandoned the fundamental evil by pursuing the path she once followed had no rich neighbors, or less powerful ones, offered enticing allurements.

The newly formed Aramæan states of Mesopotamia were reduced during the reign of Ashurnatsir-pal and the first part of Shalmaneser II.'s. This old region, for the most part, was thereby brought under Assyrian rule and made a permanent part of the kingdom. The Aramæan inhabitants, that is, the priesthood and feudal-lords, were placed on an equality with the Assyrian. Assyria, in the larger sense, then included the lands as far west as the Euphrates. The completion of this organization is the principal achievement of the second epoch of Assyrian history. The result continued until the final fall of the whole political system.

Extension beyond the Euphrates forms a new step in the development. This had been begun by Shalmaneser II. and his successors, but lasting results were first achieved during the New Assyrian kingdom by Tiglathpileser III. It was he who first deprived the lands to the west of the Euphrates of their independence and made them Assyrian provinces. But the successes attained here were by no means so great, for these states despite all that they owed in common to the old culture were, nevertheless, in population and civilization foreign to it. They were never assimilated to Assyria. The cultural life of Asia Minor there exercised its influence and erected a barrier between the civilizations east and west of the Euphrates that defied all the violent measures of politics.

In the treatment of states that were to be subjected the methods were those adopted in all ages by similar governments, whose latest representative in history is Turkey. The incessant disturbances in the cultivated regions, by nomads bent on plunder or appropriation of lands, demand that the freedom of the latter be somewhat curtailed as a guarantee of immunity from their attacks. The first step in this direction is the imposition of tribute, inasmuch as complete conquest and the establishment of the rule of the conqueror is impossible. The same procedure is then carried out with the neighboring civilized states. The king is summoned to tribute; if he yields he receives, as the vassal of Assyria, a free hand in the government of his country, but is required also to have his troops in readiness at the call of Assyria. Thus far, there is no interference on the part of the suzerain in the internal affairs of the tributary state. In cases where the demands were onerous, and the land's resources limited, the vassal was often nothing more than an Assyrian tax-gatherer who was held responsible for the prompt delivery of the tribute. The Assyrian king acknowledged no obligation to guarantee protection to his vassal against his enemies in order to facilitate his discharge of the duties imposed. If by the inducements or pressure of a neighboring state he exchanged his vassalage to Assyria for that of his neighbor, an Assyrian army appeared to call the "rebel" to account, although he may have yielded to necessity only. As a rule these vassals stood between two or three fires. They were responsible to the king of Assyria; on the other hand, the people who had to provide the heavy tribute were discontented. Thus parties arose, each of which, according to the dictates of its own interests, sought a different connection, one with Assyria, one with some other great power. In the writings of the prophets of Israel we have contemporaneous witness to such party politics. In the time of Amos the question in Judah and Israel was whether they should hold to Assyria or to Damascus and the Arabian Mutsri. Ahaz favored the former, Amos warned against the latter. After the fall of Damascus Hosea recognized only Assyria and Mutsri, so also Isaiah. After Taharqu's appearance an Egyptian party arose in opposition to the Assyrian. Between such parties stood the king, generally in a most unenviable position, for his safety depended upon his attachment to the stronger power. In the light of such conditions we may read the vacillation of Heze-

kiah, and in the activity of Jeremiah we may see
the trying situation of the last kings of Judah,
who, having to choose between Nebuchadrezzar
and the Pharaohs, were at last overtaken by their
fate.

In the very nature of things, a relation such as
this, which laid upon the vassal only oppressive
obligations, would be dissolved as soon as an
opportunity for revolt presented itself, *viz.*, when
the immediate appearance of an Assyrian army
was no longer dreaded. If it did appear the fate
of the rebel state was generally quickly sealed by
the superior military force. If the Assyrian party
did not prevail over its opponents and obtain
pardon from the Assyrian ruler by the acceptance
of the greater burdens, the country was thrown
into a hopeless war, in which the city was destroyed, the leaders put to death and the besieged
inhabitants enslaved. It is, however, to be borne
in mind that, even in such cases, the atrocities
practised in the Middle Ages, as, for example,
in the border wars of the Germans and Slavs,
were not perpetrated here. It was only the leaders of the inimical party and the responsible
princes who were punished as rebels. We see,
for example, that when Nebuchadrezzar took
Jerusalem the Chaldean supporters were left
undisturbed in their possessions.

When a state was subdued wholly by force of

arms it was deprived of its independence and incorporated as an Assyrian province. In the Mesopotamian lands this was attended with no great difficulties owing to the similarity of the population and the natural unity of the territory. But when Assyria invaded foreign countries it was hardly possible to force Assyrian rule upon their peoples, who had given proof, in their revolt, of the vitality of their own organization and institutions. Such an attempt would have had as its consequence the certain destruction of the Assyrian officials on the next outbreak of discontent. So also the deportation of the greater portion of the population would have resulted in destroying, in large part, the productiveness of the new province.

From the time of Tiglathpileser III., when Assyria was no longer able to send out colonists, an effort was made to meet the situation by exchanging the inhabitants of newly conquered provinces lying on opposite sides of the empire. The deportation of the people of Samaria to Mesopotamia and Media, and the Jews to Babylonia, is familiar from the Old Testament. Ashurbanipal, likewise, after the overthrow of Shamash-shum-ukin, undertook the repopulation of Samaria with the inhabitants of Babylonian cities. Such exchanges and transplantings are frequently mentioned in the inscriptions of Tig-

lathpileser III. and Sargon II. The policy served
a double purpose, the numerical maintenance of
the population and a more ready acquiescence in
Assyrian government. Removed from their
native soil, composed of different elements, and
unassimilated to the remnant of the old stock
among which they were settled, the newly imported peoples were forced to rely upon the Assyrian officials. The tribal and class organization
which had bound them together in the home lands,
and had brought them into conflict with their
oppressors, was dissolved, so that, for the time
being, they were incapable of resisting.

In these settlements of Assyria, effected on
these two principles of organization, a really civilized and progressive government would have
found the material out of which a new people
would have been developed, one whose interests
would have been inseparably linked with the
Assyrian kingdom. But the governmental methods of a predatory state that is dominated by the
military and priestly classes are antagonistic to
the advance of civilization. Assyria expected to
receive from the new provinces, she had nothing
to give them. The ultimate aim of Assyrian, as
of all Oriental rule, is the enrichment of the governing classes from the lowest tax-gatherer to
the governor of the state, the one below pays
tribute to the one above, and, finally, the governor

pays the king. That which the province received, if it ever received anything, was, therefore, a bagatelle in proportion to what was taken from it. The end was impoverishment and devastation. When the mother-land was no longer self-sustaining, as the result of the unjust apportionment of lands and possessions, and lived by exploiting the conquered states, its governmental methods applied to the latter must naturally prove as fatal for them.

Just as Assyria bestowed no benefits upon the vassal states in return for the burdens she imposed so she failed, in her conception of obligation to her conquered provinces, to recognize the principle of *do ut des*. The *shaknu,* or provincial governor, differed little from the former prince. The administration, however, which before was in the hands of the native born was now intrusted to Assyrian officials. The material condition of the people was, therefore, not essentially modified by this change. It is not to be supposed that the Assyrian masters extorted more from their subjects than the native rulers had coming from them; least of all was that possible in the older civilized countries. The governor who succeeded the prince inherited all his duties and obligations. His administration guaranteed to the Assyrian king a greater security since he was dependent upon the support of

the latter in the strange land. The native prince,
on the contrary, influenced by tradition and tribal
feeling, was more apt to be hostile. In other
respects the situation was unchanged. The
shaknu had to provide for the needs of the province out of the revenues and, at the same time, discharge his obligations to the crown. He had to
provide a contingent for military purposes and
furnish it with means from his province. Above
all he was required to raise and equip a provincial
guard himself, except when the empire was seriously threatened with the loss of the province.
The king had his own ''royal army''[1] which he
was called upon to support, and he tried to roll
the burden upon his officers. The governor had
also his and to it the safety of the province was
intrusted. In war time a portion of it was subject to the call of the emperor. The position of
the provincial governor was, therefore, comparatively independent. It is evident, however, that
there was a great temptation to risk an improvement of his fortune under Assyria by submitting
to another conqueror, or striking for independence in times of weakness.

If, therefore, the Assyrian ''empire,'' with its
lack of unity in population, with a government
that ignored the reciprocal support of its individual parts, disappeared suddenly after the fall

[1] *Kitsir sharruti.*

of Nineveh, making no attempt to recover and leaving not a trace behind, there is no ground for astonishment. It had been held together by an army of mercenaries and an official class—the empire vanished when they disappeared. That no one arose to charm to life again these leeches that lived upon the blood of the people is what was to be expected.

As is the case in all mercenary armies recruits are taken indiscriminately. What is offered is accepted. We may, therefore, conclude that the barbarian lands on the border supplied the bulk of the material for Assyria as the *Germanen* supplied Rome in later times, the Normans and Britons Byzantium, the Turks the Caliphate. When a state was conquered a part of the conquered army was generally added to the imperial army. This applies especially wherever, as, for example, in the Syrian states, it is to be assumed that the army was already organized on the mercenary basis.

Of the different arms, the war chariot was the heaviest, most terrible, and most distinguished. The king is always represented in it in battle. It is frequently sculptured upon the monuments, drawn by two horses, with charioteer and warrior. It is not known where this method of fighting originated. A closed phalanx with shields and lances is attested for the period of the kings of

Lagash by the "Stele of Vultures," but this is the only indication we have of the composition of the army in the early Babylonian period. The domestication of the horse, and when it became known to them, are questions closely related to the origin of the war chariot. We have no evidence of its use in Babylonia *circa* 3000 B.C., but no positive conclusion, for or against its introduction, at this time is possible from the scantiness of our material. In the Kassite period horses and war chariots play an important part as they do in the Egypt of that age. Were they introduced with the "Canaanite" immigration, or were Northern influences through Hittite and other conquests responsible for them? However that may be the Greek epic proves that the war chariot was the main reliance in Asia Minor, where Hittite civilization was the connecting link between that of Western Asia and Greece, during the last period of the Assyrian kingdom.

The cavalry was a much less important arm than the war chariot in which the nobility fought. It was never numerous and appears to have been, in the period best known to us, little in honor, and, probably, was used only for skirmishing and pursuit. An efficient horse was impossible without a proper saddle and stirrup. The main strength lay in the heavily armed infantry, who carried lances and short swords and were protected by shields, coats of mail and helmets. They were supported by a light-armed body of bowmen.

Methods of siege kept pace in their development with the necessities of the numerous wars. The usual fortifications could not as a rule long withstand the Assyrian attack. A rampart (the Roman *agger*) was thrown up against the city walls and upon this they mounted battering-rams. The brick-built walls soon crumbled under the heavy blows of the iron-capped ram. Stronger works could not, however, be reduced in this way. Shalmaneser failed before the stone walls of Damascus, and whether Tiglathpileser stormed the city or took it by other means we do not know. The reduction of Tyre, which was first taken by Alexander, was attempted by throwing up earthworks with the object of cutting her off both by land and sea, but nothing was accomplished owing to the besiegers' lack of a naval force.

Upon the king or governor devolved the duty of equipping the army with weapons as well as of furnishing its support. The construction of an armory, which always had to be well stocked with arms, was inseparable from the erection of a palace, the crowning work of an Assyrian ruler. The soldiers' support does not appear to have been the result of a payment in money drawn either from a definite tax or from the royal income. The

way in which it originated is still traceable. Originally military service rested upon possession of
the soil. While this was so in the case of the
feudal tenants who were nobles, the disappearance of the agricultural class and its inability to
perform military service led to a change; a tax
was introduced, an *aes militare,* which henceforth
the cattle-owner had to pay in lieu of personal
service. This was given to the soldiers, and it
appears indeed that each soldier kept a peasant
who had to pay tax to him. Larger possessions
would entail greater burdens. Probably later on
other sources of income than land were similarly
taxed. When the king found the support of the
entire army too burdensome he sought to shift a
part of the troops on to the shoulders of the high
officials, who naturally objected to paying the
king's troops as their own, and so the way was
paved for all sorts of janizary outbreaks. Even
in the most prosperous periods there are discernible signs of minor troubles which must have
become greatly aggravated when Assyria, shut
up on all sides within her old territory, was no
longer able to exploit and plunder the provinces.

The most thoroughgoing excavations have thus
far been undertaken in Assyria. For that reason
our information on many matters in Assyrian
history is much greater than it is in Babylonian.
Very little is known of the German excavations in

Babylon now proceeding with thoroughness and on a large scale. Those conducted by the French in Telloh bear upon ancient Babylonia, while only a small part of the finds of the Americans at Niffer have as yet been studied. From the Assyrian palaces unearthed at Nimrud and Kuyunjik we have obtained an accurate and extensive knowledge of Assyrian architecture and sculpture in the ninth and eighth centuries B.C. Ashur-natsirpal's palace in Caleh belongs to the ninth, Tiglathpileser's in Caleh, and Sargon's in Khorsabad to the eighth, Sennacherib's and Ashurbanipal's in Nineveh and Esarhaddon's in Caleh to the seventh.

It is a constant characteristic of the Orient that the pride of powerful and weathy rulers leads them to erect magnificent buildings, especially palaces for themselves. Apart from the desire for a splendid house, the visible sign of their power, there may be also a touch of Cæsarean madness in this. Apart from this the change of capital was connected with national policy; beside, the wish was always present for a private and family sepulture, for it was as necessary in death as in life to have the protection of the family-gods without which the departed spirits would be restless, homeless wanderers.[1]

---

[1] *Ina biti-shu kibir* ("he was buried in his house") is the *technical phrase* for a happy end. *Cf.* Isa. xiv., 18.—*Craig.*

We have already seen that we cannot speak of an Assyrian culture. What is found there that is not Babylonian must rather be regarded as Mesopotamian. The sculptures of Arban, however, are the only art monuments we have of Mesopotamia in the pre-Assyrian period; but in them we see an early stage of Assyrian art. Even Harran, which is indicated as the site of ancient ruins by certain visible remains, has not yet found an explorer. No conclusions as to the sculptured lions seen there are yet possible, although they probably belong to the Assyrian period. Shalmaneser II. and Ashurbanipal, and later Nabuna'id, each restored the old sanctuary of the moon-god there, and it is quite improbable that early monuments are to be found in the upper strata. But as the history of Mesopotamia points to the western side of the Euphrates, to Syria and Palestine, and as the Babylonians gave to these lands the name of Suri, thereby pointing to an age-long connection, so also the Mesopotamian culture must be considered in the light of those civilizations that flourished west of the Euphrates and adjacent to it. But here again we are confronted by a great blank. The oldest sculptures of Senjirli might belong to an age which would permit of comparisons between Mesopotamia and Syria in these earliest times. And yet barbaric productions have also appeared in times subsequent to the complete destruction of ancient civilization. The same may be said of the similar monuments of Tel-Halaf.

Our knowledge, therefore, of Mesopotamia and Assyria, obtained from the sculptured monuments, holds good only of the later times. We see them at the end of many thousand years of development with its ups and downs. And even then the influence of Babylonia is plain—the material used in their immense buildings is brick, the same as was used in early Babylonia. Notwithstanding their proximity to the mountains the Assyrians used neither quarried stone nor stone pillars. They followed the example of the Babylonians and built with clay brick, using cedar beams brought from the Amanus and Lebanon.[1] The material for their sculptures they found at their doors, and therein they had a great advantage over Babylonia where Gudea was compelled to bring the stone for his statues from Arabia and Palestine. The mountains to the north of Nineveh provided them with marble and limestone with which they could case the brick walls. That the pre-Assyrian age was acquainted with the bull colossi, which guarded the city gates and palace doors, cannot be doubted in view of the colossi of Arban. Similar works of art have not yet been discovered in Babylonia, but the *argu-*

---

[1] *Cf.* Isa. XIV., 8.

mentum ex silentio has little cogency in our present state of knowledge.

The abundant wainscoting material, and the facility with which the soft limestone could be wrought, determined the peculiarity of the Assyrian buildings. Whereas Babylonia was confined to the moulded and glazed tile, decorated with various representations, the walls of the Assyrian palaces were adorned with alabaster slabs on which the deeds of the builder were written and illustrated by the hand of the sculptor. As a rule one or two rows of sculptured slabs, some with, some without inscriptions, lined the walls on all sides. The inscriptions are one of our most important sources. The sculptures supply the only, as well as necessary, illustration of much in the inscriptions that otherwise would be undecipherable. Unlike the Egyptians with their delight in scenes from the family life these monuments represent only the things worthy of a king of Assyria. Nine-tenths of them have to do with the glorification of war, the other tenth with the royal buildings—a king of Ashur scarce understood aught else. It was not until the time of Ashurbanipal that a highly developed technique addressed itself to other objects. Representations such as we then find of the emperor feasting with his consort under the bower in the garden, are, however, rare exceptions in the long series

of battle-scenes. Here we see the tent-life, here
the king in his war chariot advancing to battle,
the furious engagement, the pursuit of the enemy,
the taking of the cities. Each expedition is por-
trayed separately, and the different scenes are
explained by accompanying inscriptions. By the
side of these we find the glorification of the king's
chase, building operations upon immense clay terraces constructed by an enormous multitude of
men, the transport of stone colossi upon sledges
on rollers. There are some exceedingly life-like
scenes from the chase among which the hunt of
the wild-asses, and the dying lioness are splen-
didly executed. But nothing is seen of family
life. The only objects worthy of the Assyrian
monarch's contemplation were the army and its
exploits; even the gods retire from view, especially in the later times. The antithesis of
kingship and priesthood appears here as well
as in the political development. The occasional
glimpses we get of common life are always in
connection with battle-scenes, the hunt, or building operations. Among these are one or two pic-
tures of tent-life and of the slaves at work on
buildings, which exhibit well the character of the
technique. The means employed in moving mas-
sive materials we have already seen in the transport of the stone colossi. In the construction of
the terraces for the buildings the earth was car-

ried in baskets upon the shoulders of long rows
of slaves. Behind every six or seven followed a
driver who plied the stick on the backs of the
loitering ones.

Art, especially in the execution of details, is
marked by advance and studious development.
Beginning with the sculptures from the palace of
Ashur-natsir-pal in the ninth century we can follow the progress made down to the new Assyrian
kingdom. The figures of the earlier artists are
comparatively stiff, and skill in presenting battle-
scenes on a large scale is wanting, whereas the
later sculptors manifest a greater freedom and
variety both in conception and execution. The
war-scenes from Ashurbanipal's palace mark the
acme of Assyrian sculpture. Assyrian sculpture
and Assyrian history advanced hand in hand. As
power and wealth increased this art favored by
Assyrian kings advanced—of any of the other fine
arts we know very little. To what extent sculpture became popular, or whether popular interest
had part in its development is not known.

Since foreign mercenaries fought the Assyrian
battles and Phœnician craftsmen built the ships,
the artists also may have been imported. The
expression "Assyrian art" can, therefore, be
used only in the same limited sense as we use the
words Assyrian people.

We have no means of determining the history

of development which unites the art of Telloh, more than two thousand years earlier, with this Assyrian art. The conception of that age, if not the execution, was more advanced. If the ideal is an essential element of art, the statues of Gudea seem to have been the product of a conception which might have resulted in work similar to that of the Greeks. Whether this is a remnant of a Sumerian inheritance that was already on the decline, or whether the "Babylonian Semites," whose work it was, were so different from their later kinsmen are questions that cannot be answered. The first possibility has also the greater probability, but that is all that can be said. The same phenomenon confronts us here that meets us in the old Egyptian kingdom. Is the stiff stereotyped art of the later period a product of the Semitic spirit that became influential through the "Canaanite" migration and destroyed in both lands the germs of free development which had been received from the older inhabitants? One thing is at least clear: the feeling and search for an ideal of beauty which, whether as beginning or end of a development, is recognizable in the art of Lagash, and of the time of Naram-Sin, has been abandoned, and a stiff, mechanical imitation of external nature has succeeded. One is the more inclined to look upon this as a result of Semitism, in view of the fact that the same spirit is present

in all things Semitic. Its defect is the utter want
of an imagination that can dream of a more beautiful world. Semitic poesy is a magnifying and
enlarging of the real world; all the surrounding
magnificence is exaggerated and distorted; that is
the end of the Semite's dreaming. He never
became other than a child whose ideal good
consists in an unlimited provision for material
enjoyment. Of intellectual delights, and the fas-
cinations of life found in the beautiful world of
the imagination he had never an inkling.

The fact that the Babylonians and Assyrians
did not study the nude human figure has been
given as the reason that their art never reached
the ideal despite the excellence of its technique.
But this explanation does not suffice. We actually possess small Babylonian statues of Ishtar
and also the torso of a large statue of a female
figure, probably also representing Ishtar, which
belong to the time of the Assyrian king, Ashur-
bel-kala. The truth is, on the contrary, that we
have to do here with a still undeveloped mind that
looked upon the human body as something base,
another proof that the Oriental never, even in
theory, rose above the immature, childish point
of view. The world and all the glory thereof
finds its expression for him in costly draperies—
beyond this his phantasy does not reach. Consequently the artist betrays his ideal of beauty in

his painfully accurate efforts to display the costliness of his master's robes. Everywhere we meet the child—who knows of nothing grander than to be "a king," and to whom a double portion of sugar is better than being right. In every work of the imagination the same defect appears—bigness not beauty is the Oriental's ideal.

The same childishness makes him cling reverently to what is ancient and traditional, and his fondness for the past blinds his eyes to the demands of the present. In so far as pertained to the representation of the gods—whereby the essence of religion is brought to view—art was governed by the revered and time-honored forms. Consequently in the developed technique of statues of the gods of the Assyrian age we can trace their origin from the old crude stone pillars worshipped by the nomads.

III—THE NEW BABYLONIAN-CHALDEAN KINGDOM

THE NEW BABYLONIAN-CHALDEAN KINGDOM

CHAPTER I

NEBUCHADREZZAR

At the death of Ashurbanipal the Chaldean, Nabopolassar, was on the throne of Babylon. To which of the small Chaldean principalities he belonged we do not know. He probably put on the crown of Bel with the good-will, or, at least, with the sufferance of Assyria. At first he sought at all events to avoid an open rupture with Ashuretil-ili, thus recognizing his suzerainty. Babylon was all that he possessed at the first; the other parts of Babylonia remained Assyrian. The details of his advance are unknown. One thing is certain, namely, that Babylon did not enter the lists against Assyria in reliance upon her own strength, but she first disclosed her plans when she entered into an alliance with Media. Moreover, as the royal house of Assyria was related by marriage to the Ashkuza, so the son of Nabopolassar was married to a Median princess.

313

We have already seen that Mesopotamia was in the possession of Nabopolassar from 609 onward, and that the destruction of Assyria was primarily the work of the Medes. When, however, this was accomplished Nabopolassar was old, or ill, and the reins of government had already passed to the hands of his son, Nebuchadrezzar II. The task of subduing the Western provinces, therefore, devolved upon him. But this could not have been attended by any insuperable difficulties, for the hatred of Assyria made it impossible for the provincial governors to assert authority after the fall of Nineveh. It was, therefore, to be expected that they would submit to the new master. Any attempt on the part of separate states to declare for independence was naturally hopeless.

In the meantime, however, another power had to be ousted from the Western provinces. Necho II. of Egypt, rightly judging the situation, saw that the hour had come to win back the provinces that from the times of Thothmes and Amenophis had been lost. While the Medes lay before Nineveh and Nabopolassar seized Mesopotamia Necho marched on Palestine and Syria, taking full possession of both. In his advance he met with no united opposition, and the single-handed effort of Josiah to block his way at Megiddo in 609 or 608 proved fateful for the Judean king.[1] Necho had

---

[1] 2 Ki. xxiii., 29.

made his headquarters at Riblah, on the Orontes, and from this point he controlled for some time affairs at Jerusalem. In 605 he advanced as far as Karchemish. He was, therefore, prepared to cross the Euphrates and, therewith, invade the territory that had been taken by Babylonia after the fall of Nineveh. At this point he was met by Nebuchadrezzar, the commander of the forces, and defeated, forced to abandon Palestine and Syria, and retreat to Egypt before the pursuing Babylonian army. Thereupon Nebuchadrezzar received, with little opposition, pledges of fealty from the governors and took possession as far as the boundary of Egypt. It had fallen to the lot of this last successful ruler of Babylonia to accomplish at the beginning of his career that which had been struggled for in vain for centuries—the West was again brought into subjection to Babylon as it was when her might and culture were at their zenith.

But this result was not won through an awakening of the power of the *Babylonian* people. Babylon was, as she had been for centuries, in the hands of conquerors who sought historical eclat for their power through the ancient renown of this home of culture. In the centuries of conflict between Assyrians and Chaldeans the oft defeated but undeterred intruder won in the end. Nebuchadrezzar, before whom Palestine now trembled, was a *Chaldean.* The Old Testament, also, in its contemporary records, designates these representatives of the last Babylonian dynasty as Chaldeans.

About the close of 605, when Nebuchadrezzar was still engaged in Palestine, he received word of Nabopolassar's death, and of disorders that aimed at crowning a Babylonian. He set out at once by forced marches for Babylon, choosing the shortest route, through the desert. Arriving at the right moment, the day appointed for the New Year's Festival, he headed the solemn procession of Bel, thereby declaring himself king of Babylon. His fame does not rest only upon the accident that he destroyed the independence of Judah, but also upon the fact that during his long reign Babylon again rose to prosperity and power.

The external evidence of this is visible even in his extensive building operations of which we read in many of his inscriptions. Babylon was rebuilt by him, after the work had been inaugurated in part by his father, Nabopolassar, and the fortification walls, towers, moat, etc., which were the wonder of that age, were erected. He constructed the "Median Wall" stretching from Sippara on the Euphrates to the Tigris, near Opis, in order to dam the water so that in case of need he could flood the whole country to the north and thus prevent the entrance of an enemy

into the territory between the two rivers. Below
Babylon a similar defence was found that prevented an attack from that quarter. He built
the great terraces which became famous as
the "Hanging Gardens of Semiramis," and he
renewed the chief temples in all the great cities.

Unlike the Assyrian kings who preface every
report concerning a building operation with a
grewsome tale of battles won, the Babylonian, and
especially Nebuchadrezzar, tells only of the works
of peace. For this reason we have practically
no information left us by Nebuchadrezzar of his
expeditions. Apart from his wars in Palestine
we know only of his fruitless siege of Tyre, which
lasted for thirteen years, and one or more Egyptian campaign. A fragment of a hymn mentions
a war against Amasis in 568. In the same connection Putu (Yavan) appears as an ally of
Egypt. In this name we have probably a designation of the Æolians and especially of Samos
that was then in control of the northern part of
the Archipelago. Pittacus, who had obtained the
upper hand by the expulsion of certain noble
houses, was ruling there at the time. Among
those expelled were Alkaios the poet, and his
brother, Nutimenides. The latter served in the
Babylonian army, and, after he had returned
home, wrote of the heroic deeds he had witnessed.
These Oriental heroes are all modelled after the

same pattern. If David had not slain Goliath[1] he would surely have fallen before Nutimenides, for, in the verse of his brother, marvels of might and skill such as this were the peculiar marks of the hero. The connection of the Orient with Greece in earliest times here again appears to view. Pittacus sought and obtained aid from Egypt; his opponents, therefore, go to Babylonia. The two great Oriental states play the same rôle in the isles of Greece that they played in Palestine, especially in Judah. Whether Nebuchadrezzar ever invaded Egypt as Ezekiel prophesied[2] we do not yet know. At all events he did not hold her long in subjection even though he may have won some victories similar to those of Esarhaddon and Ashurbanipal.

His chief pride and his claims to remembrance as a wise ruler lay in the arts of peace. There is not the slightest trace to be found in what we know of his activities of any such mental aberration as that which is recorded of him in the grotesque story of the late apocalyptic Book of Daniel, Chap. IV.

---

[1] We may, perhaps, refer to the fact, in passing, that David's claim to this honor is very doubtful. II. Sam. 21, 19, makes *Elhanan* of Bethlehem the hero, in opposition to I. Sam. 17, 4 ff. The author of I. Chron. 20, 5, noting the contradiction, changed "of Beth*lehem*" to "*Lahmi* the brother of" in the interest of harmony.—*Craig*.

[2] Chap. 29, 19 f.

CHAPTER II

THE RELATION OF THE NEW BABYLONIAN KINGDOM TO MEDIA

THE west was the only direction in which Babylonia could extend her power. East and north where the Assyrian kings were wont to wage wars disappear; Elam and Urartu are no more. The great Median kingdom now ruled there from Elam as far west as the river Halys, the boundary of Lydia. The existence of Babylonia was now dependent upon this barbarian kingdom in whose power lay the fate of Western Asia. Babylon's relation to it was much like that of Italy to the German empire of the Middle Ages. As long as Nebuchadrezzar lived the relation appears to have been friendly. In fact the destruction of Nineveh by the Medes first made the dynasty of Nabopolassar supreme in Babylonia, and it was certainly due in large measure to Cyaxares that its rulers were allowed to hold it. It would almost appear further that intermarriage with this barbarous royal house was of greater significance in Nebuchadrezzar's case than such marriages are wont to be where state politics are more highly developed. Herodotus tells of Nebuchadrezzar's participation in Median affairs when war broke out with Lydia, the third of the then great powers. During that war, in which the eclipse of the moon predicted by Thales occurred, Nebuchadrezzar assumed the rôle of peace-maker, in which he was supported by Syennesis of Cilicia. But the youthful dynasty, whose fame is coupled with the name of Nebuchadrezzar, was destined with his death to lose its glory.

AMEL-MARDUK, 561–560,

became king in 561. He is the *Evil Merodach* of the Old Testament. After two years of rule he was dethroned "because he ruled unjustly and tyrannically." This unfavorable judgment of him is given both by Berossus, a priest of Bel and Babylonian historian, who wrote in the Seleucid period, and by Nabuna'id, from which it appears that it was the judgment of the priesthood whose desires even Nebuchadrezzar never succeeded in stilling despite all of his temple-building. All that we know of Amel-Marduk is that he dealt friendly[1] with Jehoiachin of Judah whom Nebuchadrezzar deported to Babylon. He was murdered in the second year of his reign, and

NERGAL-SHAR-UTSUR, 559–556,

his brother-in-law, was placed upon the throne in 559. No attempt was yet made to go outside of

[1] *Vid.* II. Kings, 25, 27 f.

the Chaldean royal family for a ruler, but whether Nergal-shar-utsur, or Neriglissar, as his name appears in Greek, was himself a Chaldean is not clear. Little is known of him also, yet Nabuna'id ascribes to him services in the protection of the country. In addition to works of a religious character such as the repairing and beautifying of the temples he also gave attention to the construction of canals. His works of defence may be an indication that the Medes were already beginning to manifest an interest in favor of the dethroned house. He was succeeded by his son,

LABASHI-MARDUK,

who was still in his minority. After nine months he was deposed, because, as the above mentioned sources likewise agree in declaring, "he showed evil tendencies." The real cause appears, however, in the choice of his successor, a Babylonian, who, apparently, was a more docile tool of the priesthood. This last king of Babylon,

NABUNA'ID, 555–538,

is, at first sight, a remarkable individual. Without troubling himself in the least he apparently looks on while the Medes, and afterward the Persians, take possession of the land. Instead of engaging in works of defence he turns antiquarian and busies himself in the excavation of the ruins of old temples and the determining of the age of their builders. The information he has given concerning his discoveries are exceedingly valuable for us, but neither his discoveries nor the construction of new temples in which he was so zealous was of any service to his tottering throne. The Medes do not appear to have idly watched the overthrow of the friendly dynasty to which they were related by marriage. It is possible, as we have suggested above, that Nergal-shar-utsur had found it necessary to protect himself against them. Now that the breach with Babylon was complete they appear active again in Mesopotamia, which, indeed, they may have never completely evacuated. Even then at the beginning of his reign Nabuna'id manifested his real character. While the Medes besieged Harran, the old city of the moon-god, or still occupied it, Nabuna'id did nothing but indulge in pious dreams that the gods would deliver it out of their hands. And, strange to say, his dreams came to pass—Astyages was vanquished by Cyrus, and, for a time, Mesopotamia was at rest. But the gods do not seem to have revealed to the pious king that the conqueror of the Medes might prove a more dangerous enemy to him. For the time being he rejoiced over his apparent gain and hastened, with thankful heart, to rebuild the temple of the moon-god in Harran. To this end he taxed and forced into service his subjects ''from Gaza, the border of Egypt, the Mediterranean, and Syria to the Persian Gulf.'' He had become great by another's victory: that is usually a misfortune for any man.

CHAPTER III

THE FALL OF NEW BABYLONIA THROUGH THE PERSIANS

In the meantime, Cyrus, the Persian, had added to his strength. India was brought into subjection, with the territories previously reduced by the Medes, and so the only great power to which Babylonia could look for support disappeared. Then he advanced against Babylonia, now hemmed in on all sides.

In the closing years of the Babylonian empire we meet again the same conditions that have frequently appeared before in times of danger, and that appeared in Israel and Judah as well in times of national crises. Internal party strifes render defence impossible. Nabuna'id was placed upon the throne by the party in opposition to the old Chaldean royal house. He is distinctly called a "Babylonian" to emphasize his *non-Chaldean* origin. He appears to have been a "diplomat" who sought to humor both parties, the priestly and the military-official. Every one of his inscriptions shows how intent he was on winning the favor of the priests by building temples and making provision for the cultus. But this could only serve to increase the discontent of the rival party, which had the army and its strength at their command. The result was that he was shut up a prisoner in his palace and the government was intrusted to his son, *Bel-shar-utsur,* the Belshazzar of the Old Testament, to be conducted in Nabuna'id's name. Political hypocrisy had here become such a fine art that the official records do not fail to make the father, who was held a prisoner by the son, pray for the prosperity of the latter.

Cyrus, starting from Arbela and crossing the Tigris to the south of the ruins of Kalkhi, first took possession of Mesopotamia. In the following year, 546, he advanced from Elam into South Babylonia. Nabuna'id had the gods of the larger cities, Ur, Erech, etc., brought to Babylon and felt safe under their protection. Nothing is known of what happened for the next five years. In 539, however, we find Babylon surrounded. The defence by inundation, made possible by Nebuchadrezzar's Median Wall and the supplementary works to the south of Babylon, is probably to be credited with the brief respite. During these years, however, Cyrus was not able to effect an entrance into Babylon either from Mesopotamia on the north or from the regions to the south. The country round about was turned into a marsh, as Holland was in more modern times under similar

circumstances. Within this inundated region lay
the "kingdom of Babylon, large enough to support itself so long as it was not invaded." There
is a reminiscence of this in Herodotus' story that
Cyrus was engaged for a couple of years draining
the Diyala in order to accustom his army to the
drainage of canals, thus obtaining the necessary
skill for the siege of Babylon where he diverted
the Euphrates. As a matter of fact Herodotus
missed the purpose of the work which was the
construction of a passage through the inundated
region, for the Diyala empties at Opis, the terminus of the Median Wall. With this agrees the
fact that the Babylonian army under Belshazzar
actually met Cyrus there between *Opis* and *Sippara* in 539, after the passage had been constructed. The Babylonians were defeated. Nabuna'id, who was now set free in Babylon, sought
to organize a defence, but it was too late—the
army was destroyed and in the city itself Cyrus'
entrance was welcome. Babylon yielded to a Persian army under the lead of Ugbaru (Gobryas).
The great fortifications of Nebuchadrezzar were
not defended. The Persians were received as the
Assyrians had once been received,[1] as deliverers.
When Cyrus entered four months later he was
proclaimed king, and one of his first political acts
was to return the gods which Nabuna'id had

[1] P. 62.

brought to Babylon to their own cities, an act which was well calculated to win for himself the favor of the Babylonian priesthood.

Thus ended the history of Babylonia; Babylon had become a Persian province. It is true that the ancient splendor, that had so unexpectedly blazed forth again before the end, was not completely forgotten—a couple of attempts were later made to win back her independence; but these struggles were of short duration. In the provinces the same relations were maintained toward the Persians as with Nebuchadrezzar. Nabuna'id, who did nothing whatever to protect them was simply given up for Cyrus. Southern Babylonia, which Nabuna'id abandoned and whose gods he carried off, certainly regarded Cyrus as a deliverer. He in his turn was wise enough in the use of his power to loosen the reins somewhat in the provinces. He not only returned the gods to the cities of Babylonia, but he showed the same favor to many another province also that had long been subject, thus acknowledging its right of self-government, as in the case of Judah, perhaps also Sidon. So too, these provinces, which enjoyed greater internal liberties under his rule, and were less weighted with heavy burdens, must have seen in Cyrus a deliverer from the Babylonian yoke. A new epoch in the history of civilization begins at this point. Persia had already taken Asia

Minor before the conquest of Babylon and thus had come into touch with Greek civilization. From now on the struggle, which came to be determining in the development of the peoples of the Occident, is no longer upon Asiatic soil. It is true that Persia, as the heir of Babylon, in opposition to the Greeks, is in a certain measure at least in possession of an advanced culture. But this culture was more or less effete since it was no longer suffused with the fresh life of the people. It was soon surpassed by the fresh and vigorous life that appeared in Greece.

INDEX

P